The Rainbow Book of Art

PLATE 1. SASSETTA. *Journey of the Magi.* METROPOLITAN MUSEUM OF ART, NEW YORK

PLATE 2. GIOTTO. *The Flight into Egypt.* ARENA CHAPEL, PADUA

THE RAINBOW
BOOK OF ART

BY Thomas Craven

WORLD PUBLISHING
TIMES MIRROR
NEW YORK

PUBLISHED BY THE WORLD PUBLISHING COMPANY

PUBLISHED SIMULTANEOUSLY IN CANADA

BY NELSON, FOSTER & SCOTT LTD.

1972 PRINTING

WORLD PUBLISHING
TIMES MIRROR

FOR RICHIE, COEUR DE LION

Contents

List of Color Plates

following or
facing page

THE RAINBOW BOOK OF ART

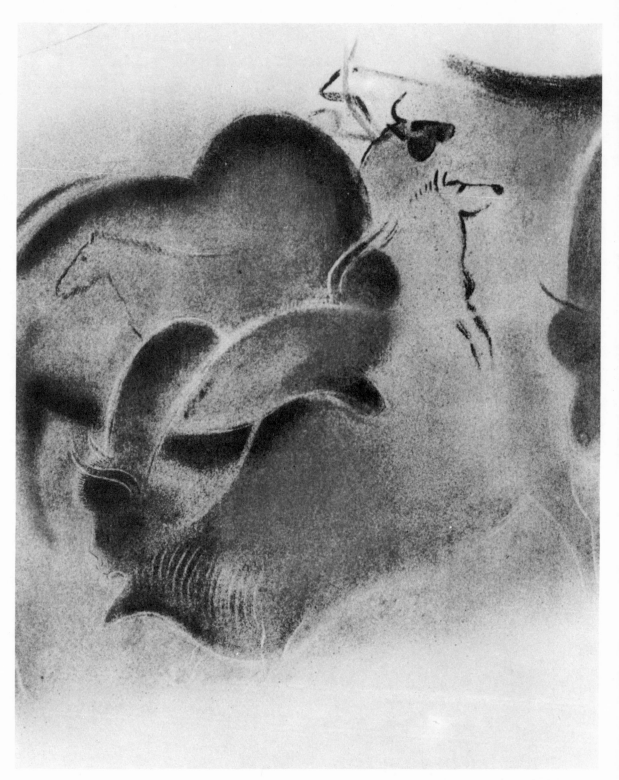

Animal Ensemble. Cave painting, Font-de-Gaume, Dordogne, France. A group from the right wall of the cavern showing a small bison with polychrome bisons painted over figures of oxen and horses traced in single smooth black strokes.

I
Before the Beginning
of Years

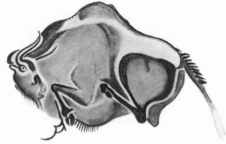

The sun had never seemed so bright to the tired eyes of Don Marcellino de Sautuola as he came out of the Church of the Sacred Heart, his little granddaughter at his heels. He had taken the child to Mass in the dark, dilapidated cathedral near Santander, on the seacoast of northern Spain, in the year 1879. The crisp autumn morning, with never a cloud over the mountain tops, gave him an idea: he would ramble over to Altamira, near by, to one of the caves which was the happy hunting ground for old gentlemen from Paris and Madrid who were interested in the past. Don Marcellino, too, was a scholar. Nudged into a trot by his grandchild, aged five, he made a beeline for the entrance of a cavern in which, so long ago that we can only estimate the date, men, women, and children with no other shelter had huddled together.

The old scholar found nothing of special concern, not even a well-chipped piece of flint, and was ready to return when he heard a scream from his granddaughter. She had discovered the entrance of a cave which had been plugged up with the litter of thousands of years, and had ducked into the hole. Don Marcellino followed her, but before long the tunnel became so small that he was unable to walk, and he stopped suddenly.

"Toros! Toros!" cried the child from some dark place—the Spanish word for bulls.

But where were the bulls? On his hands and knees, Don Marcellino crawled along to a sight that was to make history. There was the little girl gazing at the roof of the cave, pointing, and screaming, *"Toros! Toros!"* And sure enough, on smooth, flat spaces in the rocks above, he saw the most sensational animal paintings in the world—not Spanish bulls, like those bred for the toreadors of Seville, but huge bison, some as large as life, ramping and snorting and terribly alive.

Inching along behind the child, the Spanish scholar feasted his eyes not only on the bison, huge beasts similar to those butchered in the pioneering days of America, but on other animals—reindeer and mammoths among them—all painted on the ceiling of the cave and drawn with a skill that no one would believe possible, if the evidence were not above him. They are so beautiful that Henri Matisse, the great modern French painter, once said, "I could not dream of painting so well as the cave men painted before the dawn of time."

13

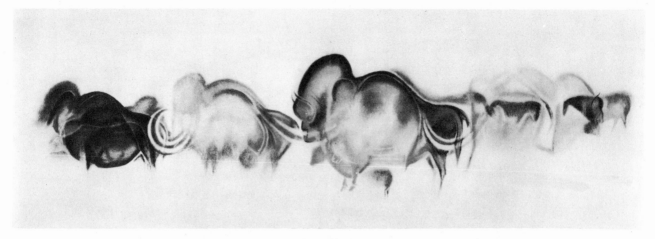

Superimposed Animals. Cave painting, Font-de-Gaume, Dordogne, France. The cave artists made animals living and real, and solved the problem of indicating one against another.

Reindeer. Cave painting, Font-de-Gaume, Dordogne, France. Fresco in red earth-colors and lampblack by cave men with the eyes of hunters and the skill of artists.

And how old? The men from Paris and Madrid couldn't make up their minds—twenty thousand, ten thousand, or fifty thousand years old? It is not too important. It was before the beginning of years, and if one should ask, "How old is art?" the answer would be, "As old as the first man who stood on his hind legs, and killed a bison, and worshiped its shadow, or spirit. As old as the first family —father, mother, and children—who crawled into the black caves and with the light of torches made of moss soaked in fat, fixed the animated shadows of wild beasts on the rocks under the earth."

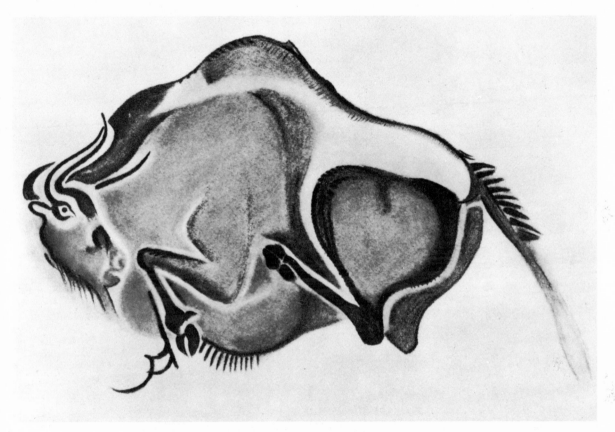

Crouching Bison Turning Its Head. Wall painting, Altamira, Spain. Painted at least 10,000 years ago in the Paleolithic or Old Stone Age, and painted with amazing observation of the form and action of animals.

Menkure and His Queen. Museum of Fine Arts, Boston. Builder of the third Pyramid of Giza, with his Queen, wonderfully preserved, and young and slim, as Egyptians wished to be presented.

2
The Dawn of Time

As a boy, I lived out West where the lone and level plains stretched on forever. Not far from town, flanked by a sluggish stream and rising sheer out of the buffalo grass, was a huge hill called Indian Mound because Indians, by the hundreds, were supposed to be buried within it. Bushels of arrowheads had been collected to support this notion. Privately, I called the hill the Pyramid of Giza. It was as high as that ancient Pyramid of Khufu by the Nile—some five hundred feet. And one side was sharp and grassless, as if the old Indians who moved the stones and earth across the river to build it, as the old Egyptians had floated their stones across the Nile, had not completed the job.

Often, at twilight, when the sun dropped suddenly into the prairies and the winds blew, I climbed the hill, and always I thought of the ancient Egyptians. They have never ceased to haunt and confuse and fascinate me. I used to see one of the Pharaohs against the setting sun, as he strode across the narrow valley of the Nile with his high priests, to worship in the temple; and I saw the Great Pyramid he had finished—his own tomb—to house his soul until it was escorted by Osiris into some flickering underworld where it would live to the end of time in the Pharaoh's own gaunt body.

The Egyptians lived, and still do, in the val-ley of the Nile, one of the longest rivers in the world. That is, they lived in the lower seven hundred miles of this river-basin—in a valley only a few miles wide, eroded by rains and cut by the river out of solid sandstone. Once a year, from July to October, after the rains had swollen the lakes feeding the Upper Nile, the river overflowed, and there was great rejoicing. For the floods enriched the valley with a deep bath of mud and made it blossom. Egypt, therefore, was a prosperous country, and when she had added to her wealth by foreign conquests and had imported captives as slave labor, she was the ruling nation of the world.

Living in a flat belt of land, with jagged stone walls on either side, the old architects realized when they began to build that nothing short of the grand and massive would make any impression.

Egypt's history, which is so long that it makes our American chronicle only a tick of the clock, is divided into thirty dynasties, named for the ruling families. These rulers, the old Pharaohs, were absolute monarchs. They could do as they pleased, so they seized the most fertile lands, built huge pyramids, temples, and statues, had the most luxurious pleasure boats on the river, and lived in handsome houses.

17

When the Pharaohs were rich and powerful, the arts flourished, and there are three such great periods: the Old Kingdom (Dynasties III to VI), which began about 3000 B.C.; the Middle Kingdom (Dynasties XI and XII); and the New Kingdom or Empire (Dynasties XVIII to XX), which came to an end in 1085 B.C. During the New Kingdom, Egypt controlled much of the Near East, but after that she was invaded by foreigners, and when Cleopatra was taken captive, the valley of the Nile became a Roman possession.

The Egyptians were a highly intelligent peo- ple and very attractive too, the men lean and strong, the women straight and slender. They lived cleanly, with a nice regard for the rights of others, and dressed simply in well-designed clothes—not much clothing since they lived in a tropical climate.

The houses of the rich were elaborate but in the best of taste. Their homes were villas with enclosing walls, swimming pools, and gardens set with cedars and fancy trees imported from Asia, trees being scarce along the Nile. The walls of the houses were composed of mats, or squares of papyrus, attached to strong posts

Hieroglyph. Metropolitan Museum of Art, New York. Figures used as hieroglyphs, when writing was in the form of pictures and symbols.

Prince as Scribe. Museum of Fine Arts, Boston. Portrait statue from about 2800 B.C., *the head of the prince powerful and realistic, the legs unfinished as in many statues.*

driven into the sand. The papyrus was a kind of reed which grew wild, twenty feet high, or more—an extremely valuable plant since it was used for making paper, small boats, and all sorts of light and strong fabrics. (Our word "paper" comes from the word "papyrus.") The interiors of the dwellings were decorated with woven stuffs like tapestry, or with glazed tiles showing the Pharaohs as they amused themselves by killing ducks, etc., or with paintings of the gods.

The Egyptians gave a great deal of attention to the idea of death; no other people ever went to such pains to avoid, or cheat, the act of dying. Other races talked about death, but the Egyptians proceeded to do something about it. The priests of the Nile manufactured a religious machine for the purpose of giving a man a ride into eternity after he had died, and they took pains that his body should not decay. The artists were endowed with the greatest subject of all—a man preparing to die or a man who, after death, was about to open the doors of heaven or hell.

The Egyptian religion was riddled with contradictions and forms of worship; it was a re-

Colossi of Ramses II. Egypt. Ramses II, in a row of colossal portraits, each 65 feet high, and adorning the front of an underground temple.

Ramses II. Metropolitan Museum of Art, New York. A Pharaoh dedicated to art and beauty, his refinement and intelligence shown in his features.

King Khafra. Cairo Museum. Perhaps the most majestic of Egyptian statues, a man of power and a ruler by divine right.

ligion of many gods. The supreme god was Amen-Ra, whose wife was Mut (mother). As the god of life or the creator, he was usually shown with the horns of a ram. He was also the sun god, and in that capacity he wore a headdress composed of a disk (the sun) with two tall ostrich plumes. The great temple at Karnak was built in his honor.

The most popular gods were the family of Osiris, his wife Isis, and their son Horus, names still used today in secret societies. Osiris presided over the underworld and, if sufficiently favored by sacrifices, would personally see to it that the spirit of the dead would return to the body, or mummy, and thus live forever in a state of bliss. His statues often show him in the wrappings of a mummy.

The Egyptians worshiped animals on a fantastic scale. Certain birds were sacred such as the hawk and the ibis, and certain animals— bulls, apes, cats, crocodiles, and hippopotamuses—and strange as it may seem, insects too were venerated, particularly the scarab, or dung beetle, which was preserved in wholesale lots. In religious ceremonies, the favored animals ranked about as high as the gods themselves. Bast was the cat goddess, sometimes portrayed with a cat's head on a woman's body. Near the town of Bubastis, this deity's special city, was a cat cemetery where hundreds of these sacred animals were embalmed and worshiped.

The boys and girls of Egypt, as a part of their education, were instructed in their deportment when death brought them to judgment. They were forced to memorize the *Book of the Dead,* a long roll of papyrus in hieroglyphs (picture writing) informing them of the etiquette of candidates who sooner or later must face the gods of the underworld.

In the making of mummies, the Egyptians have remained in a class by themselves. If the dead person were to avoid an endless excursion into the dim and lonely hereafter, with no body to occupy, his actual body, they thought, had to be preserved forever. The preserving process was painstaking, but so successful that Egyptian mummies still exist. The face was sometimes covered with a painted mask, and the finished mummy was placed in a wooden coffin sometimes carved into the human shape. If the family were rich enough, this was fitted into another coffin and finally sealed in a granite container (called a sarcophagus) for burial. The heart was put in a separate jar, sometimes shaped at the top like the person's head.

This was sealed away in the greatest tomb the family could afford, and with it a statue or two of the dead person and all the equipment and utensils he might need in the next life, including perhaps two "solar boats" for

Nakht Hunting. Thebes, Egypt. Detail from a wall painting. The prince and his family are on a hunting expedition.

his journey across heaven by day and through the underworld by night. In wealthy tombs, this equipment was a very rich treasure indeed and, in spite of all precautions, many of the tombs were robbed centuries ago. However, from a few unspoiled ones like that of "King Tut" (Tutankhamen) have been recovered the hundreds of lavish and beautiful art objects to be seen in the museums of the world today.

As if the actual equipment were not enough, the walls of the tombs were completely covered with paintings or with sculpture in low relief (that is, shallow carvings on a flat surface)—all designed to surround the new spirit with the same pleasures and comforts it had enjoyed on earth. The dead person himself was shown, often sitting before a table piled with food. A list of his titles and honors was included so that there could be no doubt as to who was buried here. With him were shown his family, his slaves, his cattle, his possessions, even scenes depicting the events of his life and his favorite activities and sports.

These scenes provide us with much of our knowledge about how the old Egyptians lived. Painted or carved in rows, one above the other, they are some of the most remarkable

Bronze Cat. Metropolitan Museum of Art, New York. The Egyptians embalmed and worshiped cats, and carved them with unsurpassed skill.

Pyramid of Giza. Giza, Egypt. Largest of the three great pyramids of Giza, in lower Egypt—480 feet high, and each of the sides at the base measuring 755 feet.

Musicians from Thebes. Copy of an encaustic wall painting, Metropolitan Museum of Art, New York. Wall painting of night life. The Egyptians loved the relaxing pleasures of music and dancing.

"action" pictures in the world. Sometimes we see a king in his chariot with his charger in a fury, as he cuts his enemy to pieces. Sometimes it is a hunter (the men of the Nile were insatiable hunters) in the reeds along the marshes, throwing a boomerang at a flock of ducks or a lance at wild bulls. And again it is only a row of geese, each one with more personality than a senator; or girls playing softball; or ladies of society attended by cupbearers and entertained by dancing girls and musicians in filmy costumes.

It was the custom of the artist, in relief carving, to set the head in profile with the eye drawn from a front view, and to pose the upper part of the body as facing the spectator, with the legs and feet in profile. This method was developed, not because the artist was unable to draw or because his vision was cockeyed, but to accentuate the most prominent parts of the body.

As you might have guessed from the ways of a people absorbed in thoughts of religion and death, the great architecture of Egypt was composed of tombs and temples. The first tombs of the Old Kingdom were mounds of earth reinforced by stones. These were followed by the mastabas, which were sloping structures of stone with flat tops like cut-off pyramids and with burial chambers under the earth; and lastly by the pyramids themselves, some of which exist today. Hundreds of pyramids arose in the Nile valley, comparatively small and crude for the most part; but as the Pharaohs grew more powerful and wealthy, the tombs correspondingly increased in size,

reaching a climax in the three great pyramids of Giza, near the city of Cairo in lower Egypt. The largest of these is the tomb of Khufu, originally 480 feet high (some of the stones at the apex were stolen later on) with each of the four sides, at the base, measuring 755 feet, and the ground area covering about thirteen acres. They are the oldest specimens of architecture on this earth.

The great pyramids are not only colossal by actual measurement—they look big, not bulging out unevenly like a fat man, but of one piece, and enormous and mighty like a giant. Their solidity makes a city skyscraper look like an impudent toothpick. And although they resemble the most primitive form of building, a pile of earth, they are marvels of engineering skill.

Blocks of stone weighing from two to fifty tons, millions of them, went into one tomb; and the outer blocks, having been smoothed

Temple of Amen-Ra, Karnak. Model, Metropolitan Museum of Art, New York. Largest of the Egyptian temples, with 134 columns 70 feet high, and an assembly hall 300 feet long.

Sphinx. Giza, Egypt. The Egyptian sphinx, a male hybrid with the head of a Pharaoh and the body of a lion, rose from the desert sands in gigantic form.

and measured at the quarries, took their places with minute accuracy. Armies of slaves dragged the huge stones up ramps of earth into position, and a Pharaoh was lucky if his tomb was ready for occupancy at his death. The pyramid was entered by an underground passage leading to a gallery and thence to the burial chambers of the king and queen. After burial, the passage was sealed by heavy pieces of stones. Connected with the pyramid by a long causeway, or sheltered road, was the tem-ple, with its corridors, chapels, and statues, where services were held before the mummy was conducted to its final nest in the deepest bosom of the pyramid itself.

The Old Kingdom was the age of the pyramid. In the Middle Kingdom and the Empire the temple came into prominence. Some of the temples were enormous, that of Karnak, for instance, with 134 columns, each seventy feet high, and an assembly hall three hundred feet long.

The most beautiful of all the temple-tombs was built by Queen Hatshepsut in a rocky background at the foot of the cliffs bordering the Nile valley. The floors of this temple were on different levels, with vast colonnades, and water was sucked up from the Nile to nourish the gardens with their imported trees. The corridors were lined with statues and the walls decorated with the activities of the famous

Queen Nefertiti. Berlin Museum. Described down the ages as the most beautiful woman of all time. The head is painted in flesh colors, the eyes are of rock crystal.

Hatshepsut. Metropolitan Museum of Art, New York. A Queen who dressed in shorts, often wore a false beard, and worked the builders of her temple to death.

queen. And she was truly a character. She dressed in a man's shorts, wore a false beard strapped to her chin, and worked her architects and builders to death.

Ancient Egypt was the cradle of sculpture, but if you had lived in Egypt and had walked slowly through Thebes or Memphis or the little towns, you could not have discovered a public monument—not one. The statues were stationed in tombs and temples and, sometimes, if a man could afford one, in the home, as a precaution, or spare, should the image in the tomb be stolen.

When I first saw Egyptian sculpture, I was astonished at the perfection of the carving, and I did not find the images strange or unfriendly—not even the sphinx, a hybrid with the head of a man (usually a king) on the body

Ashurbanipal Hunting. British Museum, London. Marvelous rendering of action in stone, the King with drawn bow, leading the pursuit of gazelles and lions.

The Pharaoh was carved to give the impression that he was every inch a king; Khafra, for example, dating from 2000 B.C., looks grim and indomitable and ready to cope with time and eternity. The kings and leaders were portrayed in wigs (in real life, wigs were worn as protection against the sun) and in loincloths deftly pleated.

To make the heads of their carvings more real, they painted them—the hair black, the lips rouged, the faces tanned to a sunburn—and the eyes were balls of painted crystal set in copper sockets. The heads of such statues were constructed with the utmost care and polished to perfection, the trunks and arms were usually chiseled out carefully, but the legs and feet were often unfinished—as if not so important. The beards of the Pharaohs look as if they were strapped to the chin, and, as a matter of fact, a great artificial beard was a symbol of high rank.

The finest sculpture was done in the Old Kingdom when the power of religious faith was highest, but during most of her long history, Egypt continued to produce sculpture that holds its rank among the best things ever done in this medium. In the Middle and New

of a lion. They seemed to me to express the wonder and the brooding and the mystery that I had experienced as a boy on the plains. The old statues of stiffly sitting Pharaohs, the heads so strong and real that they almost scare you, the queens so young and noble and slender—these come to life from the granite.

If you really believed that your salvation depended on an eternal image of yourself in stone, the chances are that you would, in the course of time, find a way to make one. After a thousand years or so of trial and error, the artists of the Nile valley figured out certain poses that never looked trivial or old-fashioned, and they learned how to carve a head that would always appear calm and profound and powerful. Thus the trunks of the seated figures are arrow-straight, with the legs at right angles; and in the standing figures, the body is erect and commanding, with the left foot always slightly forward. These postures became models, or conventions, and were used throughout the various dynasties.

Hating the very thought of growing old and feeble, the Egyptians never made a statue of an old man or woman, and never a fat one.

Dying Lioness. British Museum, London. The Assyrians carved animals howling in pain, with broken legs and blood spurting from arrow wounds.

Kingdoms the heads of the rulers are less powerful and awe-inspiring, but they are closer as portrait studies and the features are more detailed. The statue of Ramses II, one of Egypt's most splendid monarchs, is a work of almost unmatched genius, presenting to mankind the dignity and courage of a fighting ruler who admired art and culture. The heads of Queen Nefertiti, particularly the one in Berlin, leave no doubt that she was, as many authorities have written, one of the most beautiful women in all history. As the power of Egypt waned, her art declined with it, but even in the later periods under the Ptolemies, her skill in portrait sculpture was outstanding, notably in heads for mummy cases.

As supreme masters of sculpture, the Egyptians erected sphinxes as tall as pyramids and seventy-foot monuments of kings and deities for the fronts of their temples, and, on the other hand, they cut the most delicate reliefs in stone panels—figures slightly raised from the background and then painted. They also molded and glazed pottery with consummate skill, inventing a gorgeous blue glaze that remains unrivaled. They were fine jewelers, and their geometrical designs for textiles are imitated today by fashion artists.

Across the Red Sea from Egypt, east of the present republic of Israel, lies the kingdom of Iraq. The old Greeks named this valley Mesopotamia, or "the land between the rivers," the Tigris to the east, the Euphrates to the west.

By 3000 B.C. (the beginning of the Old Kingdom in Egypt) the people in this valley were already living in cities and producing works of art. They had one great disadvantage, however. They had neither wood nor stone to build with. They devised a method of making brick from clay, and of glazing the brick with beautiful colors to make a decorated outside layer on the buildings. But the clay crumbled easily with time. In Egypt the great pyramids still stand, but in Mesopotamia we must dig in clay mounds found here and there in the wilderness to discover what the old culture was like.

Babylon in the Reign of Nebuchadnezzar. Painting, Oriental Institute of the University of Chicago. Imaginary view of the city in about 650 B.C., with the ziggurats, or set-back towers, studied by American builders.

The early people in the lower valley were called Sumerians. They devised a method of writing known as "cuneiform," consisting of wedge-shaped characters which they stamped on tablets of baked clay. They accumulated a library of laws and moral warnings, and were phenomenal scientists and mathematicians, inventing the decimal system and the march of time as led by the sun, and foretelling by calculation the appearance of eclipses and even political events. The most impressive statues belong to this period; the Sumerians put together shocking heads with narrow brows, huge eyeballs, and gigantic noses.

But we are more familiar with the later people—the Assyrians in the northern part of the valley and the Babylonians in the south. These people seemed to be always fighting. The Assyrians won out about 1100 B.C. and in the seventh century, B.C. had a powerful kingdom stretching far beyond the valley, with the capital at Nineveh. In the sixth century, B.C. the Babylonians conquered again, and they rebuilt their capital, Babylon, on a magnificent scale; old engineering projects were revived, and works of art were lavishly produced until the Persians moved in about 539 B.C. and closed the history of their foes, once for all.

The Babylonians built palaces and temples and Hanging Gardens which the Greeks included among the seven wonders of the world. These gardens were extraordinarily luxurious —terrace upon terrace on artificial hills, joined by winding stairs and aisles deep enough for three chariots abreast. Lofty towers were placed at intervals and sculptured portals decorated with colossal figures in white alabaster, the forms of men and winged beasts. Upward, piercing the heavens, were colonnades—costly pillars of cedar, cornices of gold and vermilion—and between the columns were curtains of silk, purple, and scarlet shot through with strands of gold. Babylon became the symbol of splendor and wickedness.

The art of this region was devised primarily in the service of the kings. Where the Egyptians had combined the temple with tombs, the Mesopotamians combined it with the palace, and sometimes with fortifications as well. The temple tower, called a "ziggurat," was built in set-backs like many skyscrapers of today; each layer is said to have been a different color, increasing in brilliance to the summit where the sanctuaries of the high gods, purified by fires constantly burning, were open to the king and his spiritual advisers. At the burial of a king, his widow and relatives followed him to the grave and drank poison in order to join him somewhere in space.

The greater artists of the valley between the

Ashurnasirpal. British Museum, London. One of the few examples of Mesopotamian sculpture in the round, stiff as a post but formidable and impressive.

rivers were the Assyrians; they were large-scale builders who made use of arches and vaults, adorned their palaces and towers with sculpture and friezes of glazed tile, and created in stone undying evidence of their monstrous imagination and love of cruelty. They were the cruelest of the ancient peoples, always drawing blood, and most of their plastic art relates to killing or to the causes of death. As an illustration, there is a panel showing a king and queen at table—very homelike and inviting, with viands and clusters of grapes and wine—but on a trellis close by hangs the severed head of the king's enemy, recently slain and dripping blood.

In relief sculpture the Assyrians created unique images and patterns and animal forms to show the swiftness, the power, and the cruelty of the rulers. This art contains no great portraits, as does Egyptian art, and no ideal figures, as does the art of Greece. But its animals and monsters stand alone, in a strange and forbidding field of art into which none but the fearless may enter.

Winged Bull. Metropolitan Museum of Art, New York. Winged monster with a man's head and the body of a bull, and five legs, four in profile and the fifth visible from the narrow front.

Venus of Milo. Louvre, Paris. Most beloved of all statues, this large-bodied goddess of love has become accepted as the symbol of the nobility, composure, and purity of womanhood.

3
The Glory that Was Greece

Ancient Greece, without her colonies, was not much larger than the Greece of today—about the size of Scotland; yet from this scrawny patch of earth arose some of the most distinguished human beings thus far to adorn our planet. The poet Shelley once exclaimed, "We are all Greeks! The framework of our ways of teaching, our athletics, sciences, poetry, philosophy, politics, and above all, our arts, these were the work of a handful of blond democrats living in or near the city of Athens!"

The mainland of Greece was, and is, a mountainous country with a jagged coastline, and a great gulf separating Athens from Sparta. There were mountains everywhere, no rivers to amount to anything, very thin soil, and a short list of crops—grapes, olives, some grains. There were currants for marmalade and goats for cheese; and, important for our book, quarries of beautiful marble and ideal sites for temples and statues of the gods. The sea was within reach of everyone, and an athletic god, like Apollo, with a sudden hop could land in Italy, or with a skip and a jump, in Troy-town, in Asia Minor. Naturally then, the Greeks went to sea and returned with sculptures from Egypt in their galleys and winged monsters from the land between the Asiatic rivers. You may have read in Homer how, all because a woman named Helen had been kidnaped, they launched a thousand ships and burnt "the topless towers of Ilium."

The old Greeks were a wonderful race, reasonable and sensitive in high degree; and they believed that the arts were bestowed on them from heaven for the glory of the gods favoring them and for the enrichment of their daily lives. In every branch of human activity—from the preparation of food to the preparation of war, from the adornment of the body to the adornment of their cities and shrines—they were unexcelled. Their sculpture and architecture are the closest to perfection that man has attained, and that is not all—they designed exquisite necklaces and helmets that put those of our soldiers to shame. They remain the most artistic people in the history of mankind.

In matters outside the arts, the Greeks were not always noble. Indeed, they were capable of acts of barbarism and practices hardly less than repellent. They did not believe that work was especially meritorious—they thought it better to have someone else do it for you, a slave, if possible. What we call the rights of the common man they disregarded. They controlled the increase in population by exposing infants on mountain tops to the vultures, and saw nothing wrong in suicide. They served a sort of cocktail called the hemlock, a deadly

31

Parthenon. Athens. Built from 447 to 431 B.C. *under the direction of Phidias, and partly destroyed in 1687 by an explosion. The view shows the Doric columns and remnants of the metopes and triglyphs above them.*

potion, to philosophers judged dangerous or subversive. They had a low opinion of women, confining them, as a rule, to the kitchen, and dressing them alike in pleated, though beautiful, robes. Family life, in the modern sense, was unknown, and children were bundled off to public nurseries to be educated by the state.

As in Egypt and Mesopotamia, virtually all works of art were produced in the service of religion. But in contrast to the solemn and immensely fearsome gods of the Nile, those of Greece were glorified men and women, superior to ordinary mortals in physical beauty and cunning, sometimes very noble, but always human and not always without deceits and trickeries. The temples of Greece were shrines dedicated to this deity or that; the statues were carved as symbols of the ideal beauty, divine power, or wisdom of the gods; and domestic articles such as spoons, vases, mirrors, and chairs were ornamented with figures of Athena or Zeus or some other resident of Mount Olympus.

The names of the top-flight Greek deities are known the world around, but here are a few, in case you have forgotten your history: Aphrodite (or Venus, as she was called in Roman mythology), goddess of beauty and love; Apollo, god of music, athletics, and the chase; Ares (or Mars), god of war; Artemis (or Diana), the huntress and goddess of marriage; Athena, goddess of wisdom, and the arts of war and peace; Demeter and Persephone, mother and daughter, goddesses of the harvest; Dionysus (or Bacchus), god of wine and the drama; Hephaestus, sacred to mechanics; Hermes, the messenger; Pan, a minor god, but very popular as lord of the woodland; Pluto, ruler of the underworld; Poseidon, god of the sea and of rivers; and the father of the celestial crew, old Zeus, the hurler of thunderbolts.

In the morning hours of history, certain Greeks on the island of Crete produced a civilization of extraordinary refinement, a luxurious mode of living with vast palaces, bathrooms equipped with hot and cold running water and flush toilets, gambling rooms decorated with frescoes of ox-eyed girls serving drinks to trim matadors who had killed unbelievably long and snorting bulls. At a later date, about 1500 B.C., the Spartans built temples with sculptured walls and gates. The classic Greeks traced their artistic ancestry back to prehistoric times, and many cultures mingled and made war and peace to arrive at the final glory of the Greek genius.

In the field of architecture, the Greeks did not direct their best energies into the building of homes and shops. Their houses were unattractive shelters—little better than stuccoed boxes concealing a back yard, or patio—and their commercial buildings were not much more impressive. They ruled out of art everything even remotely related to buying and selling, and an artist guilty of introducing politics or propaganda into his work was summarily dosed with hemlock. True art was created in the name of the immortal gods and for the exaltation of the human soul.

The Greeks were acquainted with the arch and the dome, but they did not seem to consider such devices necessary. They used walls, columns, and a low-pitched gable roof—nothing more. The three orders of Greek architecture are universally known, the character and dimensions of each being regulated by the style of the column: the Doric with the simple cushion for the capital, which is that part of the shaft next to the lintel; the Ionic, with the double scroll, or volutes, at the top; and the Corinthian, distinguished by its sprouting of chicory leaves at the capital.

In the fifth century, B.C., the whole area was Greek, from the homeland—the marble-topped island in the Mediterranean frog-pond —to Italy on the one hand and the Asiatic coast on the other. When the Persians, under Xerxes, razed the city of Athens, the Greeks began courageously to rebuild it; and under the leadership of Pericles, they voted to restore the Acropolis, the highest part of the city. There they erected the Parthenon, the temple sacred to Athena, often cited as the only perfect work of architecture erected by the genius of man.

The Parthenon is generally believed to have been designed by Phidias, pre-eminent among Greek architects and sculptors, and director-general of the program to restore the Acropolis. The fame of Phidias, unfortunately, rests largely upon the word of the Greeks, since not one original statue once accepted as his work has come down to us; his monumental figures, the pride of his countrymen, are known today only in small copies. We feel sure that he reconstructed the Acropolis by ransacking the treasuries of the Athenians and dependent is-

Parthenon. Restored model, Metropolitan Museum of Art, New York. The perfect building in proportion, design, workmanship, and mural sculpture. The columns were tinted in golden browns, and all the sculptures were colored.

lands. If we make a guess at the value of ancient money in modern terms, we might estimate that the Parthenon cost $4,500,000, and the gold-and-ivory statue of Athena by Phidias, in the front chamber, $6,000,000; that the total restoration of the hilltop cost $58,000,000, and that 90 per cent or more of the national

Maenad Leaning on Her Thyrsus. Roman copy of a Greek relief, Metropolitan Museum of Art, New York. Nymph, of the cult of Bacchus, holding the thyrsus, or staff of the god of wine. The exquisite carving of the drapery was greatly admired by the classical French sculptors.

Girl with Pigeons. Metropolitan Museum of Art, New York. Tablet, or stele, used as a gravestone. The profile, the simply designed birds, and the girl's serenity are in the purest Greek style.

income was earmarked for works of art! This would be inconceivable in the United States today.

In its final development, the temple was a rectangular structure, surrounded by a double row of Doric columns, a portico at front and back, and a colonnade on either side. In the front chamber, or *cella*, the cult statue of

Horsemen, from the Parthenon frieze. British Museum, London. Small animals as shapely as goddesses, carved in low relief, or two and one-half inches from the background.

Athena was placed, and in the back room the sacred treasures were assembled. The rites of worship and the cooking of sacrificial animals were performed outside to safeguard the spotless interior from cooking grease and body odors.

The building was composed entirely of marble, even to the hand-carved, translucent tiles on the roof. For twenty years the slaves of Phidias quarried the sides of Mount Pentelicus, for the superfine marble that went into the Parthenon—pure white marble slightly warmed by golden oxides. All the blocks of the walls were so precisely hewn and polished and fitted, one with another, that no mortar was used to hold them fast. This masterpiece of building was 228 feet by 101, and 65 feet high, and the proportions of the columns, the walls, and, in fact, of every bit of marble, out-side or in, were taken into account for the sake of the beauty and harmony of the whole structure.

In the gable ends of the Parthenon were statues referring to the birth and career of Athena; and in the *metopes,* or square blocks above the walls, the Centaurs and Lapiths were represented in dramatic conflicts. Under the eaves ran a frieze, or ornamental strip, 525 feet in length, a carving in low relief of warriors on horseback, humble folk on foot, girls carrying olive branches and other objects, and sad old men holding jars of liniment, all moving to the altar sacred to Athena. In this procession, running around the temple, were perhaps the choicest creations of all, the small-size horses, tense and alive, rearing and charging, horses of breath-taking beauty, with personality and fire in their nostrils, as smooth

The Fates, from the Parthenon. British Museum, London. Removed to London in the nineteenth century against the poetic wrath of Lord Byron. The rippling drapery and beautiful carving explain "the glory that was Greece."

It is one of the major tragedies of history that so much of Greek art has disappeared—the existing temples are in ruins; no trace of the super-statues of Phidias is to be found; and the bulk of the smaller statues is known to us only in copies by the later Greeks and Romans, though fortunately many of them are wonderful copies.

The Greeks had mastered the working of metals as early as 2000 B.C. and of casting figures in bronze at the same time. Along with these, they loved to model little figures in bright red clay, and to keep them on the mantel as tributes to the household gods. Their crowning achievements were in marble,

and shapely as the goddesses—and carved only two and one-half inches deep on the marble slabs.

The Parthenon is a simple work, as fundamental as the sea, and not much different in plan from the log cabin in which Abraham Lincoln was born. But every year, modern builders, engineers, and artists discuss the beautiful proportions of the temple and delve into the secrets of its perfection.

The building stood on a hilltop, and to appreciate its full splendor we must keep in mind the fact that much of it was colored. The white walls were untouched, but the columns were faintly washed with brown wax; the gable ends were painted blue; and the statues were colored to counteract the deathly tombstone look of the raw marble. What a sight the Hermes by Praxiteles must have been, standing in the sunlight on a pedestal of the Acropolis! The body was waxed into a sun-tan; the eyebrows were blue, the lips scarlet, the hair bright red dusted with gold!

But, alas, the Parthenon was used as a powder magazine by the Turks in 1687 and almost ruined by an exploding shell. In 1802, Lord Elgin, an English millionaire, acquired the remaining statues and presented them to the British Museum, an act which inflamed Lord Byron to furious poetic curses.

Wounded Amazon. Metropolitan Museum of Art, New York. The Amazons, mythical antagonists of the Greeks, were women warriors with the strength of athletes and the beauty of goddesses.

Birth of Aphrodite. Museo delle Terme, Rome. Central figures of the Ludovisi Throne—the goddess of love rising from the waves into the arms of her handmaidens.

Praxiteles. *Torso of Hermes. Olympia Museum, Greece. Softly contoured to give the illusion of living flesh. The only extant Greek statue unreservedly assigned to a specific Greek artist.*

the carving of which, after two centuries or more, approached their standards of perfection. The artists studied the human body closely and observed the ripple of muscles in action; they studied the athletes in the Olympic games—the first contests were held in 776 B.C.—and caught the rhythm of the human body as it raced, swam, boxed, or was poised to throw the discus. From the end of the seventh century, B.C., to the close of the fifth, a flawless array of figures in marble came to life. Cold stone yielded up the illusion of living flesh, of bodies serene and noble—some of

Old Market Woman. Metropolitan Museum of Art, New York. After carving goddesses, the Greeks began to depict everyday people. Here, an old crone returning from town with fruit and chickens.

Zeus and the Giants, from Pergamum. Berlin. Detail of a combat between gods and giants, Zeus and Athena participating, a ferocious encounter with the gods as terrible foot soldiers.

them majestic giants such as the Zeus and Apollo of Olympia. In all these, the artists avoided as a plague all that was violent, or forced, or eccentric—always keeping in mind an ideal form toward which their best brains were advancing.

In the fifth century, B.C., the Greeks, all things considered, produced the greatest sculptors the world has seen, only one man of different stock measuring up to them, Michelangelo the Florentine. On the temples (or, more exactly, as a part of the temples) on the Acropolis, on other hilltops and sacred groves near the sea, at the Temple of Zeus in Olympia, with its austere nine-foot statues of Zeus and Apollo so placed as to be seen from the ground level 60 feet below, they created sculptures for future generations of artists to emulate.

The "big three" among the sculptors were Polyclitus, a marvelous technician who composed his bronze athletes by a scheme of mathematical ratios; Myron, renowned for fig-

ures in action; and Phidias, already named, the builder of colossal figures in gold and ivory.

The Egyptians, as we have seen, produced portrait figures of unrivaled grandeur; the Assyrians gave us religious symbols in the form of fantastic monsters; but it remained to the Greeks to cultivate the beautiful and to create figures to satisfy, in the mind of the artist, a notion of the ideal. Though working from living models, they were religious men seeking the expression of ideal beauty—a figure flawlessly proportioned, a face exalted and serene, a profile worthy of a goddess—now called the "classic profile." You know it well from the *Venus of Milo,* the most beloved statue in the world.

After the fall of Athens, in the third century, B.C., the continuation of Greek art was transferred to Egypt, to Antioch in Syria, and to Pergamum near Smyrna. The glory that was Greece spread from kingdom to kingdom and was, in the course of time, imitated and altered by the Roman conquerors. The final flowering is labeled the Hellenistic period, which, in contrast to the Olympian calm of the classic days, is riotous with physical energy and violence.

The finest sculpture of the Hellenistic age comes from Pergamum, where, about 160 B.C., King Eumenes II caused a stupendous monument to be built on a hillside to celebrate his military successes. This great white altar was painstakingly removed by German archeologists to Berlin, its present home. Below the platform of the altar ran an unbroken frieze, 400 feet long by 7 feet high. The frieze was carved into a furious combat to which the Germans gave the awful name of *gigantomachia,* or battle between gods and giants; it shows high gods and second-team gods arrayed against superhuman warriors, strange shapes of man and beast combined, and fighting dogs thrown into the tussle. It is sculpture that writhes and bleeds and howls with rage.

The famous *Laocoön,* now in the Vatican, was the work of three sculptors in the first century, B.C., and greatly admired by Michelangelo. Laocoön was the Trojan priest who, when the wooden horse was propelled to the gates of Ilium, remarked that he feared the Greeks even when bringing gifts. At this, Athena, a champion of the Greeks, lost her self-control and dispatched two serpents to kill the priest. The Vatican group represents the man with his two sons in their death struggle against the snakes.

Greek painting of the classic period must be accepted on faith alone. Not a single sample of the leading masters has been preserved —only a few legends connected with names which were placed as high on the roster of art as those of the sculptors. We have the tale of Zeuxis, a showy fellow who made a fortune in painting, and his rival, Parrhasius, who also had a talent for publicity. Parrhasius delineated an Olympic runner so convincingly that the spectators saw the sweat oozing from his painted pores; and Zeuxis, not to be outdone, painted a bunch of grapes so true to nature

that a pair of swallows darted into the roofless exhibition room and pecked at the fruit. And we are told that Apelles, because of his picture, *Aphrodite Rising from the Sea,* was applauded as genuinely as the masters of sculpture.

Painting in Greece reached its peak in the fourth and third centuries, B.C.—in wall decorations revealed to us by Roman copies. A copy in mosaic of a fourth-century fresco in which Darius is routed by Alexander at the *Battle of Issus,* is an action picture of the first magnitude—and a large-size hint of the ability of artists in the classic days. The best surviving fresco, the *Aldobrandini Wedding,* shows a semi-religious ceremony with the usual hocus-pocus supposed to indicate divine mysteries. The work was painted about the time of the birth of Christ and has captivated classic Frenchmen like Poussin as well as modernists

Laocoön. Vatican, Rome. The old Trojan priest and his sons, condemned to death by Athena, champion of the Greeks, are in a convulsive struggle with the serpents, the messengers of destruction.

Lady Playing the Cithara. Wall painting, Metropolitan Museum of Art, New York. Greco-Roman wall painting from Pompeii in the first century B.C. *has the closely observed figures and the illusion of depth centuries ahead of early Italian murals.*

The objects shaped and ornamented by the Greeks were a part of the routine life of the people: vases to hold fruits and flowers, decanters for wine, storage jars for olive oil, table china, and sacred utensils of many varieties, decorated with religious subjects. Associated with pottery, which is usually called a "minor art," were innumerable objects in metal—masks, cups, daggers, and armor—all fashioned with exquisite handicraft—and household appliances such as mirrors, goblets, lamps, and candlesticks, made holy, as well as useful, by free designs from the doings of the gods above.

There is no end to the artistry of the

like Picasso because of its severe, geometrical style.

In a branch of art which used both pictures and ornamental patterns, the Greeks were supreme—in pottery and vase-painting. Here we are not obliged to take the word of the Greeks for it—we have in the museums thousands and tens of thousands of examples, many of them as fresh and fine as the day they were lifted from the kilns. The first examples go back to the luxury-loving Cretans, about 2500 B.C., who fancied huge urns and vases of every size and capacity, and decorated them with circles, segments, and sharp lines darting here and there.

For a full century, from 600 to 500 B.C., the old potters worked in the black-figure style; that is, with dark figures against a red background, and after that in the reverse style, or red figures against a black surface; and finally, in the most beautiful designs ever traced on clay, in dark outlines on a snow-white background.

Prize Fighter. National Museum, Rome. Bronze figure from about 50 B.C. *The muscular torso and the cauliflower ear are age-long attributes of boxers.*

rippling down to the feet. And the Amazon warriors, the followers of Diana, and a few prize-winners wore the loveliest of all garments —the brief, pleated tunic, seen today over a pair of trunks on young figure skaters.

Bronze Hydria (water jar). Metropolitan Museum of Art, New York. The kitchen utensils of the Greeks were works of art, faultless in proportion and discreetly ornamented.

Greeks: their jewelry, for example, was almost the last word in refinement and craftsmanship; and their coins, bearing, for example, the heads of Zeus or Athena, or showing some nymph and satyr, were as carefully prepared in a small way as the friezes of the Parthenon. Though women were kept in their place, they knew how to dress. For plain women, there were plain garments girdled and good to see; for favored women, a kind of tunic draped across the bust, drawn in at the waist, and

Black-figured Amphora. Metropolitan Museum of Art, New York. The making of pottery was a national industry in Greece, with dark figures used against a white ground, as in this amphora, or the opposite. The decorations were taken from the legends of the gods, and thus religion came into every home.

Colosseum. Rome. The sports palace of the Romans, and the model of the stadium as developed by American universities.

Arch of Constantine. Rome. The most imposing of the triumphal arches erected by the Romans to frame the parade of the conquering legions.

4
Roman Grandeur

You can say, "he works like a Trojan," and that's a compliment; you can tell her she "has a Grecian profile," and that's a form of flattery; but there is another metaphor which, if properly used as it was recently used with reference to Sir Winston Churchill, says even more with so little. The figure of speech is, "He's an old Roman," and there is no need to explain it. The old Romans were proud and resolute and strong, and to their basic virtues they added their powers of organization, their vision of a world empire, and their genius for building on the foundations of grandeur.

The Romans began to build almost as soon as the founders of their capital, as the story goes, were suckled by wolves: first, their homes; next, the cities they had sacked in conquest; and thirdly, the foreign states they captured, one by one—the city-states of colonial Greece in the Mediterranean Sea. After Greece fell apart, the Romans took over, and the whole of their known world—with half-known regions in what is now England, and in Gaul which was "divided into three parts" —was under the dominion of the great city on the seven hills.

The Roman Empire was not built in a day, a year, or a century. Long before its rise, an area in central Italy (now Tuscany, the cradle of western painting) had been settled by peo-

ple we call Etruscans. The Etruscans came there, or some of them anyway, we think, from Asia Minor, bringing a culture of their own. They produced beautiful works of art, especially in bronze, which were later collected and highly prized by some of the Romans themselves. The Etruscans welcomed newcomers and new ideas and, inspired by the talents of Greek refugees, began to produce art objects for the export trade, pottery, in particular. Into the settlement of Etruscans came the tribes from the Tiber River, at Roma, and the mixture tempered the Roman thirst for conquest with the Etruscan thirst for art.

As Rome established herself as the center of civilization, it became clear that her destiny in the arts was to be realistic in sculpture and utilitarian in architecture, as she had been imperialistic in government. With the collapse of Greece, artists and scholars fled thither and yon, and the Romans, offering money and jobs, attracted Greeks by the thousands. As a consequence, Roman sculpture and architecture were partly shaped by Grecian influences. But the old Romans were not just a collection of militaristic bullies who bowed low before the superior artists of Greece. From the outset, the Romans held sane ideas about art, and proceeded to test them in practice, their most impressive contributions being

43

Pantheon, Rome. Reconstructed model, Metropolitan Museum of Art, New York. The Greek temple, as the Romans worked on it, with the addition of a dome, an extra story, and many statues.

in architecture. Here they labored and created on a Gargantuan scale, blending utility with beauty, and practicality with mass-production —always guided by a stern sense of design.

The Romans are frequently called the "Americans" of the ancient world, but it would be more accurate to say that the Americans are the disciples of the Romans; our commercial structures, our college stadiums, railway stations, apartment houses, and water and sanitation systems are descended from the examples set by the men of Rome.

The Romans were the first to use concrete in large amounts. The patient, block-polishing Greeks had fitted one stone with another, but the Romans had only to dump concrete over rubble and dress the surfaces with marble or granite. The monumental constructions of the Roman Empire are familiar to all of us: the basilicas, or halls of justice; the temples, such as the Pantheon, the shrine of all the gods;

miles and miles of aqueducts, built of arches standing upon arches, with a pipe line on the top to bring fresh water to the hot populace; colosseums for prize fights and spectacles; elaborate tombs, villas, and bathhouses surpassing in size and equipment anything before or since. One of the largest bathhouses had accommodations for 3,500 unwashed Romans, with steam rooms, massaging decks, swimming pools, and loafing salons—with central heating throughout and sanitation that might have been (and probably was) advertised as "completely modern."

Roman architecture was a development of the Grecian post and lintel, that is, upright supports for a crosspiece. With this primary setup to build on, the men of the seven hills adapted spacious domes from the Eastern Empire, arched or vaulted ceilings, and a rather garish use of ornament which the Greeks would not have allowed. The old Romans had a sense of grandeur which carried them into engineering achievements matched only by the inventions of modern science. In order to hold up the 135-foot dome of the Pantheon, they built walls 20 feet thick; in faraway Spain, a colony, they reared an aqueduct over and through a mountain range; and their paved roads into the northern wildernesses are traveled today by Fords and Fiats and Jaguars. Such achievements were not exactly beautiful according to Grecian standards of modesty and perfection, but they affirmed another kind of beauty—the massive and practical, faultlessly controlled by the needs or functions of people. The fine old Pennsylvania Station in New York City, solid and sooty, is modeled on a Roman bathhouse; and the stadiums attached to our athletic fields, the oval bowls, and horseshoes are modeled on Roman amphitheaters.

Central hall, Baths of Caracalla. Rome. The remains of the vast domed rotunda, the meeting place of the Romans after they had luxuriously bathed in adjoining pools.

Pont du Gard. Nîmes, France. Arch upon arch, 160 feet above the ground, the old Romans provided a colonial pipe line for fresh water.

Augustus Caesar, from the Prima Porta. Vatican, Rome. Covered with decorations, lofty and self-contained, the Emperor assures his troops that he is one of the immortals.

tion than we find in the old lower East Side of New York, or the Latin Quarter of Paris, where often a bathroom is still a luxury.

The Romans were great organizers of art, great practical builders, as they were also eminent politicians and lawyers and tough-minded rulers who held together the mutually hostile states of the world for a long time. They were also great sculptors, but, as you have guessed, not in the Greek style, a fact that has impelled Grecomaniacs to underestimate them. When I was very young, with a lady-tutor in Greek to ensnare me, I was taught to believe that the Athenians were divine artists but that the Romans were merely competent, unimaginative hewers of stone. True indeed, they never approached the Greeks in ideal, or spiritual creations; but they have left us, by and large, the most firmly built and masculine portrait statues in the eternal

The domestic architecture of the Romans was far superior to that of the Greeks, or any other ancient people. Like the Americans, who hark back to them in so many ways, they loved apartment houses, both in town and country, with rows of two- or three- or four-room suites, advertised by the real estate brokers as offering all the latest conveniences—split-level floors, playrooms, cocktail bars, breakfast nooks, sun parlors, garbage-disposal units, and, for those who could afford it, courtyards for badminton, playgrounds for children, and swimming pools for commuters. Even the poorest of clerks had warmth and comfort, though the slaves lived in cells, or cubicles, without windows. The poorer classes had more comforts and better sanita-

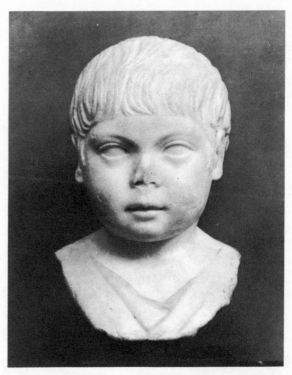

Portrait of a Child. Museum of Fine Arts, Boston. The Romans portrayed children with understanding and affection, simply and fondly, but without false sentiment.

Caracalla. Metropolitan Museum of Art, New York. The marble face comes to life in masterly style, hard and truthfully observed with no condescending graces.

gallery of art. They were realists, not like the Egyptians, always striving to make a god out of a Pharaoh without sacrificing his handsome personal appearance—but to carve an everlasting memorial to a leader, every inch a man, short-haired and intelligent, strong-featured, strong of body, and clad in the trappings of a hero. They devised appropriate ornaments for their temples, and with the common sense that set them apart, left their purely practical buildings sparsely decorated. In one department of sculpture they easily outclassed the Greeks: in the heads of children. The Roman artists seemed to love and understand children, while the Greeks, for reasons unknown to me, kept the moppets out of art, as they kept them off the streets.

Much of the painting in the Roman Empire was so completely Greek in style (or even executed by imported Greek artists) that it is called Greco-Roman; it is actually Greek painting done on Roman soil. However, as time went on, foreign styles were digested and some completely Roman ideas emerged, to form what is known as Roman painting. The best records we have of ancient painting are those preserved in the towns covered by lava in 79 A.D., the year Mount Vesuvius literally blew its top and suffocated three adjoining cities. In Pompeii and Herculaneum, fifteen miles from Naples, were unearthed some very celebrated wall paintings in excellent condition—paintings which mark the close of an ancient civilization and the upsurge of a new order of things. In Herculaneum are excellent murals of mythological scenes. The notorious wall paintings of Pompeii are in a style which went out of fashion with the decline of Rome. Many of them represent scenes which, in modern society, would not pass police inspection. It should be noted, however, that in technical skill, these paintings are far from elementary in use of light and shade and perspective.

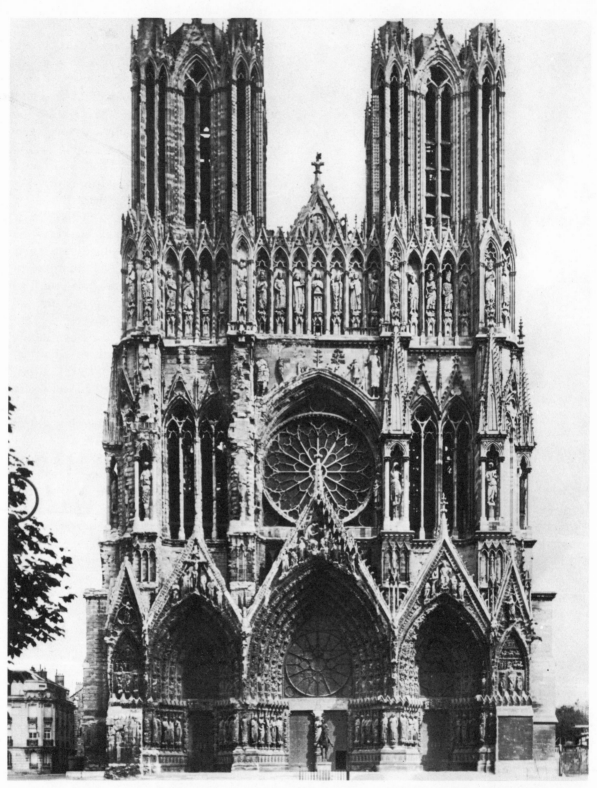

Façade, Cathedral of Notre-Dame, Reims, France. The Gothic church façade with pointed arches, spires, rose window, deep portals, and elaborate sculptural ornament.

PLATE 3. SANDRO BOTTICELLI. *The Birth of Venus*. UFFIZI, FLORENCE

PLATE 4. PIERO DELLA FRANCESCA. *The Battle of Constantine*. CHURCH OF SAN FRANCESCO, AREZ

5

Between the Dark and the Daylight

As the grandeur of Rome faded and fell and the pagan emperors strove to save their washed-up gods by forbidding the worship of the Lord Jesus, the followers of Christ went underground—literally. To escape persecution, they descended into the Catacombs, or abandoned quarries, and in these dank tunnels gave their dead a Christian burial, celebrated the forbidden Mass, and joined together, hand and soul, to preach in secret the new Gospel. In the consecration of their faith, they turned to art; and on the stuccoed walls of the caverns made pictures and carvings in very low relief. They were opposed to statuary as something too close to the popular pagan art, but they accepted painting as a helpful way of underlining the teachings of Christ.

They had no imagery of their own. I mean they had no figures, or forms, which could be instantly recognized as symbols of their faith; and so they adopted many figures straight out of the Greco-Roman myths. Thus we have, in the first four centuries, A.D., a style called Christian art, although the term should be extended to include all religious art from the Catacombs, through the victory of Constantine the Great, to the end of the Renaissance. In the first centuries of Christian art, old forms and motifs and serviceable pagan gods were collected and revamped to serve the Christian Gospel.

Much of the Catacomb painting belongs to the kindergarten of art, and much of it is of no interest except as historical evidence of the struggles of oppressed zealots. Instead of the myth of Cupid and Psyche, we must behold the union of the soul with God; instead of the ancient and beloved image of the good shepherd returning with the lost lamb, we have Christ, the Good Shepherd, bringing into the fold the sheep that had strayed. And here, I must bring up a curious bit of symbolism.

We know from the New Testament how often the lowly fishermen figure in the narratives as the disciples of the Lord. And it so happened that the Greek word for fish IXΘΥΣ was an anagram of devout possibilities. These letters when used as the initials of separate words, form a little creed or confession of faith, Ἰησοῦς Χριστὸς θεοῦ Υἱὸς Σωτήρ—which reads, in our own tongue, *Jesus Christ, Son of God, Saviour*. It is not surprising, therefore, that in the art of the primitive church, the fish is prominent as a sacred symbol, referring directly to the Saviour. In the beginning, Christ was shown as a beardless youth, the Redeemer taken from Pan, the shepherd, or from Orpheus, the tamer of wild beasts; and

49

Christ the Good Shepherd. Lateran, Rome. A sculpture of a favorite pagan image converted into a Christian symbol of the Good Shepherd returning the errant lamb to the fold.

cence, with a population at the time of Justinian, 527–567, of a million inhabitants. At the Hippodrome, wild and tame animals were raced together, by wild and tame drivers, men and women alike; and it was there that Justinian, the Emperor, had his first glimpse of Theodora, the daughter of a tamer of wild animals and herself an actress, not a polite occupation in those days. She was twenty years old, and he married her. As she clutched the power he brought her, she grew vain and haughty, but she was shrewd and intelligent. In their reign the arts flourished and formed the new Byzantine school.

Perhaps the finest specimen of Byzantine building is the *Hagia Sophia,* which means divine wisdom, or St. Sophia, as it is generally named, a church in Istanbul erected by Justinian, who employed 10,000 laborers for six years (532–538) in building it. The plan of the church, like all the early churches, was adapted from a Roman basilica, or court of law; but in the history of architecture, St. Sophia is the synonym of a new type of building—the construction of the dome. The Egyp-

from the very first paintings on the walls of the Catacombs, we may see the growth of Christian symbols which were to provide artists a working scaffold for a thousand years or more. Catacomb art used to be regarded as crude and childish, but it is now greatly admired by artists recognizing the need for a religious backbone to painting.

Christian art came into the daylight when the Emperor Constantine officially embraced the new faith and moved the capital of the Roman Empire to Byzantium, renaming the city, after himself, Constantinople. For a couple of centuries the art of the Christians groped along, gradually throwing aside its pagan trappings, and finally disappearing into two schools—the Byzantine and the Romanesque.

Today, the city on the Golden Horn is called Istanbul; but in its early history, as Constantinople, it rose to its first magnifi-

Wall painting. Catacombs, Rome. Catacomb painting with crude symbols of the Good Shepherd, Adam and Eve, and the Temptation.

St. Sophia. Constantinople (Istanbul). The finest specimen of Byzantine building, with marble walls, mosaics, delicately carved columns, and golden vaultings.

tians and Greeks were no strangers to the dome, but both rejected it; the Romans used it, with the arch, as part of their science of building; but it fell to the Byzantines to build and mount the dome most beautifully—to erect the vaults of crystal glass reflecting the radiance of eternity.

To settle a dome, or hemisphere, on a circular base is not so difficult, but to make a dome behave on a square foundation is really a tough problem. The Byzantines solved it. If you make the diameter of the dome equal to the sides of the square, the corners will remain uncovered; if you enlarge the diameter so as to cover the corners of the foundation, the dome will be too big to rest on the sides. What the Byzantines effected may be illustrated by a simple example. Take half an orange, and put it on a plate, flat side down. Then cut a vertical slice off each of the four sides, and the orange will resemble the dome of St. Sophia. The vertical cuts forming semicircles on the sides are like the arches which rest on the corners of the foundation; and the dome, thus constructed, rises lightly in its splendor. The curved triangles supporting the dome at the corners are called pendentives, if you happen to need a good word.

Byzantine architecture rises to ethereal glory in St. Sophia, with its great central dome fixed on strong arches and united with the half-domes. It is not too impressive from without, but the interior is spacious and soul-lifting, with marble walls and mosaics; the capitals of the columns are delicately carved, and the vaultings covered with squares of gold. When the church was rededicated on Christmas morn, 563 A.D., a local poet wrote: "At last the holy morn had come, and when the first beam of rosy-armed light, driving away the shadows, leaped from arch to arch, all the princes and people hymned their songs of praise and prayer, and it seemed as if the mighty arches were set in Heaven."

Among Byzantine buildings we must not forget St. Mark's at Venice, with its acres of mosaics, carvings, and enamels, or the churches at Ravenna, in Italy, where Dante sleeps and Byron loved his young countess. In the sixth and seventh centuries, A.D., Ravenna was the home of a colony of Byzantine artists who built four churches. I have seen many of the great churches of the world, but one of them, Sant'Apollinare in Classe, at Ravenna, is the most moving of all, sternly simple, almost as finely proportioned as a Greek temple, and brightened by exactly the right amount of mosaic color. A second church, Sant'Apollinare Nuovo contains perhaps the most beautiful mosaics in Western Europe.

Mosaic art is composed of little cubes of

St. Mark's. Venice. The gorgeous architectural style of Byzantium in the old days, the exterior extraordinarily rich to harmonize with a lavishly decorated interior.

Nave, S. Apollinare Nuovo. Ravenna, Italy. One of the finest of early churches, with two aisles separated by rows of ornamented columns, and above them mosaics of angels, saints, and martyrs.

blackest of centuries, when there was no sculpture and little painting to speak of, kept art alive in the edifices of great churches, in mosaic decorations and manuscripts, and in metal work of remarkable quality. And we must thank the Byzantines for the bulk of the symbols which found their way into Christian

Justinian and His Court. S. Vitale, Ravenna, Italy. The Emperor bringing gifts to the new church at Ravenna, and attended by his bishops, priests, and courtiers.

colored glass or stone embedded in cement, and is seldom ventured today, unless we take account of the tile work in bathrooms or railway stations. It is as simple, in some respects, as an old manuscript worked out in glass, and it allows for no shading of tones and little perspective. It is best on a big scale, and seen from a distance. If you should suddenly behold the *Procession of the Virgins,* in Sant'Apollinare Nuovo, or in San Vitale, the mural of *Justinian and His Court* and the *Retinue of Theodora* with the beautiful portrait of this famous queen, you would understand the majesty of mosaic art in the hands of the old masters.

We used to read in our history books of the "Dark Ages" in Europe, a vague term generally used to point out the chaotic state of the Continent from the fall of Rome to the solidly established Christian art at the beginning of the Renaissance. The term is now discarded largely because the art of the Byzantines has been revalued and raised to its deserved rank. The highly trained and devout men of Constantinople, toiling for Christianity in the

Empress Theodora and Her Retinue. Mosaic, S. Vitale, Ravenna, Italy. The majesty of old mosaic art, as shown by the wild, intellectual Theodora with her retinue.

art—the traditional figure of Christ, the pattern of the Crucifixion, the Holy Trinity, the Annunciation and Resurrection—all of which, even to the placement of the figures in space, were a heritage used by the Florentine painters from Giotto to Raphael.

At this point, as we approach the medieval builders of France, and after them, the countless artists of the Renaissance, it would be well to specify one condition absolutely necessary to the birth and growth of art. So far as its purpose, its true meaning, and its usefulness to mankind are concerned, it is neither a secret nor a solitary occupation. The greatest movements in art—the periods in which it has really influenced the lives of everyone—have occurred when men, women, and children worked together to lend comfort and beauty and exaltation to the soul in its path from the crib to the hereafter. It takes two to make a work of art: the artist and those for whom he creates; and no artist of any significance has ever produced, or ever will, anything solely to please himself. To be sure, he does not lower his standards, but he keeps in mind the fact that his picture or statue dramatizes the beliefs and emotions shared by everyone—not by the specialist alone. The artist who works for himself alone works for nobody.

As Rome declined, and the Christians struggled to bring the word of God to the people, the arts were in a pitiful state. It is not too much to say that in this dark and often hopeless period, the Church kept the arts alive. In Western Europe, especially in France, it was the monks who came to the rescue of art. The old monasteries were the centers of architecture, sculpture, the illumination (or adornment) of sacred writings, and stained glass. We must not overlook the Irish monks of the seventh and eighth centuries, who shall be named the foremost of manuscript-makers. The Irish *Book of Kells,* an illuminated copy of the Gospels in Latin, is a landmark in the spread of Christian art and religion.

The monks erected buildings with beautiful arcades and courts, and developed the art of stained glass for the windows of their churches. They took the drafty Roman basilicas and converted them into Christian churches, in a style now called Romanesque. The best examples of Romanesque building are the Benedictine Abbeys, originally governed by monks who took the oath of poverty, chastity, and obedience. These abbeys were designed with short, squat columns and low, massive walls to support a roof made of barrel vaults—that is to say, a roof shaped like a barrel cut in two in its longest diameter. In the front were deep recesses for doors, or portals, framed in round arches and adorned with statues—and above them, towers, or spires.

A number of the old Romanesque monasteries are in existence today, principally in France, and not as sights for tourists, but as the working headquarters of the Cistercians and the reformed Trappists who live in silence and support their cause by manual labor.

Romanesque architecture was stout and heavy, with massive walls to shoulder its bellied vaults and fat towers; and it was rugged, too, with its portals, rounded arches, and cloisters, altogether of a very substantial type of beauty. It was an art for the monasteries; but as Christianity became the spiritual nerve-center of the towns, and people actually crushed each other squeezing into the abbeys, the old architects began to modify their buildings to accommodate their flocks. As they sought to improve on the Romanesque style and increase its scope, lo and behold!, they found themselves, in the eleventh and twelfth centuries, at Chartres and other places, in possession of a new style called Gothic. The word Gothic, oddly enough, was a term coined in derision by Raphael, who favored the classical and rejected this style as something barbaric, and hence northern or "Gothic."

The Romanesque, or half-Roman architecture, was almost the exclusive property of the monasteries; the medieval castles, with their moats, towers, walls, and dungeons—and the crying widows of slain knights—were the retreats of feudal lords; but the Gothic struc-

West Portal, Church of St. Germain. Amiens, France. The fifteenth-century Gothic carvings from the Church of St. Germain exhibit increasing technical skill at the expense of rugged fervor.

Isaiah, Jeremiah, Simeon, Saint John the Baptist, and Saint Peter. North portal, Chartres Cathedral, France. Friendly, human figures rising in their niches like venerable long-stemmed flowers.

tures were made by and for the people. Although the Gothic style was also used for town halls and municipal buildings in the Low Countries, it was used mainly for the church, or "Gothic cathedral." In the principal church of a diocese, the bishop had a throne or chair called the *cathedra.* It was logical that this church, and then any important church, came to be called a cathedral.

Today some skeptics would have us believe that the cathedrals were built by laymen of the town and not by artists trained by the Church. They may have a point there, since all the workmen of those days belonged to guilds, or unions. But the truth remains, as solid as a Gothic portal, that the cathedral was conceived and directed by the Church fathers, and built by masons, painters, and sculptors, who contributed their talents not

only for the pay they received—which was nothing much—but to have a place for the salvation of their souls. In the twelfth and thirteenth centuries, the houses of God were built by co-operation of the whole community. Hear these words from an abbot, in 1115, describing the building of a church.

"Who has ever seen the like? Princes, powerful and wealthy, proud and beautiful women, bent their necks to the yoke of carts which carried the stones, wood, wine, oil and lime—everything necessary for the building and the men working at it. One saw as many as 1,000 people, of both sexes, drawing wagons, pressing forward in the emotion which filled their hearts. Nothing could stop or delay them—and from dawn to dusk the sound of hymns arose."

The Gothic church was the result of many tendencies, some of them going back to the Roman builders, but it became a new form of architecture in its final state, the first since the Greeks. It provided a means of supporting a lofty vaulted ceiling by intersecting arches; and as the walls of the church rose higher and higher, with a heavy roof above them, and the strength of the walls was lessened by many openings for windows, something had to be added to keep the walls from tumbling down. An arched prop, or crutch, erected outside the church, and called the flying buttress, was the answer to this prayer.

The Gothic cathedral was built in the form of a cross, with three or more deeply set doorways or portals, two spires as a rule, enormous windows of stained glass, and pointed arches above the portals and windows and in the vaulted ceilings. The spires pointed to the heavens, and so did all the arches, as well as the ceiling of the great nave, or main part of the building. Everything conspired to lift the soul of the worshiper to the throne of God.

France and England are particularly noted for their beautiful cathedrals. In France, the great churches were consecrated to the Virgin Mary—*Notre Dame*—in Paris, Chartres, and Laon, for example. The great churches were

Façade, Notre Dame. Paris. The most finished of the Gothic style of cathedrals, with two wide towers of equal height and a façade appropriately ornamented.

open to everyone—not to the privileged few as were the temples of Egypt and Greece—and the atmosphere of the interior was close to the solemnity of heaven. The vast windows, illustrating Biblical stories, were made of stained glass, an art that is almost obsolete. The designs of the old windows had the nobility of mosaic patterns translated into glass—mostly panes of red and blue, through which the outside light was changed to tones of purple.

But the indescribable glory of the cathedral is the sculpture. The old churches were drenched with sculpture. It is estimated that the cathedral at Chartres, north of Paris, displays 10,000 carvings; they do not look as if

they were added to the building like the frosted figures on a wedding cake, but as if they were a part of the building and as necessary as the arches and windows.

The sculptures, of course, were Biblical and followed, as far as possible, the instructions of Vincent of Beauvais, the great encyclopedist of the age of St. Louis. Vincent wrote a book of four divisions: *The Mirror of Nature,* or the creation of the world on different days with the names of animals and plants; *The Mirror of Knowledge,* the story of man's fall and salvation through a Redeemer; *The Mirror of Morality,* a classified list of virtues and vices; and *The Mirror of History,* which de-

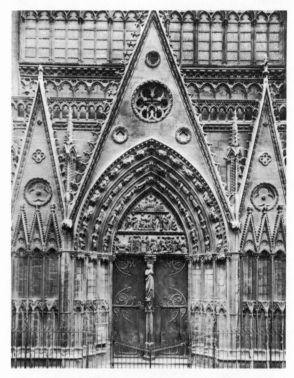

North Portal, façade, Notre Dame. Paris. One of the three doorways, or portals, of the famous cathedral, minutely decorated with Biblical figures.

Christ in Glory. Tympanum, west portal, Chartres Cathedral, France. West portal showing Christ in Glory above the door, one of the 10,000 figures adorning the cathedral.

scribes a living humanity, struggling and suffering and making progress under the eye of God.

As Victor Hugo said, the spiritual history of the Middle Ages was written in the stones of the cathedrals—in statues designed to clothe the idea of Christianity in forms which all could appreciate and to instruct the faithful in great truths. To enter the cathedral was to experience a great uplifting, like the partaking of a sacrament. The cathedral was a poem of religious light colored by the stained windows; it was the symbol of faith and love, and within it the worshipers felt the mystical union with the body of Christ and the mingling of soul with soul.

The medieval figures are far from the ideal beauty created by the Greeks, but they have a beauty all their own, more neighborly and human. Set in a background where everything

Virgin of the Portal. South side, Chartres Cathedral, France. The Virgin Mary dominated the Gothic cathedral, one portal always reserved for her image.

is pointed, they seem to grow out of their pedestals or rise like flowers from a bed—slim and long, with prominent eyes, the men with curling hair and beards, the lady saints with long braided hair and delicate lips breaking into a little smile. The prophets of the Old Testament are like living men, and Christ, after the agonized statues of the earlier centuries, became more tranquil, with a sort of comforting majesty.

The lives of the twelve apostles, with popular beliefs and legends, were told in stone, and the saints were often carved as workmen from one of the guilds. But the dominating figure of the whole of Gothic art was the Virgin Mary, to whom most of the cathedrals were dedicated. One entrance was always adorned with her image, sometimes with half-closed eyes, and smiling lips—sometimes with a shy, plump face like a village maiden transformed by visions of heaven.

Because of the great Gothic artists and the daily force of Christianity the thirteenth is often called the greatest of centuries. It was an era in which men were bound together by the same idea; when their views on all subjects from wars and politics to art and religion were in harmony. There was only one Church, and one form of worship, one system of education, one type of beauty, and one scheme of law and order. It is no wonder that such an era should have produced some of the most inspiring art the world has seen.

Christ Blessing or "Le Beau Dieu d'Amiens." West front, Amiens Cathedral, France. Gothic sculpture at its best, the "Good Lord of Amiens" blessing the town consecrated to His precepts.

Antonio Pollaiuolo. *Hercules and Antaeus. Bargello, Florence. An example, in sculpture, of the artist's handling of the nude in action, the figures painstakingly studied and portrayed with great muscular energy.*

6

The Renaissance in Italy

The word *renaissance* means rebirth. It is something to be achieved only by a miracle. And something like a miracle occurred in the arts in Italy toward the end of the thirteenth century and during the two centuries which followed. After the pagan gods had been put to death permanently and St. Francis had carried the teachings of Christ into the hearts of the humble, and after the scholars had rediscovered the treasures of Greece and Rome, there was such an awakening and flowering of the arts as the world has never seen again. In this so-called Renaissance, the city of Florence was the center.

Florence was a small, square city, old and rich and proud, with fighting towers and palaces as solid as rocks; and a very prosperous city because of her wool and silk industries, her banking houses, and her guilds which controlled all branches of labor, from the butchers to the sculptors, from plumbers to painters. It is worth noting that all the guilds imposed religious observances on their members; that they demanded the highest standards of workmanship and guaranteed the products; and that the artists, while a separate division, were lumped together with the doctors, and held responsible for their wares.

In Florence, where there was so much art, there were no art schools. A talented boy was apprenticed to a recognized master and thoroughly trained in the business—and it was an organized business—of making pictures, carving statues, or designing buildings. At first he was no better than a janitor, or valet; then he was taught carpentry, metal work, masonry, the grinding of colors, and other crafts. Every day he was made to draw from a model. If he had the stuff in him, he was chosen—often in his teens—as the master's assistant, with a small salary; and when he was mature enough to satisfy the examiners, he was admitted to the guild of St. Luke, under which the painters operated, and duly licensed as a practitioner.

The apprentices were taught that every art had its basis in the crafts, and it would be hard to find a Renaissance artist worth remembering who was not a licensed master in three or four occupations—and a skilled mechanic in the bargain. If he deserved it—that is, if his originality justified his training—he was drawn into open competition, traveling from town to town to build churches or halls, to paint the story of Christianity on the walls of churches, or to carve sacred images. It was a man's work, and a profession with large returns in money to outstanding artists.

As the arts circulated, public demand increased: in fourteenth-century Italy, there

61

Duccio. *Entry into Jerusalem, scene from back of The Majesty. Opera del Duomo, Siena. Showing the decorative style of the Sienese with Christ and His Apostles receiving garlands at the city gate, and Gothic Italian towers in the background.*

prophets as he imagined them—rugged and formidable, tender and shy, as earthy as a close friend, or high and mighty and sitting among the clouds.

Florence was a community of contrasts; alive with new ideas and not afraid of experiments; rich in things of the spirit and of the senses; hardened by warfare and commerce; humanized by the philosophy of St. Francis; unreasonably proud, aggressive, and revengeful; capable of the extremes of good and evil; absorbed in the making of money, but, as her culture grew, bestowing more attention on the arts than any other city except ancient Athens.

Before the Renaissance, however, the great center of art in Italy had been, not Florence, but Siena, a rival city some forty miles to the south. The Sienese artists, clinging to the Byzantine style, produced the last great painting of medieval times—rich in color and decorative patterns and executed with exceptional refinement. The faces of their brooding, unreal Madonnas, often set in a background of real gold leaf, are unforgettable; and the work of

were hundreds of churches, town halls, guild halls, public buildings, private palaces, houses, and monasteries—all to be designed and decorated with paintings and statues. The great art of the Italian Renaissance was part and parcel of a great subject, the story of Christianity. But it never occurred to the men who employed the artists—the popes and prelates, the counts and prominent families—to question the artist's convictions if he happened to admire the pagan arts of Egypt, Greece, and Rome. In fact, many pagan subjects were used. And it never occurred to the artist that he was not an independent person, at liberty to represent the Lord or the Virgin or the

Giotto. *The Deposition. Arena Chapel, Padua. The trials of the spirit expressed in simple, sculptured figures, each pose and gesture relating to the body of Christ.*

Masaccio. *The Tribute Money. S. Maria del Carmine, Florence. The incident, from St. Matthew, reveals the Lord instructing St. Peter to take the tax collector's coin from the mouth of a fish.*

their masters, like Duccio, Simone Martini, and Sassetta (see Plate 1), is highly prized today. But in lesser hands the style became repetitious and lifeless, and new ideas were in the air.

The Florentines took the waning Byzantine tradition and filled it with a blood stream rich in red corpuscles. The man who had the genius to inject new life into the dying forms was named Giotto. He was the first personality in the new movement whose identity is a matter of historical record, and his position, after seven centuries, is still among the sovereigns of painting.

Giotto was the first of the Italian masters to draw from nature. That in itself was a revolution, though today life-drawing is one of the fundamentals. Giotto, in his own lifetime, practically abolished the flat medieval style, the rigid Byzantine image, by bringing art down to earth, by observing the habits and postures of men and women as they went about their business. When he had to draw a saint he made him a human being—a little flat, at times, as he wrestled with the old style,

but never a staring pattern on a wall. He struggled all his life with the technical problem of making figures massive and solid—in our language, three-dimensional—and his figures have the weight and bulk of sculpture.

Giotto was born in 1266, a few miles north of Florence, in "a wilderness of hills populated by goats," according to Leonardo da Vinci. His father was a shepherd, and the boy, with the curiosity of a peasant and the eye of a born artist, began to observe the shapes and movements of a lamb that pleased him, and to sketch the animal on a flat piece of stone. Thus, he formed the habit of drawing at an early age.

There is an old story, now disputed, that a famous Florentine painter named Cimabue happened to pass through the lonely country and to see by the roadside a small boy scratching a picture of a sheep on a stone. Impressed by the boy's efforts, he took him to his workshop in Florence and made him an apprentice. In any case, the boy was trained in architecture, sculpture, and painting, and was soon at ease in the medium of fresco, a form of wall painting in which water colors were brushed on wet plaster, becoming a part of the surface as the lime in the plaster dried and crystallized.

We know much about Giotto's art, but the events of his life have not been recorded with full certainty. He lived in a time of trouble and the shedding of blood—when two fierce political parties fought for supremacy. He saw assassins at work and the agony in the faces of women as they bent over the bodies of the murdered and hurt. And when he was given tragic subjects to paint, he made them human and dramatic by the added authority of experience. As his powers grew surer and bolder, he brushed aside the cobwebs from the art he had inherited and brought it into the daylight, painting faces that were not masks or patterns but faces that brightened with smiles or grew tense and dark in sorrow.

In his early twenties, Giotto was acclaimed the most original artist in Italy, and was called to the town of Assisi to decorate the walls of the upper church with episodes from the life of St. Francis. These murals are on view today, some in a faded condition, some poorly restored, but they are clear enough to show us that the artist, in his first trial, proved himself one of the great storytellers in paint. On his return to Florence he married a young woman who bore him eight children described by his friend Dante as "lumps of deformity as ugly as their father." He was now in full command of his powers, with more work than he could take care of, an increasing income, and houses in town and country. "And all Italy," an old writer tells us, "was on tiptoe to see what he would do next."

At the age of forty, he moved to the little town of Padua to undertake the most ambitious job of his life, the decoration of a church called to this day the Arena chapel (see Plate 2), because it was built on the remains of a Roman theater. He covered the entire interior

Uccello. *The Rout of San Romano. National Gallery, London. Vividly modern in a design alive with clashing planes, radiating lines, and geometrical horses.*

PLATE 5. FRA ANGELICO. *The Coronation of the Virgin.* SAN MARCO, FLORENCE

PLATE 6. LEONARDO DA VINCI. *Mona Lisa*. LOUVRE, PARIS

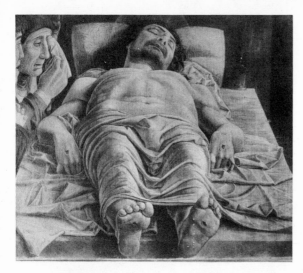

Mantegna. *Dead Christ. Brera, Milan. A technical tour de force—one of the most re-markable illustrations of foreshortening in the records of art.*

with frescoes, and achieved one of the world's masterpieces of painting in scenes forming a panorama of the principal events in the story of Christian faith—the life of the Lord, the saints, martyrs, and disciples who lived and suffered by and for their faith.

In these murals, Giotto introduced intimate touches heretofore foreign to art, such as Joachim's little dog trotting out to meet him; the newborn Mary making a face as her eyes were washed; the infant Jesus sucking his thumb; and a fat barrel-maker tasting the wine at the feast at Cana. He told these stories in pictures as simple and moving as the words of the Gospel, and painted them with the confidence and affection of one who loved all human creatures.

During the twenty-five years left to him, af-ter he had finished the Padua commission, he worked in various cities, and, in 1334, was named the master builder of Florence. As an architect he designed the bell-tower of the cathedral; and as a sculptor he ornamented the base of the tower with some of the finest of early Renaissance carvings. He died loaded with honors, and the people of Florence, who loved him, gave him a sumptuous burial in the Cathedral of Our Lady of the Flower.

Among the followers of Giotto were some second-rate storytellers, typical of the small souls who tag after a great man. But along came Hulking Tom Masaccio, as he was nick-named, who put the new style of painting squarely on its own feet. This young tramp of genius died in his twenty-sixth year, but lived long enough to paint, in the Church of the Carmine, in Florence, a series of frescoes in which the figures are bathed in light and air. Giotto's figures, despite their solidity, seem to stick to the background, but Masaccio's stand apart with plenty of elbow room around them.

Masaccio painted, in the *Expulsion of Adam and Eve* from the Garden of Eden, a miserable pair of sinners who are examples of everlast-ing shame and suffering. He stripped man and woman to the skin and left them to weep and shiver; he was a creator of the tragedies that cleanse the soul. He has been called the master of masters for the reason that all the great Florentine artists, including Michelangelo and

Botticelli. *Madonna with Six Angels. Uffizi, Florence. Also called "The Madonna of the Pomegranate," and one of the most appealing of the artist's melancholy virgins.*

Fra Filippo Lippi. *Madonna, Child, and Two Angels. Uffizi, Florence. The Madonna—the artist's wife was probably the model—is portrayed with a tender interest in the charms of Florentine women.*

Fra Angelico. *Angel Musician, detail from Madonna dei Linaiuoli. S. Marco, Florence.*

Leonardo, went to his chapel as students to learn how to draw, and to see how Hulking Tom had managed to give his figures not only solid bulk and form, but unforgettable grandeur.

After Masaccio, Italy produced so many famous artists that it would require a volume merely to list them. An old historian reckoned the number to be about 16,000, the term artist meaning all craftsmen who rose to distinction. It is not surprising, therefore, that Italy produced so many works of art, and fed the museums of the world with paintings and sculptures for centuries. The most famous masters of the Renaissance will appear in the chapters

Verrocchio. *Bartolommeo Colleoni. Venice. The stern power of the young Renaissance as contained in a statue generally called the greatest equestrian sculpture in the world of art.*

School of Andrea della Robbia. *Virgin Adoring the Christ Child. Bargello, Florence. The Virgin in Adoration, from the workshop of Andrea della Robbia, who worked with pictorial skill in glazed terra cotta.*

which follow, but there are many men of genius whom we cannot pass by.

Among the crowd of sculptors, I must single out Jacopo della Quercia, whose sharply defined and powerful figures guided the hand of Michelangelo; the beloved white and blue enamels of the Madonna and angels by Luca della Robbia; Andrea del Verrocchio, whose statue of the bandit *Colleoni,* at Venice, has every right to be called the greatest equestrian statue in the world, with a similar heroic bandit by Donatello, in Padua, a close second; and Lorenzo Ghiberti, whose bronze doors for the Baptistery at Florence were cited by Michelangelo as "worthy to adorn the gates of Paradise."

Speaking of Donatello, it is written that, as a boy of seventeen, he was consulted by juries in awarding art commissions. He was driven

Donatello. *Niccolo da Uzzano. Bargello, Florence. One of the most powerful and realistic of all portrait busts, and one that offers no flattery.*

Antonio Pollaiuolo. *Fighting Men. Engraving, Metropolitan Museum of Art, New York. The artist, a student of anatomy, depicts the human body in fierce, muscular energy.*

Mantegna. *Adoration of the Shepherds. Metropolitan Museum of Art, New York. A Christian subject presented with the austerity and grandeur of ancient Roman sculpture.*

by what the Italians called the "terrible fury," and by an observation of life so searching that his statue of Christ was called a "crucified peasant." He had a passion for the statues of ancient Rome, the study of which he combined with his fresh studies from nature. He was sane and strong and daring; and all his carvings—his children, youths, warriors, and old men so wizened they looked skinned alive —are so charged with energy as to make them neither old nor new, but living on and on.

Among the painters of Italy, I shall name a half-dozen whom I look at nearly every day— in photographs of their work unavoidably— and always with renewed admiration.

Paolo Uccello, a barber's son, was a math-

ematician and a student of perspective (the devices used by artists to give depth to a scene as the objects within it disappear in the distance). He would sit up all night drawing polyhedrons with eighty faces, and other oddities; and when his wife begged him to go to bed, he would cry out, "O what a delightful thing is this perspective!" He brought into painting, for the first time since the murals of the Romans, battle scenes with clashing planes and projecting lances, and chunky horses, simplified like hobbyhorses.

Andrea del Castagno was a man of ungovernable passions and ferocious energy—so swaggering indeed with rages and devilish threats that he was for many years suspected

Andrea del Castagno. *The Last Supper. S. Apollonia, Florence. A hard and wiry conception of the Lord's last meeting with His Apostles, and with the most robust figure of Christ in Italian art.*

Ghiberti. *Sacrifice of Isaac. Panel, east door of the Baptistery, Florence. Extolled by Michelangelo as "doors worthy to adorn the gates of Paradise."*

of murdering his best friend in order to rob him of some painting secrets. For hard power that was never relaxed, he had no equals among the Renaissance masters, and the figure of Christ in his painting of the *Last Supper* is the most vigorous and masculine in Italian art. With much joy he accepted the invitation to paint on the front of the town hall, in Florence, the figures of a gang of conspirators who were hanged heads downward. He painted the traitors as they were suspended, and in the words of an old writer, "in the strangest attitudes and with an art that was varied and exceedingly fine." For this he was ever afterward called "Andrea of the Hanged Men."

Antonio Pollaiuolo, son of a chicken breeder, was painter, sculptor, engraver, and anatomist, all in one. His knowledge of the nude figure was enormous, enabling him to represent the tension of muscles and the effects of action on the structure of the body. His subjects, mainly from mythology, made use of this knowledge, and the most complicated poses were as child's play to his talents. He was not only a great artist, but a great teacher, and the athletic wildness and violence in his work typified one aspect of the Renaissance in Italy.

The fame of Piero della Francesca burns more brightly today than it did when he was alive and working in his home town of Arezzo, a sunburnt spot in central Italy. Like his master, Uccello, he was a tireless student of mathematics and the science of perspective. Piero loved wars and battle pictures (see Plate 4), parades and festivals, and strange people in unusual costumes. He had an orderly, exact mind, and his large frescoes were put together with such mathematical precision as to lead many to believe that he was in possession of a magic formula. He is celebrated today by artists seeking to discover the secrets of his carefully planned murals—his solid figures painted from clay models; his cool, quiet landscapes, running back into vast distances; and the beautiful architecture of his decorations.

Piero's pupil, Luca Signorelli, was far from

Signorelli. *The Souls of the Damned. Cathedral, Orvieto. One of the frescoes of "The Last Judgment," with nude forms darting through space and cowering sinners awaiting the voice of doom.*

cool and serene. He was, in fact, the byword for terrific agonies and fiery duels between the righteous and the damned. He worked night and day and took delight in drawing the human body. It is related that when his son was killed, a youth whom he loved tenderly, he caused the body to be stripped of clothing, and without shedding a tear, painted the boy's portrait so that he might keep close to him the image of what God had taken away. In his sixtieth year, he painted the *Last Judgment*, in the cathedral at Orvieto. In this forsaken town, you may see today the *Souls of the Damned* and the *Resurrection,* pictured in nude bodies swirling through space, skeletons, angels, and demons, with a force that will stagger you. Signorelli also painted some of the handsomest angels in art—"handsome" rather than "beautiful" because angels, originally, were masculine.

Andrea Mantegna, son of a farmer, was like an old Roman born again, with his deep respect for the nobility and power of his ances-

Gozzoli. *Procession of the Magi. Riccardi, Florence. The three wise men bearing gifts, painted in a processional mood with gorgeous costumes and banners. The three riders are portaits of three of the Medici.*

family man who painted Madonnas and saints as though they were members of his own household. Quite different was the beloved Fra Angelico (see Plate 5), who prayed before taking up his brushes; no other artist has expressed, with such sweetness and truth, the Christian faith, with its heavenly bliss and the joys of suffering. His pupil Benozzo Gozzoli covered wall after wall with illustrations of the picturesque court life of the Renaissance. And that all-around master of all mural jobs, Domenico Ghirlandaio, if he were alive today, would decorate college halls and factories and churches, with athletes, laborers, and saints— and he would never do the greatest work, perhaps, but he would never do a poor one.

There is not space for more than a word or two about the architects who took the styles of ancient Rome and adapted them to new types of building. In Rome, you will see St. Peter's, the largest of churches, with a dome designed by Michelangelo, and many Renaissance structures showing the influence of the ancient planners. In Florence, the palaces resemble military fortresses slightly dressed up, and in Venice, the private houses and palaces have an oriental splendor with embroidered decorations and a great deal of color.

tors. He studied the statues of the ancient artists, and traveled everywhere to see how people of all classes lived. Like many other Renaissance artists, he modeled his figures in clay before painting them, but the paintings themselves are not copies of sculpture—they have the fierceness and grandeur of the old Roman marbles, and the vitality of living Italians.

The Madonnas of Sandro Botticelli, son of a tanner, are almost as popular as those of Raphael, and his pagan pictures such as the *Birth of Venus* (see Plate 3) delight people of all tastes. Botticelli was a strange mixture, half-pagan, half-Christian, and so sensitive that one of his rivals swore that he had no skin at all. He had, perhaps above all Renaissance painters, that quality of charm which makes him the pet of both critics and public.

Fra Filippo Lippi, a barber's son, the holy monk who eloped with a nun, was a jovial

Ghirlandaio. *Birth of the Virgin. S. Maria Novella, Florence. The birth is treated as a family matter, with everyone co-operating and comely young girls in attendance.*

St. Peter's. Rome. The vast interior of the largest church in Christendom. St. Peter's set the standard of church design for three centuries.

Strozzi Palace. Florence. Built with Florentine severity to serve as the house and fortress of a proud and fighting family.

Leonardo da Vinci. *Self-portrait. Red chalk, Turin Library. The one-and-only Leonardo at sixty, grave and a little skeptical, and much older than his years.*

7

Leonardo da Vinci

The name of Leonardo da Vinci rings through the ages with the golden notes of wonder and enchantment. He is the subject of more speculation than any other artist; he came closest to the divine touch, "that which creates flawlessly, like God himself." The words are his own; but he was critical too, and human, and said, in his last illness, "When I thought I was learning how to live, I was only learning how to die." He did not solve the riddle of living, but he grew wiser by trying, and it is not too much to say that he had the finest mind that ever served a suffering mortal.

Did you ever, on a sleepless night, addled by dreams, wish that you could control the forces of nature? If you dreamed of being an artist, you would stroke the paper with pen and ink, and a Madonna or a cat or a flower would leap into being miraculously; if a scientist, you would contrive fearful engines for the destruction of your enemies, or impossible craft for racing through the heavens. It is common for all of us to yearn for such magic powers, but one man, Leonardo, actually seemed to possess them. And he used them, not crazily for profit, but by logic, insight, imagination, and reflection—all woven into the tissue of his wonderful brain—for the glory of the race.

In his thirtieth year, Leonardo, a Florentine, applied for work at the court of the Duke of Milan, and the letter he sent is one of the most incredible examples of self-examination ever written by a job-seeker—or anyone else.

"I have," it began, "a method of constructing very light and portable bridges, to be used ... in warfare—fireproof and easy to remove.

"For sieges, I am prepared to remove the water from ditches, and to make an infinite variety of scaling ladders and other engines.

"I have also most convenient and portable bombs, proper for throwing showers of missiles, and with the smoke thereof, causing great terror to the enemy.

"By means of excavations, I have ways of reaching any given point, even though it be necessary to pass under rivers.

"I can also construct covered wagons, secure and indestructible, which will break the strongest units of the enemy and behind which the infantry can follow in safety.

"I can make mortars and field-guns of beautiful and useful shape—entirely different from those in common use.

"For naval conflicts, I have numerous instruments, offensive and defensive, and I can also make smoke screens of powders and vapors.

"In times of peace, I believe I could equal any other in works of architecture. I can pre-

75

Leonardo da Vinci. *Adoration of the Magi. Uffizi, Florence. An unfinished painting with wonderful figure studies and intricate excursions into perspective design.*

children—nine more sons and two daughters, all of them jealous of the first-born and eager to do him wrong.

Leonardo's wonderful mind began to shine out very early. He loved to examine the formation of rocks, and to follow the courses of rivers; he was captivated by flowers, faces, and flying birds, excelled in mathematics, and was forever drawing and modeling figures in clay. At seventeen, he was not only the star pupil but the assistant of Verocchio, an admirable teacher as well as the great sculptor who made the statue of *Colleoni,* at Venice. He remained with his master till his twenty-fifth year, and then opened his own shop. Between the ages of twenty-five and thirty he

pare designs for buildings, public or private, and conduct water from place to place.

"Furthermore, I can execute works in sculpture—marble, bronze, or terra cotta. In painting also I can do what may be done, as well as any other, whoever he may be.

"And, if any of the above-named things shall seem to any man impossible, I am perfectly ready to make trial of them in whatever place you shall be pleased to command."

Surely no other man, however given to boasting, ever made such claims for himself, but the most remarkable thing about the letter was that it was true.

Leonardo was born in the village of Vinci, west of Florence, in 1452, the son of a lawyer and a peasant girl of sixteen. His parents were not married, and as often happened in those days, the mother gave up the child and was married off to another man—in this case a carpenter. At the age of thirteen, the boy was received in his father's home at Florence, a household that kept growing as the father married four times and filled the place with

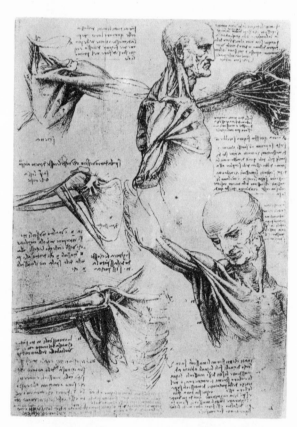

Leonardo da Vinci. *Analysis of the Shoulder Girdle. Drawing, Windsor Castle Royal Library. The artist, after dissecting many corpses, explains graphically the relation of muscles and bones in terms of movement.*

Leonardo da Vinci. *Studies of Cats. Drawings, Windsor Castle Royal Library. Like the Egyptians, Leonardo was a profound student of cats, sketching their agility and grace in every conceivable posture.*

little for the past, never bowed to the Greeks or Romans, and learned, for the most part, by observation and experiment. Among other things without number, he dissected thirty corpses, and made the first drawing of an unborn child and a series of anatomical sketches which are not only true to life but beautiful to behold.

At twenty-one, Leonardo made the first drawings of landscape, and discovered the colors of shadows; and not much later, he developed what is known as *chiaroscuro,* a way of using darks and lights so as to make an ob-

Leonardo da Vinci. *The Virgin of the Rocks. Louvre, Paris. First of two versions, with science and sentiment perfectly blended, and the faces enchantingly refined. The pointing fingers, indicating the presence of God, were taken from an old symbolism.*

painted many pictures, only three of which have survived: *Saint Jerome,* in the Vatican; the *Virgin of the Rocks,* in the Louvre; and the *Adoration of the Magi,* an unfinished experiment in the Uffizi, at Florence. In these years, his income was fairly large, and he kept a stable of horses and several house-servants.

His fame increased, and with it, step by step, the gossip of his supernatural talents. He did not scatter the legends himself, but he did not deny them—he did not care. He could not stoop to quarrel or condemn. He wore fine clothes of his own designing; his manners were lordly; his mode of living resplendent. Far from being soft or overrefined, he was a daring rider and his strength was the talk of Tuscany: he could break stallions and bend a horseshoe with his bare hands. Unlike Michelangelo, and most of his associates, he cared

Leonardo da Vinci. *The Last Supper. S. Maria delle Grazie, Milan. Probably the most celebrated picture of the western world, and painted, Leonardo said, to reveal the emotions of the participants by facial expressions and postures.*

ject firm and full and real. He sketched criminals as they were hanged, and children at games; and his pen and ink studies are of the most delicate and lovely, and at the same time, the most spontaneous and precise representations in any art—anywhere—whether the subject be a human heart, a woman with a cat, a child, a horse, a skull, or a military tank.

The Duke of Milan, to whom he addressed the famous letter, snapped him up immediately, and gave him a house and vineyard, and a list of his duties as artist. Leonardo was required to paint the ladies of the court, to supervise festivals, design costumes, invent floats and fripperies, and make himself ornamental at special events—items which bored him profoundly, at times. When free he acted as a sanitary engineer, and built the first heavier-than-air flying machine; though unsuccessful, it was almost modern in idea. For sixteen years he constructed and tested models

for a great equestrian statue; he wanted, not a heavy motionless group, but a rearing horse of fury and action, but the statue never developed beyond clay models.

In the dining-room of the Church of St. Mary of the Graces at Milan, he painted the *Last Supper* (the last meeting of Christ and His apostles) which is certainly as widely known as any picture in existence. Leonardo argued that it was the purpose of painting to reveal the emotions of people by means of their expressions and postures, and he wrote in his *Notebooks* a careful description of the apostles in his *Last Supper:* One of them has laid down his glass and suddenly turned his head. Another twists his fingers, knits his brows, and leans toward his neighbor who spreads out his hands and opens his mouth in amazement. Another whispers in his companion's ear; another upsets a cup on the table; and one watches, while another apostle blows

Leonardo da Vinci. *Madonna with Saint Anne. Louvre, Paris. Two figures strangely related, and the Christ Child playfully employed. In the background is a fantastic Italian landscape.*

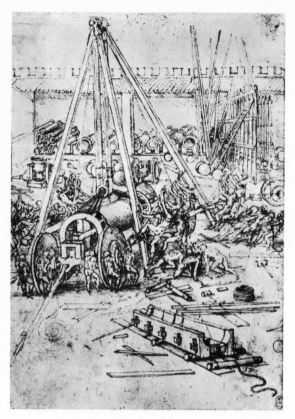

Leonardo da Vinci. *The Arsenal. Drawing, Windsor Castle Royal Library. The artist invented many engines of warfare, including the tank, and fantastic weapons now realized by modern science.*

out his cheeks, and a second shades his eyes with his hand.

He spent four years on the picture, making hundreds of studies of characters—sometimes working all day long; again, putting down only a couple of strokes. As he crossed the city of Milan, gorgeously dressed, crowds followed him, as today they gape at a movie star, and whispered, "There he goes to paint the *Last Supper.*"

Alas, for the painting, its nobility and grandeur have almost faded away! Leonardo, always experimenting, painted it in tempera on a damp wall. The colors refused to stick, and today the mural is only a spiritual ghost of its original majesty.

In Milan, and elsewhere as he changed residence, Leonardo kept a record of his reflections as an artist and scientist in his *Notebooks,* five thousand pages of manuscript written, for some mysterious reason, in reversed or mirror writing, and adorned with sketches of almost everything—animal, vegetable, or mineral. It is not likely that ever again will any man be so prophetic, so deep-delving as he, yet always the great artist, who can impress each object with the clearness and charm and living radiance of his own personality.

He was the founder of the sciences of engineering, geology, and anatomy, and a master of optics; he was a cartographer, or mapmaker, and his maps of Italy are still useful; the tank of warfare, roller bearings, the pocket-handkerchief and the wheelbarrow are his; and he designed new styles of domed architecture and recommended underground canals for the sanitation of cities. Not long ago more than two hundred scale models of his practical machines were exhibited in New York.

When the French conquered Milan, Leonardo drifted on to Venice where the nightclub type of gaiety wearied him, and thence to Florence where he served as military engineer for Cesare Borgia. His mural for the Council Chamber, a scene of horses in violent action, because of some chemical mistakes, ran down the walls and is no more. He did not grieve. He was busy with the portrait of *Mona Lisa* (see Plate 6).

This portrait, as everybody knows, is that of a robust young woman, her hands (perhaps the most shapely ever done in pigment) in her lap, and her broad face and high forehead framed in a flowing veil. The background is a greenish-blue vista of shadowy peaks and a winding stream. The tantalizing smile, so subtle that it disappears in coarse reproductions, has made sages quarrel and poets sing. *Mona Lisa* is a mystery woman—but the puzzle of her identity is not more baffling than the mystery of a painted form so beautifully fashioned and enduring that it cannot grow old and die like the woman whose likeness it bears.

Leonardo wandered to Rome to work for

PLATE 7.   MICHELANGELO BUONARROTI. *Creation of Adam*. SISTINE CHAPEL, ROME

PLATE 8. RAPHAEL. *Madonna of the Goldfinch*. UFFIZI, FLORENCE

PLATE 9.   TINTORETTO. *Miracle of Saint Mark*. ACADEMY, VENICE

PLATE 10. JAN VAN EYCK. *John Arnolfini and His Wife*. NATIONAL GALLERY, LONDON

Leo X, who did not know how to employ him, and at the end of two wasted years, he crossed slowly over the Alps into France, the guest of Francis I. He was given quarters in a chateau in Touraine, and his last years were passed comfortably among people who appreciated his qualities. He grew old prematurely, with hands paralyzed; and, unable to paint, he continued his researches in science. In his sixty-seventh year, he commended his soul to God and was received in Heaven by St. Luke, the patron saint of artists.

Leonardo da Vinci. *Study of a Woman's Hands. Drawing, Windsor Castle Royal Library. In the painting and modeling of the hand, Leonardo was never excelled.*

Michelangelo. *Head of David. Academy, Florence. Head of the eighteen-foot figure known as the "Giant." Hewn, incredibly, from little models in wax, first the right arm wielding the hammer, and then the left.*

8

Michelangelo

Michelangelo Buonarrotti is the superman of art. He was a sculptor worthy of a seat among the ancients; and in the field of painting, against his will, he brought forth the greatest single-handed achievement in all art—the mural decorations in the Sistine Chapel, in Rome. Besides the genius he was born with, he had the resolution—the will power—of a regiment, and not once did he deliver an inferior piece of work, or an easy one. In his pride, and aware of his powers, he accepted every commission offered him, putting to shame all his rivals.

Yet he was not a happy soul. No man is happy who seeks to improve the universe. His complaints were not the cries of one defeated by life, but the agonies of a genius whose achievements, no matter how great, could never match his dreams of what he wanted to do. From the day of his birth, near Florence in 1475, he was doomed to pay the price for the gifts the fates had wished upon him.

He loved above everything else to carve in marble, and said, in old age, "Nothing was right with me unless I had a chisel in my hand." He spurned the softer pleasures of life, and cared nothing for the charms of women. He felt that he was put on earth to accomplish and, from his fifth year, worked day and night, learning to draw and to cut stone. At

thirteen, he was a pupil of Ghirlandaio, one of the most successful painters in Florence, and in the workshop of this master was trained in the business of fresco painting.

When Lorenzo the Magnificent, head of the Medici family and ruler of Florence, offered the use of his gardens to the most promising youth in town, Michelangelo was awarded the honor. His heart leaped up, for in the gardens, with their treasures from Greece and Rome, he could study the antique and develop the vast schemes already forming within him. He learned every detail of his craft, using his left hand as easily as his right. At sixteen, he carved in low relief (that is, in figures but slightly raised from the background), a *Madonna and Child* of amazing strength and beauty. Lorenzo, observing the boy's ability, took him into the palace of the Medicis, and treated him as a son. He lived with his patron for two years, had a studio of his own, and enjoyed the company of the poets, artists, and philosophers who came to the palace.

The young genius worked unceasingly. All day he hewed marble and at night made drawings or studied the sculptures of the ancients. To outstrip Leonardo da Vinci, whom he disliked for no good reason, he dissected corpses secretly and mastered the anatomy of the human figure, but this stinking business ruined

Michelangelo. *Study of a Sibyl. Red chalk, Metropolitan Museum of Art, New York. The most valuable drawing in America. The Sibyl was constructed from a male model, the artist preferring the muscular development of athletic men.*

for it, *terribilità*—in huge figures in action, or ready to burst into action. At twenty-one, he found himself the sole support of a good-for-nothing family, and he thought it his Christian duty to shoulder the burden. In time, he bought a villa for his father and provided for shiftless brothers and numerous relatives, never too busy or depressed to listen to their tales of woe or to advise them on everything from head colds to marriage. He went to Rome and made money—but lived like a dog, eating lightly and sleeping in his working

his appetite for food and drink. With other young artists he went to Masaccio's Chapel to study, and while drawing therein, often quarreled with a bully named Torrigiano who has left us a record of one encounter.

"It was Michelangelo's habit," said Torrigiano, "to make fun of all of us who were busy in the Church. He thought he could draw more boldly and beautifully than any of the boys, and one day, when he gave me a bawling-out, I answered him with a crack on the nose that flattened the bone and cartilage into a biscuit and gave him a beauty mark that he carried to his grave."

At eighteen he was the foremost sculptor alive. He was already beginning to express the force of his genius—the Italians had a word

Michelangelo. *Moses. S. Pietro in Vincoli, Rome. Intended for the uncompleted tomb of Pope Julius II. The artist loved the inflexible character of Moses, the great Jewish leader.*

clothes in a foul room, and seldom taking a shower, for he had a superstitious horror of getting wet.

In his twenty-fifth year, he carved his *Pietà,* a figure of the Virgin Mary with the dead Christ in her arms, a masterpiece that brought him the fame he had earned—the most glorious Virgin Mary in stone, serene in her feminine strength, serene in her suffering spirit. When asked why he made the Mother so youthful, he replied, "Women who are pure in soul and body never grow old."

He accepted commissions right and left, and threw the city of Florence into an uproar by carving a nude figure of *David* from a block of marble discarded by other sculptors as too flat and long. The figure was an eighteen-foot giant carved to the very limits of the block, with a little bump of uncut stone on the top of the head to show his bumbling rivals how exactly he had calculated. No one knows, for certain, how he did this monumental job—but it is likely that he made some little studies in wax —about eighteen inches high—and then, first with one arm, and then the other, removed the marble that imprisoned the *David.*

Together with Leonardo, he was appointed to decorate the Grand Council Chamber of Florence. The subject gave full play to his powers—a group of naked foot soldiers suddenly called to battle from the river Arno where they were bathing. His full-size design for the fresco (called a "cartoon") was known as "the great drawing," but, unluckily, it was cut to pieces and stolen by jealous artists.

In Rome again, he was engaged—one might almost say taken into custody—by Julius II, the warrior Pope who treated artists like soldiers. But Michelangelo understood the Holy Father and gave him as good as he received, and the gruff pair hit it off very well. It was agreed that the young sculptor should construct a tomb for his employer, and the plans were stupendous. The story of this undertaking is called "the tragedy of the tomb," because the original plan for a monument three stories high, adorned with some forty figures,

Michelangelo. *Pietà. St. Peter's, Rome. Carved in the artist's twenty-fifth year. The Virgin was portrayed so youthfully because, Michelangelo said, "Women who are pure in soul and body never grow old."*

dwindled away year by year; it ended up in a single figure, the *Moses,* now in a church called St. Peter in Chains, in Rome. What a statue! A sculptured image in which the marble can hardly hold back the wrath, the power, and the passion of the old leader of the Israelites!

Michelangelo quarreled with the Pope over one job and another, and was finally commanded to decorate the ceiling of the Sistine Chapel—a scheme suggested by the architect Bramante, who secretly hoped the assignment to Michelangelo would fall through, thereby leaving the way open for a young painter named Raphael.

"They thought they would cook me!"

Michelangelo. *Dawn. Tomb of Lorenzo de' Medici, Florence. A woman of many trials in slumbering despair, her large figure magnificently carved to embody the sadness of the human race.*

His battles with sculpture had been huge and terrific, but they were as nothing to the tortures awaiting him in the Sistine Chapel. Fortunately, he was physically in the best condition of his life, thirty-three and tough as steel.

He devised an architectural framework for the ceiling, with compartments of various shapes and sizes, and in these spaces painted 343 figures, 225 of which would be from ten to eighteen feet high, if they were standing up. Adam, for example (see Plate 7), is a thirteen-foot giant, naked and powerful, the most beautifully constructed nude in all painting—and it was put on the wall in three days! The figures were all drawn from life—with strong men posing for the females—and enlarged into "cartoons," or stencils, scaled exactly to the size of the areas to be frescoed.

At first, Michelangelo used assistants, but he fired them all—they were too slow and dumb—and then he toiled alone save for the mechanics who, each day, prepared the wet

Michelangelo exclaimed. "I hadn't worked in fresco since I was a boy and I told that to Julius. I also reminded him that painting was not my trade; that it was a woman's chore. But he bade me shut up, and added that he was the one to judge my abilities."

Sick at heart and disgusted, the artist surveyed the Chapel, 132 feet by 44, with a vaulted ceiling 68 feet above the floor. The walls had already been frescoed, and it was his task to work upward through the curve of the vault and thence across the flat expanse of ceiling. He had a scaffold set up and estimated the size of the space to be covered—about 10,000 square feet. His mind began to warm, in spite of himself; his energies sang out in confidence. His imagination turned toward the beginning of things and the making of man, and he forgot the hot-tempered Pope, the crafty architect, and the sweet cherub Raphael who, like himself, had an angel's name.

Michelangelo. *Day. Tomb of Giuliano de' Medici, Florence. The mightiest figure in sculpture since the Egyptians, and a figure inspired by the woes of Italy.*

Michelangelo. *Libyan Sibyl. Sistine Chapel, Rome. One of the pagan forms brought by Michelangelo into the Sistine Chapel.*

of great artists. In spite of this, his work in the Sistine Chapel hurt him permanently. In one of his sonnets—he was also a poet—he described his condition after lying on his back for years. He said that he became stoop-shouldered, that his eyesight was damaged, that months went by before he could lower his chin, and that he was never without pains in his neck. As a reward, he had carried the art of painting to a new height.

The subject of the creation had been used by artists throughout the Middle Ages, but Michelangelo painted it so that it truly seems to be the handiwork of God. If you could only see the murals when the Pope of today is celebrating Mass with the Sistine Choir co-operating: God, the Father, sailing through the heavens; the origin of the sun and moon; the temptation of Eve and the expulsion of Adam and Eve from the Garden of Eden; and on either side of these, rows of prophets, and pagan athletes, and sibyls who foretold the coming of Christ. Other artists had painted Paradise as a place with ponds or flowers, little watered gardens with birds and lilies. But

plaster for him to paint on. On his back, day after day, his head wrapped in a towel, he made pictures of the creation and fall of man, always forced to remember that the figures had to be seen at a distance of seventy feet. Sometimes, it was too cold for plastering, and he knocked off—read Dante and the Bible, and made life-size drawings for his figures. Twice he had to pursue the Pope to the ends of Italy in order to beg money due him. For four years he was a slave on a scaffold. Then one day he wrote to his father: "Tonight, I finished the Chapel I was painting. The Pope is pleased."

Michelangelo was scrawny and undersized, with a broken nose, a wrinkled brow, a little forked beard, and a mop of hair. He had, however, the vitality that seems to be the property

Michelangelo. *Temptation of Eve and the Expulsion of Adam and Eve. Sistine Chapel, Rome. The first pair of mortals tempted by the serpent and expelled from the Garden of Eden.*

Michelangelo. *Delphic Sibyl. Sistine Chapel, Rome. An ancient Greek figure, in a Christian setting, who emphasizes the impending tragedy of Italy.*

Michelangelo's Paradise was no more than a few rocks, a tree here and there, and a tuft of grass. It was the only kind of Paradise suitable for his men and women; for he created a race of supermen—not circus giants, but men and women with the figures and faces we associate with the highest types.

Thirty years afterward, he returned to the Sistine Chapel to paint the *Last Judgment* on the end wall. The painting provided two hundred additional figures, not one repeating a former pose.

In the latter part of his long life, he labored each day, as he had always done, in sculpture and painting, and as if those were not enough, in architecture, poetry, and engineering. He saw nine popes come and go and slaved for all of them. He carved the statues in the Chapel of San Lorenzo, at Florence. As an architect, he designed the dome for St. Peter's, still the world's largest church.

Weakened by gallstones and fevers, he worked too hard, and at the expense of his health. "I live alone," he cried, "like the pith in a sunflower. My teeth rattle; my face would scare a scarecrow; in one ear a spider spins his web, in the other, a cricket chirps all night. I cannot sleep. This is the end to which my art —my glory—has brought me!"

He began work on his last monument, his last work in marble, the *Deposition* (or taking down of Christ) *from the Cross,* in which Nicodemus was carved after his own gnarled visage. He was not up to the task and, in a fit of rage, tried to demolish the group. He worked at night by the light of a candle stuck in a cup of heavy paper; and surprised, one

Michelangelo. *Jeremiah. Sistine Chapel, Rome. Patriarch and prophet, one of the artist's supermen, and a monument of brooding power.*

night, by the sudden visit of a friend, he began to tremble and the candle dropped to the floor. "Soon," he remarked, "I shall fall like this lamp—and the light of life will go out forever."

Michelangelo. *Head of God, the Father. Sistine Chapel, Rome. The most convincing conception of the Almighty in Christian art.*

Michelangelo. *Head of Adam. Sistine Chapel, Rome. Head of the thirteen-foot figure of Adam, the first man, as he is called into being in his athletic glory.*

A slow fever began to burn his heart out, and he made his will, leaving all he had to his undeserving family, not only his estates but his strongbox containing a large fortune in cash. He died in 1564, the year of Shakespeare's birth.

Raphael. *Self-portrait, 1506. Pitti Palace, Florence. Raphael at twenty-three, "his face extremely sensitive, his expression very modest," an old writer assures us.*

9

Raphael

Above my desk hangs a print of a little group called the *Three Graces,* painted by Raphael at an age when he would have been a high school boy, had high schools existed in his time. I look at the print every day or so, and it never fails to quicken my blood. It is a boy's inspired notion of the beautiful—the clean and classic loveliness that Edgar Allan Poe understood so well when, as a boy of fourteen, he sang of "the glory that was Greece." And throughout his brief career, Raphael never paused, not even a moment, in his working devotion to the beautiful in art.

He died on his thirty-seventh birthday, and his body lay in state beside his great canvas, the *Transfiguration of Christ,* once the most popular picture in the world. The whole of Rome flocked to his funeral, and all Italy wept: the best-beloved artist of the Renaissance had gone to his Maker. For centuries Raphael was revered as the archangel of painting.

Raphael Sanzio was born in Urbino, in 1483, the son of a second-rate court painter who was also a second-rate poet. In his eleventh year, his talents were much talked about, and at sixteen, he entered the studio of Perugino, one of the most capable and honored painters of central Italy. At eighteen, he was painting as skillfully as his master, in portraiture and altarpieces alike. He absorbed from

Perugino the secrets of placing figures in celestial settings, grandly and neatly.

At nineteen, he was on his own, and at one-and-twenty, with a more than modest reputation behind him, went down to Florence where the top-flight rivals, Leonardo and Michelangelo, were battling it out for supremacy. It was not a likely moment for an outsider to shine, but Raphael, though a little delicate and too good-looking, was no sissy. On the contrary, deep within was a will to conquer that was not to be thwarted. His drawings, compared with those of Michelangelo, were loosely put together, and he plunged into the study of anatomy and the movements of the human figure. At the end of three years—for he was extraordinarily gifted—he had made himself a draftsman of the first water. He looked long and ardently at *Mona Lisa,* and from that masterpiece acquired gracefulness of modeling and learned how to capture the sweet, puzzling beauty of a woman's smile. All his life he borrowed from others, but what he took he made over into his own style, expressive of the magnetism of his rich personality.

In Florence, between the ages of twenty and twenty-five, Raphael produced a series of *Madonnas* which won for him immediate fame, and which have remained the standard idea of the Mother of God (see Plate 8). These *Madonnas* bring before us a woman fair to

91

Raphael. *The Transfiguration of Christ. Vatican, Rome. Found unfinished at the artist's death, and placed, in state, beside the body. The lower part of the canvas is the work of Romano.*

teacher, Perugino, washed down the Vatican drains. Though sensitive, he was very determined, and went to work with energy. With his corps of assistants, he covered *Stanza* after *Stanza* (room after room) with meetings of pagan and Christian folk—the ancient groups representing Philosophy, Law, Poetry, and History in a stage setting called the *School of Athens;* the opposing groups forming a Christian drama, the *Dispute of the Sacrament,* which had to do with the ceremonies of the Christian religion. Some of the frescoes clearly showed the influence of Michelangelo, but the Pope did not mind. Nor did anyone, save the great man who lay on his back on the scaffold.

"This young upstart," cried Michelangelo, "has been sneaking into my chapel. Throw him out!"

Raphael. *Saint George and the Dragon. Mellon Collection, National Gallery of Art, Washington, D.C. Painted at twenty-one, when the imaginative world of Raphael was chivalrous and poetic.*

look upon, but also filled with the glory of the inward soul, a woman with the purity and comeliness of the people of Paradise. And they are, if you look at them intently, blonde Italian girls whom Raphael knew and loved and glorified.

The fighting Pope Julius II, needled by Bramante, the architect, summoned Raphael to the Vatican. The artist, twenty-four years old, charmed the churlish old pontiff—and everybody else except Michelangelo, who was at that particular time at work in the Sistine Chapel. No empty walls being available, the impulsive Pope commanded the frescoes in some of the rooms to be erased; and Raphael, a tender soul, wept to see the murals of his old

Raphael. *The School of Athens. Vatican, Rome. The supreme mural decorator and portrait master brings to life a galaxy of great men from the antique world.*

Raphael's fame mounted so rapidly that, before he knew it, he was operating a fresco-factory with fifty assistants to fill the orders. Despite poor health, he accomplished an enormous amount of work. He designed mosaics and tapestries, headed a committee to preserve the relics of ancient Rome, was one of the architects of St. Peter's, and even tried his hand at sculpture. He was one of the foremost portrait painters, and his murals in the Vatican set the standard for wall paintings for hundreds of years. No one has surpassed Raphael in putting figures together in vast spaces so suitably and conveniently.

In the register of artists, Raphael stands out for a very simple, but also for an everlasting, reason. He thought up, and designed and created, the most beautiful people, young and old—men, women, children—ever to spring from the imagination of man. And surely, in this atomic age when beauty is somewhat forgotten, we should all look again at the young man whose heart and talents were dedicated to the cause of beauty.

He lived in splendor, and women of all classes ran after him. He was engaged to the daughter of a cardinal, but his true love was *La Fornarina*, the baker's daughter, who posed for him, and who was the model for the Virgin in the *Sistine Madonna*.

Worn out by overwork, Raphael caught a fever that never left him, and after ten days of unholy temperatures, on Good Friday, 1520, he gave up the ghost.

Raphael. *Study for Madonna and Child. Silverpoint, British Museum, London. Showing the delicacy of Raphael as his pencil stroked the human face into a living expression.*

Raphael. *La Donna Velata. Pitti Palace, Florence. The veiled lady is supposedly "La Fornarina," or the baker's daughter, the object of Raphael's deepest affection.*

Raphael. *Pope Leo X with Cardinals. Pitti Palace, Florence. The Pope with Cardinals Giuliano de' Medici and Lodovico de' Rossi, his nephews. Painted with uncompromising characterization.*

Raphael. *The Sistine Madonna. Dresden Gallery. The Madonna with St. Barbara, Pope Sixtus II, and angels—the most beloved of all Madonna paintings.*

ael. *The Dispute of the Sacrament, The
uta. Vatican, Rome. Discussion of the
monials of the Christian religion and the
fication of the Sacrament. The standard
ural painting for centuries.*

Crivelli. *Virgin and Child. Metropolitan Museum of Art, New York.* Typical of the artist's Madonnas, wry-faced and a little prim, but quaint and gentle, in a decorative setting.

PLATE 11. PIETER BRUEGHEL. *The Wedding Dance*. DETROIT INSTITUTE OF ARTS

PLATE 12. PETER PAUL RUBENS. *Rubens and His First Wife*. ALTE PINAKOTHEK, MUNICH

10
Bride of the Adriatic

We remember General Grant as a great American, terrible in war, but otherwise a modest, massive, lovable personality, sparing of words and as honest as the day is long. As President of the United States, the General was far from successful—the dupe of crooked politicans—and at the end of his unhappy years in Washington, to relax his frazzled nerves, he made a famous tour of the world. Plain-spoken, without pretensions to culture, and as practical as Robinson Crusoe, this curious American of genius arrived at the city

Doges' Palace. Venice. Open loggias with pointed arches and sculptured columns make the palace one of the finest in Europe.

known as the Bride of the Adriatic. One of his remarks will not be forgotten.

"Venice would be a first-rate city, if it were drained," he said. "My engineers on the lower Mississippi could do the job."

The idea of a city with its foundations under water, a city built on mud flats, with lagoons everywhere, a Grand Canal for the main street, and little bridges every block or two, seemed absurd to the Middle Westerner.

Today, after fifteen hundred years, Venice stands knee-deep in water, as she has always done, perhaps the most beautiful city in the world. When the fading Roman Empire was riddled by Attila, the Hun, in the fifth century, a tribe of refugees in northern Italy fled to the salt marshes at the head of the Adriatic; and there, amid a hundred islands, Venice was born, rising from the waves like the fabled goddess of love, and destined to become the pagan center of the Italian Renaissance.

Venice had little in common with the rest of Italy. With her back to the peninsula, she looked to the East, and it was from the East that she gathered her wealth and her love of splendor and gorgeous recreations. Her ships sailed the Mediterranean to the Orient, returning with rich cargoes of silks, rugs, jewels, and slaves (black and white) for the auction block.

97

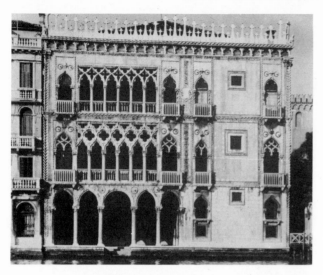

Ca d'Oro. Venice. Superb example of the elegance and tracery of the Gothic palace architecture of the fifteenth century.

Some of her captains were out-and-out pirates, and some of her rulers were highwaymen, even "sticking up" one of the holy Crusades for profit.

Unlike Florence, the lagoon city was well-behaved and peaceful, without foreign invaders or civil uprisings. Venice was governed by a council of aristocrats whose names were inscribed in the Book of Gold, and if any foolhardy schemer made so bold as to conspire against the secret policies of the nobles, he was found the next day in the stagnant waters of a dark canal with a dagger in his throat. The nobles were shrewd men and very polite until crossed—and most understanding of the arts of pleasure. They were dedicated to the enjoyment of life—to the glorification of things most appealing to the senses.

At the close of the fifteenth century, the liberal Venetians advertised their city as the "jewel casket of the world." The Grand Canal was crowded with black, flat-bottomed gondolas, or water-taxis; and in the fashionable, sometimes gaudy, shops, merchants of many nations—Turks, Moors, Greeks, Arabs, Jews,

S. Maria della Salute. Venice. The old church with its two domes is a celebrated example of the richness of the Baroque spirit.

Caravaggio. *The Calling of Saint Matthew. S. Luigi dei Francesi, Rome. The artist selected his religious characters as boon companions, or plain everyday people.*

Caravaggio. *Fruit and Foliage. Ambrosiana, Milan. Detail from a large canvas, and a realistic still-life not surpassed by the moderns.*

Carpaccio. *The Dream of Saint Ursula. Academy, Venice. The peaceful chamber of a maiden saint in the morning light, with an angel appearing in a dream, to announce the girl's martyrdom.*

and Germans—haggled over their silks, laces, enamels, and blown glass.

The architecture of the city was elaborate and exquisitely designed: St. Mark's with its domes and mosaics; marble palaces decorated with carved columns and frescoes; private houses shining through the dazzling mists in rainbow colors, with banners and flags flaunted from curved balconies. Idle, undieted women lolled on the roofs of houses, playing with dogs and doves and parrots, or bleaching their hair in the sun, since the Venetian gentlemen also preferred blondes. Muscular girls competed in boat races; chambermaids were decked out like princesses; there was no end to the pageants and processions, and the carnival season lasted for months.

In such a background of color and costly amusements, the Venetians paid less attention to intellectual matters than did the Florentines. They gave us no poets, scholars, or historians, few sculptors worth recording, and not too many painters—but some very great ones. In Florence, as we have seen, an artist was an architect, goldsmith, painter, and sculptor, all in one; in Venice he was a painter, pure and simple, required not only to execute religious subjects but also to celebrate the charms of the city.

Giovanni Bellini. *Feast of the Gods. Widener Collection, National Gallery of Art, Washington, D.C. The old Greek deities recorded in very earthy fashion—not more godlike than Venetian revelers.*

The art of painting came rather slowly into Venetian life. While the merchants were establishing trade relations with the East, there was little demand for painting, and it was not until the Ducal (Doges') Palace was built, in 1365, that the absence of artists became embarrassing. No local painter was capable of decorating the palace in appropriate style, and outsiders had to be called in. These visitors, trained in northern Europe, opened the eyes of the Venetians to the light and color of their city, and also introduced a form of oil painting much more suitable to damp climates than the fresco.

One of the early Venetian painters was Carlo Crivelli, but he was Venetian by residence rather than by the character of his

Giovanni Bellini. *Madonna with Saints. S. Maria dei Frari, Venice. Most splendid and formal of the artist's altarpieces—a queenly Madonna with saints and a couple of Venetian senators.*

Giovanni Bellini. *Doge Leonardo Loredano. National Gallery, London. One of the prize-portraits of Venice, nobly conceived, beautiful in color, faultlessly executed.*

work. He was a product of the Paduan school led by Mantegna, and persisted in using tempera colors while his rivals were struggling with the new medium of oil pigments. Crivelli was essentially a Madonna painter, and his skill with tempera (powdered colors held in solution by yolks of eggs) has never been surpassed. He caressed his pictures into designs as lustrous as enamels. His Madonnas have a wry, original, "prissy" look, unlike the more comely Virgins of the other Venetians.

Although the Venetians, as a school, brought non-religious subjects into Italian art, and although they were pleasure-loving, the painters, to a man, were truly religious, accepting commissions from the Church as a matter of course, and carrying them out beautifully. Encouraged by the rulers, they took painting into portraiture, pageantry, legends, and pastorals—into any lagoon or country garden where life was untroubled and satisfying. They avoided the harshness of life, and the miseries, and concentrated on soothing joys and relaxations.

The Venetians really came into their own

Gentile Bellini. *Corpus Christi Procession in St. Mark's Square. Academy, Venice. Religious parade with choristers and candle-bearers, dignitaries with sacred relics, sight-seers, and overlords on the balconies.*

Correggio. *The Marriage of Saint Catherine. Louvre, Paris. The Christ Child putting a ring on the finger of St. Catherine, the Virgin and St. Sebastian smiling at the gesture.*

Giorgione. *Adoration of the Shepherds. Samuel H. Kress Collection, National Gallery of Art, Washington, D.C. Generally accepted as the work of Giorgione when he was veering from sacred themes to idyllic landscapes.*

Carpaccio. *English Prince Leaves His Father and Greets Saint Ursula. Academy, Venice. Two episodes in the legend of St. Ursula—on the left, the English Prince taking leave of his father—on the right, the Prince greeting Ursula.*

when the Bellini family appeared, father and sons. Jacopo Bellini, the father—we might call him "the old man," and it would be no slander—was a character. He went down to Florence to exhibit some pictures, and was thrown into jail for beating up a hoodlum who, as a loyal son of Florence, tried to deface his canvases. Jacopo is remembered, in art, for his endless curiosity in all sorts of occupations, and for his sharp, carefully outlined sketches of buildings and animals—drawings which won the admiration of Leonardo da Vinci.

Gentile Bellini, son of the old man, was a painter of portraits and of narrative pieces. His *Corpus Christi Procession,* a view of St. Mark's Square during a religious festival, is a reflection of the Venetian love of display— with a crowd of choristers and candle-bearers, dignitaries fetching up reliquaries (sacred objects), groups of sight-seers, and in the ringside seats on the balconies, the overlords sipping wine and looking very high-class indeed.

The star of the family—"the big Bellini" as he was flippantly called—and the first of the great Venetian masters, was Giovanni, official

Carpaccio. *English Prince Greets Saint Ursula (detail). Academy, Venice. The departure of the newlyweds on their pilgrimage.*

artist to the Republic. He lived to the ripe age of eighty-six, painting better each year, and creating a new type of Madonna—quite an accomplishment in Italy. His portraits hold up in the company of masters like Titian and Holbein, and his allegorical scenes are still fresh and arresting; and, to cap it all, he was the first true painter of landscape in Italian

Giovanni Bellini. *Saint Francis in Ecstasy. Frick Collection, New York. Essentially a landscape, and one of the first. It was painted to reveal the light, color, and forms of nature.*

art. His *St. Francis in Ecstasy,* regardless of the title, is a pure landscape, composed to reveal the light and color and forms of nature instead of the doings of man. His *Feast of the Gods,* now hanging in the National Gallery of Art, Washington (thanks to the quarter of a million dollars paid for it by Andrew Mellon), presents the old Greek deities as a very commonplace crew, not more dignified than a group of Venetian revelers.

If Bellini pictured the gods as tipsy Vene-

tians, he did so with a certain smoothness and harmony and beauty. A century and a half later, Caravaggio tried his hand at a similar gathering, and his gods were hardly more dignified than a group of lawbreakers lined up in the police court. Caravaggio painted religious characters as if they were everyday people, his *Calling of St. Matthew* being a case in point. He was a technical wizard, as his still life called *Fruit and Foliage* proves.

Vittore Carpaccio, a disciple of Gentile

Veronese. *Rape of Europa. Doges' Palace, Venice. The Greek girl Europa, as played by a beautiful Venetian model, is carried off by Zeus in the guise of a bull.*

Veronese. *The Marriage Feast at Cana (detail). Louvre, Paris. A detail, presenting all kinds of revelers, for which the artist was reprimanded by the Church.*

Veronese. *The Marriage Feast at Cana (detail). Louvre, Paris. Detail from the finest of four great Feasts at Cana by Veronese—250 diners at a table resembling a Venetian banquet. The artist himself plays the violin.*

Bellini, devised narratives in paint, bringing St. Ursula (a charming Venetian maiden, as he drew her) into nine episodes concerning the Princess of Brittany who agreed to marry a titled Englishman on condition that the English king accept Christianity—and more—that he provide an escort of eleven thousand maidens in a pilgrimage to Rome.

A native of Parma, in northern Italy, but associated with the Venetians, was Antonio Allegri, known as Correggio, who amazed the men of his own time—and many since—by his incredible skill in perspective and his soft, sleek, lifelike modeling of the nude figure. Correggio was a dome painter, one of the first. As cupolas came into style, and painters were asked to depict figures seen from the floor level, Correggio demonstrated his ability to paint saints and angels in all manner of odd postures. Besides his domes, he painted Madonnas and scenes from mythology, both the Christians and the pagans coming out as beautiful examples of flesh and blood.

Giorgione, a brilliant young Venetian who died in early manhood, composed his pictures with so much eloquence of form and color that they have been called "music on canvas."

He too painted religious pictures, but he will be remembered as long as painting is an art for his pastorals—or outdoor scenes in which a few happy souls, some clothed, some not, seem to be glad that spring is upon the world. Giorgione was a poet in paint, one of the greatest, and many of his pictures are purely imaginary, or idyllic moods, charged with the light and color of the Venetian spirit.

Paolo Caliari, more recognizable as Veronese (from his home town, Verona) celebrated Venice at the height of her charm and splendor. He was the champion of the physical beauty of mature men and women, painting alluring blondes in blue and silver and nobles of strength and magnificence in grand architectural settings. He was the greatest decorator ever to lay brush to canvas. And no one, except Tintoretto, has come within reach of him in the management of crowds, the best example being the *Marriage Feast at Cana,* in the Louvre. In this stupendous blaze of worldly pomp, he portrayed, as Ruskin wrote, "the Lord and his disciples at table, and then

Guido Reni. *Aurora. Palazzo Pallavicini, Rome. The god of day, surrounded by dancing hours, and preceded by the goddess of dawn.*

proceeded to fill the canvas with fools, dwarfs, musicians, drunken Germans and other oddities, not to mention his own friends and various sinners"—a throng which shows the world, as only an artist can, how people, high and low, looked and behaved.

In Veronese, the beautiful city of Venice had a magnificent interpreter. She had two other painters, not yet named, of such stature that they are reserved for the next chapter.

Guardi. *View of Venice. Grenville Lindall Winthrop Collection, Fogg Art Museum, Harvard University, Cambridge. The lagoon city at the close of the eighteenth century, by an artist who painted from a gondola.*

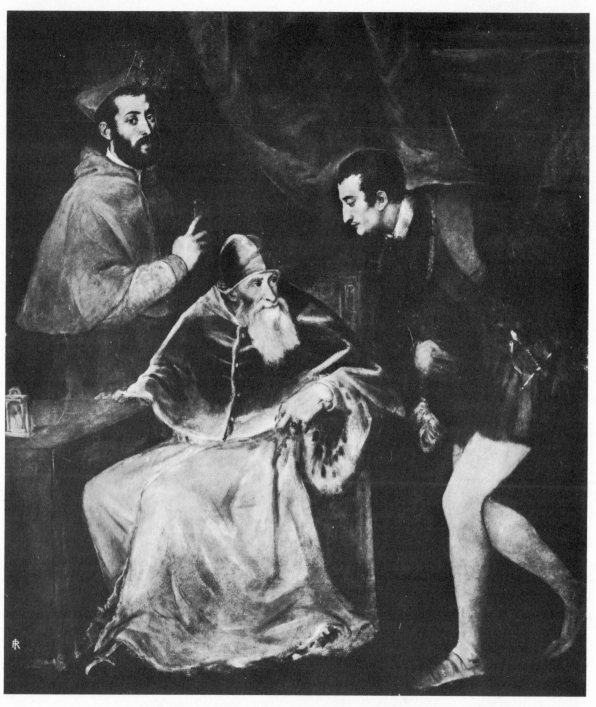

Titian. *Pope Paul III and Nephews. National Museum, Naples. The aged Pontiff weighing, by turns, the merits of his nephews, smooth flatterers and traitors.*

II
Titian and Tintoretto

In the long roster of painters, you will find none more fortunate than Titian, the great Venetian. He lived on and on, without doddering or chattering, as the aged sometimes do, with his common sense intact and his bargaining powers sharper with time—a well-balanced soul, painting in his ninety-ninth year with more boldness and originality than in his youth. He kept himself in good health, never stooping to gluttony or other excesses and never wasteful, an excellent host but always with one eye on the cost of the feast. When honors poured upon him from Germany, Spain, and the Netherlands, he accepted them graciously, and returned to his studio to work and study.

Titian was born, in 1477, at Cadore, an Alpine district seventy miles north of Venice. He went down to the Adriatic in his youth to study with Giovanni Bellini. Though talented, he did not seem precocious. From Giorgione, who was his fellow student, he learned the craft of the new oil-tempera medium, and was quick to grasp the popular appeal of Giorgione's fanciful landscapes and outdoor groupings. The two Venetians worked together without jealousy, and so close was the partnership that a number of their early paintings may have been the work of one or the other, or of both in collaboration. Not much is known of Titian's career before thirty, except that he was industrious but unhurried and that he was deliberately preparing himself to become the leading artist of the day. The moment arrived at Giorgione's untimely death and Titian made capital of it.

For half his life, with uncanny skill and sureness of touch, Titian applied his glowing style to portraits, fancy pieces, and religious themes. He made his men and women so ample and resplendent that the very light in which they are revealed seems to come from within the figures themselves and not from some distant source. No one knows how closely his portraits resembled his sitters, for in those days there were no camera likenesses for comparison; but it is a fact that after he had finished his portrait of Paul III and had put the canvas on the terrace to dry, the passing crowds solemnly halted and made the Sign of the Cross, as if they were in the presence of the Pope himself. It was his custom to finish his portraits without models, slowly revising the drawing and color into an image far more beautiful than any one model can hope to be and beyond the claws of time. He seldom painted an old man—death made the Venetians uncomfortable.

Titian, in business affairs, had the heart of a western horse-trader, never missing the

Titian. *Portrait of a Young Englishman. Pitti Palace, Florence. The Venetian ideal of aristocratic breeding, a pensive lordly figure esteemed by the dictators of gentility.*

ment. The picture, unluckily, was destroyed by fire the year of Titian's death.

At the age of forty-five, not too eagerly, Titian married Cecilia, a barber's daughter, who presented him with three children; one of them, Lavinia, was very dear to him, a strapping handsome girl who posed as Venus or Salome, according to his needs. His wife died five years after their marriage and he did not weep. With her out of the way, and with an international reputation and more commissions than he could handle, he bought a house in the suburbs of Venice. Here he lived splendidly. His studio looked across terraced gardens out to the open sea; kings and passing princes were honored to dine with him; fair women ornamented his parties, and it was whispered that a curly redhead both delighted

chance to collar an extra ducat. To increase his income, he wangled the post of painter to the State, no small honor, with certain tax exemptions allowed and the services of an assistant. It is a little distressing to note that he collected regularly the stipend for an assistant who was never employed. The official appointment was granted on condition that he paint a battle picture for the Hall of the Grand Council. For twenty-five years, while drawing his salary, he stalled the committee of the council, painting a Doge or two to keep them quiet; and the committee, in the face of his great fame, were afraid to throw him out. At last they cracked down on him, and gave him exactly one week to begin the battle piece or refund all unearned money. The prospect of losing revenue spurred him into action, and he composed, so the old chroniclers assure us, a battle of such boldness and surging magnificence as to make the town mad with excite-

Titian. *Charles V on Horseback. Prado, Madrid. Detail from the equestrian portrait of Charles V. Titian, at seventy-one, painted the old Emperor with an Impressionist touch.*

Titian. *La Bella. Pitti Palace, Florence. The imperious Duchess of Urbino, wife of the artist's wealthy patron, sumptuously gowned in velvet of peacock blue.*

and even acknowledged by Michelangelo who said that "the Venetian would have been a great artist, if he had only learned how to draw"—meaning, of course, to draw in the Florentine style.

At the age of ninety, he sent off fifteen canvases to Philip II of Spain, with a typical wheedling letter. It is worth quoting:

"In these pieces, your Majesty, I have put all the knowledge God has given me, and which has always been and ever will be dedicated to the services of your Majesty. That you will please accept this service as long as I can use my old and weary body, is my prayer; and though the burden is heavy, it becomes lighter, as by a miracle, whenever I remember that I am living to do something grateful to your Majesty."

His wailings about old age were uttered to drive a harder bargain with the Spanish monarch. The truth is that Titian, his eyesight weakening, and his hand no longer steady, was painting in an astonishing fashion—the

and angered him. It was to please this girl that he mixed a special combination of high colors into a tone that is still called Titian red, and still favored by the girls of Venice.

Midway in his career, Titian hired an agent named Pietro, or Perry, Aretino, the first publicity agent in the history of art, and an unblushing blackmailer. Aretino, however, was not a commonplace scoundrel. He loved music and painting, and came to the aid of all sorts of unfortunate people, and he was unfailingly honorable as Titian's agent. By his eloquence—he knew all the tricks of the trade —he tripled the income of the painter and persuaded the great Emperor Charles V and his family to pose for their portraits, as well as many nobles and cardinals.

In his seventieth year, Titian journeyed to Rome where he was welcomed by the Pope,

Titian. *Bacchus and Ariadne. National Gallery, London. The god of wine leaps from his chariot to console Ariadne, now forsaken by her false lover.*

colors slapped down in broad streaks, with colored lights breaking into dark shadows— a style opening the door to a modern French movement called Impressionism.

The old man continued to paint. His friends were carried off in hooded gondolas to rest in the uplands forever. He got no fun from wine or pheasants, and redheads no longer amused him. No more did he sing of the glory and delicacy of Venice; and with shuddering brush he painted a city ruined by barbarians from the North. He portrayed himself, an ancient goblin in a skullcap; and finally created a great dramatic picture, *Christ Crowned with Thorns* —far from the pagan, poetic scenes he had done with Giorgione, when all the world was young.

To his last breath, he could not overlook the cost of things. It was his hope to be buried in the Church of the Frari, but as payment for the privilege—if burial anywhere is ever a privilege—he offered to paint a *Pietà* for one of the chapels. Can you imagine an old man, one hundred years behind him, painting a picture for the price of a tomb? Titian tackled the

Titian. *Venus and Adonis. Metropolitan Museum of Art, New York. One of Titian's many versions of a popular subject. The goddess of love hopes to detain an attractive young huntsman.*

job with the resolution of youth, but before the canvas was completed, the plague crept over the poisonous canals and carried him to the hills.

When Titian was a mere fifty-six he had his first encounter with another great Venetian, whom most of us know only by his nickname.

The Italians, who cherished painting as something sacred, bestowed on artists a show of homely affection such as Americans lavish on athletes. They addressed their artists by nicknames—the Baby Bottle, or Tom the Tramp—as we refer to the Brown Bomber or the Yankee Clipper. And the artists, the majority of them, like our boxers and baseball players, springing from the lower social strata, loved their monikers and lived up to them.

In 1518, in Venice, a boy was born, christened Jacopo Robusti. As a small boy, Jacopo ran errands for his father who tinted fabrics for the Venetian markets. The father, being a dyer, it was almost inevitable that Jacopo should be called "the little dyer," or Tintoretto, a name familiar to all, for it is inscribed in the seventh heaven of the glory of art.

The little Venetian was not only born into the business of coloring fabrics but was also

Tintoretto. *Bacchus and Ariadne. Doges' Palace, Venice. The floating goddess of love bestows the chaplet and ring on Ariadne, with the lightness and grandeur of Tintoretto's brush.*

born an artist, and when he began to decorate the walls of the shop with huge pictures in singing colors, his father sent him to Titian to be trained. The story goes that Titian, hard-boiled where his own prestige was concerned, examined some of the boy's drawings and forthwith sent him on his way. True or false, the story has an obvious moral. Titian, a re-strained and orderly painter, had no time for the bold and independent spirit of the little dyer, and, it is unpleasant to add, never a good word for the young artist as he rapidly came into notice.

There was no further apprenticeship for Tintoretto. He was by nature the captain of his soul, and mastered his profession by work-ing day and night. At twenty-five he had his astounding powers in hand, and if any single expression could be found to describe his gen-ius, it might be "controlled audacity." He was sensational, and the Venetians, almost fearful of his energy, gave him another nickname, "the Thunderbolt." He was a dramatist in paint, a great draftsman with a brilliant sense of color. "One can never do too much draw-ing," he often remarked, and he invented a special contraption for lighting small clay models which he sketched in all sorts of pos-

Titian. *The Entombment. Louvre, Paris. The two Marys, and disciples, in Venetian gar-ments, turn to the form of Christ in the light of the setting sun.*

tures. He came into the luxury-loving city like a tempest, decrying the lazy splendor of those who wished to ride up and down the canals forever, as if they would finally moor their gondolas at the gates of heaven. He warned the Venetians that without faith and drafts-manship their painting would crumble; faith was needed to keep the subject matter holy, while drawing was a cable to bind one's con-victions together.

Tintoretto was one of the world's most prolific painters, and before he was thirty had painted four of his finest pictures: the *Worship of the Golden Calf,* the *Presentation of the Vir-gin,* the *Last Judgment,* and the *Miracle of St. Mark* (see Plate 9). These are illustrations of sacred stories. In his time artists had no fear of the word illustration, which today generally suggests a picture that is all right for its pur-pose, but not a work of art. In the great days of Italian art, most of the pictures were illus-trations, or interpretations of religious stories.

In Tintoretto's pictures there was nothing doubtful or uncertain. He drove his meaning home like a bolt from above. Like Shake-speare, he cut into the heart of the situation in bold strokes. In the *Presentation of the Vir-gin,* for example, the situation is viewed as if he had been an eyewitness of the drama. The

Tintoretto. *Christ at the Sea of Galilee. Sam-uel H. Kress Collection, National Gallery of Art, Washington, D.C. The action is accord-ing to St. John, but with dramatic agitations that make it very modern.*

little girl, silhouetted against the sky, stands at the top of a wide staircase, while below her we see her mother with watchful children and a row of cripples and beggars. The *Miracle of St. Mark* illustrates the story of a Christian slave condemned to death by a pagan master for praying at the shrine of St. Mark. The slave is stretched out on the ground, but the very instant the deathblow is to be delivered, St. Mark descends from heaven to shatter the instruments of torture. Here, again, one feels that the artist must have been at the scene, sketchbook in hand, and to add to that impression, Tintoretto included himself among the spectators.

In a city dedicated to exciting pastimes, Tintoretto spurned fashionable living. He was a man of simple tastes, devoted to his family, a jolly host, and carefree with his purse. One of his seven children, his favorite daughter Marietta, wearing the equivalent of blue jeans, helped him square up his big pictures. His wife was the daughter of a nobleman, and once in a while, to please her, he would dress up as formally as a Grand Councillor on parade, and take her out to dine at the Golden Terrace. Though gentle and even-tempered, he would fight, if necessary. It is told that when

Tintoretto. *Presentation of the Virgin. S. Maria dell' Orto, Venice. Painted by the artist, as an eyewitness, with the little Virgin against a bright sky, the mothers and cripples below.*

Aretino, the scoundrel who managed Titian's affairs, came to sit for a portrait, Tintoretto casually unsheathed a sword and placed it by his easel; and the blackmailer, always boastful of his dueling, was meek for once.

If there was a competitive job in the guilds, Tintoretto would bid lower than anyone else. When payments came in, he scattered his earnings among the poor and oppressed. First, he loved his art, as a tornado loves a landscape, and then his children for whom he made ingenious toys and games.

His work included religious pictures, scenes from history and mythology, and portraits, and in his capacity to get a commission finished speedily, he was equaled by one man alone, Rubens. In two months he finished two elaborate compositions, each with twenty figures. When the Charity School of St. Roch advertised for designs for a ceiling decoration, Tintoretto, having secretly obtained the exact dimensions of the space, turned up, not with sketches, but with the finished picture. The other contestants called him a cheat, but the regents of the School accepted the painting. To add to their astonishment, he presented

Tintoretto. *Worship of the Golden Calf. Samuel H. Kress Collection, National Gallery of Art, Washington, D.C. The pagan idol becomes the center of interest in a scene of startling lights and shadows.*

PLATE 13. JAN VERMEER. *The Cook*. RIJKS MUSEUM, AMSTERDAM

PLATE 14. **REMBRANDT VAN RIJN.** *Portrait of Himself.* NATIONAL GALLERY, LONDON

PLATE 15.   HANS HOLBEIN, THE YOUNGER.   *Erasmus of Rotterdam*.   LOUVRE, PARIS

PLATE 16. EL GRECO. *Toledo in a Storm*. METROPOLITAN MUSEUM OF ART, NEW YORK

the decoration to the School as an offering to the Saint who cared for the plague-stricken, and volunteered to decorate the entire School for whatever sum the regents could afford, offering three paintings a year. The offer was accepted and punctually each year, for twenty-five years, he produced the three paintings, among them the great *Calvary*, the *Temptation* and *Crucifixion*, and narratives by the score.

Always up to his chin in projects, Tintoretto painted vast scenes in which beautiful nudes

Tintoretto. *Paradise (detail). Doges' Palace, Venice. A fragment of the "Paradise," the largest painting on canvas in existence—74 by 30 feet, with 500 figures.*

Tintoretto. *A Venetian Senator. Frick Collection, New York. A senator who had been a sailor, hence the glimpse of the sea and the light turned on a weather-beaten face.*

float through the air with the greatest of ease. His battle pieces, because of the dampness, have turned dark but the clashing energy of the warriors is still in evidence. At the age of seventy-two he began to work on one of his last pictures, the *Paradise,* for the Hall of the Grand Council, as a token, he said, for the good life the Lord had granted him, and to prepare himself for the life to come. The great picture was completed and affixed to the wall shortly before he died, the largest painting on canvas in existence, 74 by 30 feet, with 500 figures! When asked the price, he answered, "Whatever you think is fair." The nobles named a figure. "Too much," he replied and insisted on taking less, thus winning a higher place in paradise for his labors and his generosity.

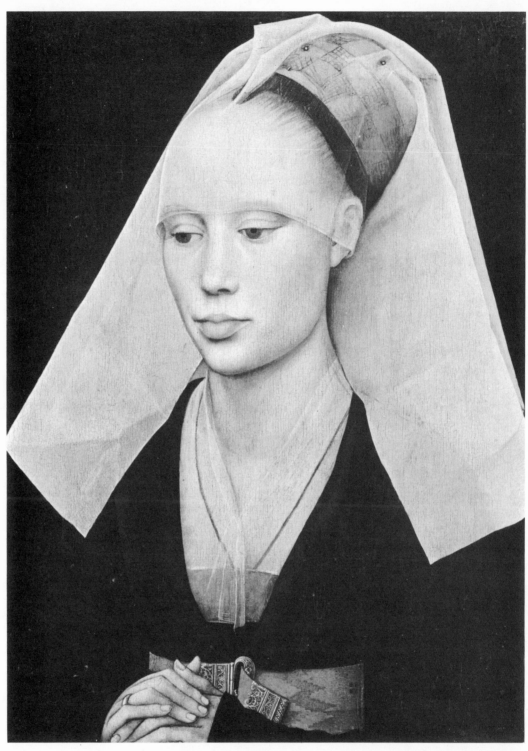

Van der Weyden. *Portrait of a Lady. Mellon Collection, National Gallery of Art, Washington, D.C. One of the glories of northern portraiture, the features modeled like sculpture. The headdress, rings, and slender fingers indicate a woman of high birth.*

I2

By the Cold North Sea

Thus far, in the course of painting, the Italians have had all the attention, and some of us, I dare say, are inclined to think that the art of painting was their unique invention and exclusive glory. The Italians themselves have not discouraged this notion, and during the Renaissance when some northern, or Flemish, pictures were exhibited in Italy, Michelangelo rose up in wrath, and we know how he could rage.

"You call these things paintings!" he screamed. "Little bits of litter here and there, all cleverly tricked out to fool the eye—trees and hills, canals and hedges, and a few saints and prophets thrown in to please the priests. Women will like these tidy, trivial scenes, especially the very old and the very young, and likewise sad nuns and friars who love to sniffle. But where is the measure and reasonableness of great painting, as we, in Florence, recognize and practice it? Where is the might of the angels of the Lord, and the shame of sinners? The sublimity and noble proportions and power that open St. Peter's gates to our art?"

Michelangelo, needless to explain, spoke with the fervent patriotism of the Florentines who swore there was something in the very atmosphere of their city favorable to the birth of divine genius. But as the world has grown older and the styles and techniques and achievements of the various nations have been interchanged and studied, we have come to appreciate all kinds of art and to understand how each one came about and under what influences it was created. We know that the arts grow and flourish as races and peoples grow and flourish, and that wherever human beings live intensely, have strong beliefs and fight for them, love and worship and rejoice and die, some kind of art will arise to bring men and women closer to one another and to animate their convictions. We also know that the arts, like trees and birds and people, are conditioned by the climate and physical characteristics of local or geographic areas. I have tried to bring out some of these distinctions in discussing the Florentines and the Venetians, but when we come to the Low Countries bordering on the North Sea, the differences from Italian art are extraordinary—as Michelangelo was quick to discover.

In Italy, with its warmth and sunshine, the buildings were conducive to wall decorations in fresco, and the churches and public halls were filled with large paintings before which people would gather as before an altar. On the other hand, in what is now Belgium and Holland, the damp climate made frescoes impossible, and painting became more and more

115

Town Hall. Bruges. Municipal architecture in the late Gothic style of the Low Countries, rich in detail and beautifully executed.

cities were hives of industry; there were 40,000 members of the textile union at Ghent, for example, and Bruges, the chief port, had more shipping than the city of Venice, 150 vessels coming to anchor in one day!

"In those days," writes an old historian, "the squares of Bruges were adorned with fountains, the bridges with statues in bronze, the public buildings with all manner of Gothic carvings, and the spotless houses hung with paintings and tapestries."

"These Gothic people," according to a traveler from Italy, "are courageous and sociable; they eat, drink, and make merry, but they work with marvelous patience. They work hard for money, and they know how to get the most for their money, and they are cold and self-possessed, the women behaving themselves when given freedom, and loving their homes—not always the case with the Italian girls when they are allowed to run."

When the great Albrecht Dürer visited Antwerp, he was amazed at the splendor of his re-

secular (that is, concerned with non-religious subjects), and smaller in scale, in order to find a spot on the walls of private houses. The Netherlands produced an incalculable number of small and intimate canvases—some in the shape of folding altarpieces for churches, but most of them portraits, miniatures, and domestic scenes such as canals with windmills, cattle, fish and fishwives, tavern doings, and fresh green landscapes, all of them designed as substitutes for nature—to brighten up the long and dismal winters in a soggy background. By following their own noses, the Flemish artists developed a style all their own.

It was five hundred years ago when the Van Eycks and their followers made pictures so fresh and staunch in color and so perfect in technical finish as to give the illusion that they were born yesterday. At the end of the fourteenth century, Flanders was booming and the

The Belfry. Bruges. The celebrated Gothic tower with the chimes that still ring out, hour by hour, day and night.

Brueghel. *A Peasant Wedding Feast. Kunsthistorisches Museum, Vienna. One of several pictures exhibiting the joys of gluttony, and the uninhibited vitality of the Flemish peasants.*

ception as a guest of the painters at the guild headquarters. At a procession held on Lady Day, he wrote that "there were 400 triumphal arches, each forty feet long and decorated with allegorical paintings. The whole town was gathered together, and I saw the various unions pass in review—the guilds of the goldsmiths, painters, masons, butchers, carpenters, sculptors, sailors, and weavers, and in advance of them, all the religious orders in their special uniforms, and a great body of widows, who made lace to support themselves—in white linen and very pitiful to look upon. At the end came the canons of Our Lady's Church, with priests, scholars, and treasures, and twenty persons bearing the image of the Virgin Mary with the Child Jesus; and floats with ships, and The Three Kings, and youths and maidens representing various saints. The procession took more than two hours to pass our house."

The Flemish people were sober, hard-working, and pious, not overrefined by the standards of Venice, but loving their homes and neighbors—and once in a while ready for a riotous brawl. They had earned the right to a little fun. For centuries, they had struggled to drain swamps, mend the wounds of war, fight floods, learn to spin and weave and paint, al-

ways hoping for a higher reward in Heaven. Suddenly they found themselves fed and clothed in fine raiment, living in strong squat little fortresses that endure as works of art.

The Flemings bent their minds to the everyday business of living, and in their continued curiosity in commonplace affairs, we may find a clue to their enormously refreshing art. They had no desire to look on the world from a mountain top. All they wanted to be was human. They loved their children, surely, and their children's dogs, and tiled, steaming kitchens and fattening foods; and they loved their canals—not for pleasure as in Venice, but as routes for barges laden with merchandise—and they loved the thousand and one quaint costumes, toys, mirrors, and knickknacks making up their routine.

The Flemish people were Catholics and they depicted the Biblical characters as plain people like themselves, often in a style based on old manuscripts decorated by the monks. Their artists were realists and craftsmen, and in a very short time, by sustained observation,

Brueghel. *The Harvesters. Metropolitan Museum of Art, New York. One of a series of paintings designed to represent the months of the calendar. The peasant laborers are resting, and the golden grain shines out against a poetic background.*

Jan Van Eyck. *Portrait of a Man. National Gallery, London. Marvelous Flemish craftsmanship, with the common man portrayed to the last line and hollow, but with a modeling and completeness no camera can touch.*

they solved most of the troublesome problems of picture-making.

About 1420, the Van Eyck brothers appeared with a new method of oil painting which was to determine the direction of art in the centuries to come. Oils had been used before as a means to protect colors, but they were the first to mix oils with the pigments. Upon an underpainting of tempera (the familiar method, using egg yolk) they applied several coats of colors, diluted with transparent oil glazes. The result was a beautifully lustrous surface with the tempera underpainting shining through clearly, and with no dry blobs or undigested patches.

To their countrymen, this was a miracle, and the bones of the right, or painting arm, of Hubert, the elder brother, were tucked in a costly casket and deposited in St. Bavon Cathedral, at Ghent.

It was for St. Bavon's that Hubert, assisted by his brother Jan, painted on hinged panels the altarpiece called the *Adoration of the Lamb,* one of the masterpieces which carry the majesty of art from here to eternity. The *Adoration* contains most of the elements ob-

Jan and Hubert Van Eyck. *Adoration of the Lamb, detail of interior panel. St. Bavon, Ghent. The White Lamb on an altar encircled by small angels; far off, the New Jerusalem.*

Jan and Hubert Van Eyck. *Adoration of the Lamb. St. Bavon, Ghent. The great altarpiece unfolded—above, Christ, flanked by John the Baptist and the Virgin Mary, angels, and Adam and Eve—below, the White Lamb with Knights of Christ at the sides.*

Jan Van Eyck. *Singing Angels, from Adoration of the Lamb. St. Bavon, Ghent. Full-throated Flemish angels singing their hearts out for the Sacred Lamb.*

Hubert Van Eyck. *Playing Angels, from Adoration of the Lamb. St. Bavon, Ghent. A lovely organist with an orchestra of angels welcoming the King of Heaven.*

jectionable to Michelangelo, to whom a single tree was the sign of a forest and a couple of rocks and weeds a convincing landscape: it contains saints and mysteries and little figures here and there, with long shadows on the vivid green of the turf, and rivers winding around

thoughtlessly, and clipped hills—and goodness knows what else. Other great works of art may stun you or take your breath away, the Sistine Chapel, for instance, or Tintoretto's thunderbolts, but nothing on earth is quite so enchanting as this vision of the Apoc-

Van Dyck. *James Stewart, Duke of Lennox. Metropolitan Museum of Art, New York. Van Dyck, star pupil of Rubens, paints a Duke in brilliant style.*

Ghent. Retreating far away is a great meadow of Easter daisies, with orange trees and roses intermixed, and a file of martyrs, Knights of Christ, Just Judges, and Holy Women. Far away there is a ridge of darker hills, and then the new Jerusalem, sharp against a skyline of bluish mountains.

All this is clear as crystal, the colors sealed by the oil glazes against the dampness of Ghent. All the little things put together add up

Bosch. *The Ship of Fools. Louvre, Paris. Illustration for a book of the same title, portraying an incident in the voyage of wayward men and women to the Isle of Folly.*

alypse. A new dawn comes up under a pale sky. In the central panel we behold Christ, noble and ruddy like a Flemish gentleman, John the Baptist, a hairy character in a green gown, a piquant Virgin Mary, and choirs of full-lipped Flemish angels singing and harp-playing. In the right and left panels are Adam and Eve, naked and scrawny, a pair of northern sinners. In the lower tier, we look into a vast lawn embroidered with spring flowers; the Fountain of Life; the White Lamb on an altar encircled by tiny white angels; prophets, apostles, philosophers, priests, and citizens of

Van der Weyden. *The Magdalene, detail from the Deposition. Prado, Madrid. Revered, of all northern Magdalenes, as the noblest personification of sorrow.*

to a great vision on the part of the two gentle brothers who looked upon the world and found it good.

Jan Van Eyck, the younger brother, is famous, separately, because of his portraits—and what faces he put on canvas! His sitters, however, were not vain, and uttered no complaints when he made their plainness distinguished by his drawing and coloring. He set down all the wrinkles, warts and blemishes, and the drooping chins which women, then as now, try to hide. His masterpiece, *John Arnolfini and His Wife* (see Plate 10), five hundred years old and as fresh as a new-laid egg, is one of the most desirable pictures in captivity. A small painting, 30 by 20 inches, it is the portrait of a little shrimp of a man in a top-heavy beaver hat and a fur cape, holding hands with a meek consort in a wimple and a

green robe that flows and overflows. You had best look at this picture with wide-open eyes. The wooly dog, of course, is not hidden, or the pairs of slippers, or the mirror on the wall, which reflects the couple. But you might examine the frame of the mirror, with its ten distinct miniatures of the Passion, and cast about for a string of amber beads, some shriveled oranges on the window sill, the one candle burning in the candelabrum, and on the wall above the mirror, in Latin and with the flourish of a schoolboy, the signature: Jan Van Eyck Was Here, 1434.

Another painter, Rogier Van der Weyden, was a man of unusual culture, a French-speaking Fleming who had traveled in Italy. He was less earthy than his rivals—in fact, likely to be very elegant, as you will see in his

Memling. *Madonna with the Red Apple. Hospital of St. John, Bruges. A Belgian Madonna with a high forehead, downcast eyes—healthy and modest.*

Brueghel. *The Blind Leading the Blind. National Museum, Naples. The old parable of civilization stated in savage northern style—the blind leaders staggering with their blind followers to their doom.*

Portrait of a Lady, a sharp-edged painting with the features modeled like sculpture, and with the hands small and thin-fingered to signify gentle birth. Van der Weyden's *Deposition,* now in Spain, with its stricken figures and the agonized Magdalene, stands worthily with the great *Depositions* of Italy.

Visitors to Bruges do not easily tire of the old Gothic buildings, the canals, the celebrated Belfry, and the pictures by Hans Memling. Every time you enter a medieval landmark, you are face to face with a Memling. This painter, a German by birth who spent his working life in Bruges, was a craftsman with a steady, gentle touch as he brought his figures to life in hard pigments. His *Madonnas* have the Flemish look: the foreheads high, the eyes drooping in short downward glances, the expressions modest and charming, not starchy, not sugary.

As we approach the sixteenth century in the Low Countries, we have the spectacle of

Flemish painters traipsing diligently over the Alps into Italy, and returning with just enough heroic stuff in their befuddled minds to ruin the fine old Flemish tradition. They tried to be Titians and Tintorettos and succeeded only in making themselves ridiculous. In the midst of this predicament, a robust and remarkable character arose, a sort of Mark Twain of Flanders, by name Pieter Brueghel.

Brueghel, the old man—he had a painting son who went to Italy and became very feathery and ladylike—was once regarded as a clodhopper with a talent for odd and humorous paintings. Now he ranks with the top-flight artists of the western world, a broad-shouldered, broad-visioned, substantial painter interested in the habits and behavior of people, notably the peasants, and in the soul troubles of all his countrymen.

Brueghel never passed up an opportunity to paint crowds—not mere crowds, but multitudes and cataracts of people, swarming and surging for food and drink, for love and a let-down from toil, and for a truce with their Maker. At first, following the goblins and monsters of the medieval artists, he portrayed the peasants as if they were half-tipsy animals afraid to be decent; and he also portrayed them as searching for the better land, in a kind of Pilgrim's Progress.

As a young man, Brueghel climbed over the Alps and looked at the Mediterranean and the arts of Italy. It was a magnificent vista, but it did not change him. He knew where he belonged. He was a Northerner, a link between the Van Eycks who pictured the miracle of the *Lamb* and the great man who was to come, Peter Paul Rubens.

Besides painting his peasants, with their

feasting and ponderous dancing (see Plate 11), and those strange multitudes scrambling up the hills to the Crucifixion, Brueghel composed some of the mightiest of landscapes. In his own style, with never so much as a bow to Bellini and the Italians, he planned a series of twelve landscapes to symbolize the months. Five of these were completed, such as *Dark Day* and *Hunters in the Snow*, pictures of winter with its frozen stillness, of the sports of Northerners, and of the snug houses, the barns, the animals, and seasonal labors—landscapes as dramatic as those of Rubens.

In the later Gothic days of the Low Countries, a painter lived and worked under the forbidding name of Hieronymus Van Aaken. He was a popular artist while he lived, and

Brueghel. *Hunters in the Snow. Kunsthistorisches Museum, Vienna. A frozen winter landscape relieved by the sports of men, the figures drawn in silhouette against the snow.*

Bosch. *Christ Bearing the Cross. Ghent Museum. A screaming mob, hideously caricatured, surrounds the figure of Christ in a close-up picture.*

In that part of the Low Countries now called Holland, beginning with Frans Hals, a national outburst of painting occurred which was over and done with in two generations. It was a local uprising during which Holland was stockpiled with painters, and a good picture was fair exchange for a keg of beer or an Edam cheese. And most of the paintings were done while troops were marshaling and cannon roaring, while the Spaniards were trying to grind the Dutch under their heels.

Hals, drunk or sober, was a "pro," as we say, one who makes his living by his profession, and at his best, in streaks and patches that flow and unite and remain where they belong, he made his models immortal—his fishwives and crackpots, his feasting soldiers and woebegone women in charge of charity homes. In one swift glance, he caught the faces of his

suddenly, in our own twentieth century, he has been praised exceedingly under his more common signature, Jerome Bosch, or simply Bosch.

Bosch painted religious pictures and allegories that will amuse and astonish and sometimes repel you. He brought the drama of Christianity not just down to earth but into the caverns under the earth, where monsters are bred and devils keep them company, and where the world is savage and horrible. His savage canvases delighted the sour Philip II of Spain who devoted a room to Bosch's insanely fantastic creations—half-fish and half-men, toads with the faces of women and men flying with the wings of bats, and huge insects straddling tablespoons. Nothing seems to make sense and yet everything is painted in a clear and beautiful style. Bosch is in the limelight today because the Surrealists, trafficking in the weird and the disconnected images of the dream world, point to him as their spiritual ancestor.

Hals. *The Merry Company. Metropolitan Museum of Art, New York. The feasting topers and a girl have had too much to drink and are excited about it.*

Hals. *Hille Bobbe. Kaiser Friedrich Museum, Berlin. Also called "Molle Bobbe"—an old Holland witch with the bird of lunacy on her shoulder.*

portrait of the board of regents.

He delineated all kinds of people, from the members of the civic guards to the town loafers—and if you are interested in the men and women of seventeenth century Holland, you have only to look at the gallery of portraits into which Frans Hals put his heart and soul and his slapdash genius.

The solid citizens of seventeenth century Holland did not regard an artist as anybody in particular. Artists lived poorly, accepting any odd job coming their way; and Jan Steen, who should have been a popular idol, left five hundred unsold pictures to the world, any one of which today is more valuable than government bonds of large denominations.

Jan Steen was born at Leyden and educated in the university there. He set out to be a

sitters, the solid fighting men who resisted the Spaniards and the tipsy crew who sang with him in the taverns. He was a spontaneous artist, if ever one lived, splashing his colors here and there with a recklessness that seemed to be only the good luck of an inspired toper; but, actually, they were the sure-fire shots of one of the most dazzling performers in the business, a craftsman who knew precisely where each smear of color was essential.

In his day-by-day career, wretched and hilarious by turns, Hals, frankly, was wanting in self-discipline. He said he didn't need it, that he did very well as God made him. There is a well-founded suspicion that his first wife died after a beating he had given her, when he was drunk; but he married again and brought up ten children, several of whom tried to be painters. While his second wife lay in her deathbed, Hals, eighty years old and living shabbily in an old men's home, painted the

Hals. *Portrait of a Man. Frick Collection, New York. Speaking characterization of a portly Dutch burgher in his best clothes.*

Hals. *Banquet of Officers of the Civic Guard of Saint George. Frans Hals Museum, Haarlem. The Civic Guards portrayed with consummate dash and skill—one turns down a glass, through which a plate of oysters is visible, and above which is a hand squeezing a lemon.*

scholar, and then a brewer, and failing as both, finally managed to keep alive by running a tavern. Steen was more than a heavy drinker with a talent for painting. He was a serious student of the Dutch people whom he painted with sympathy and understanding—not only the doctors and apothecaries, but the prodigal sons and daughters, the crowded households, and the heavy little children who were always in the picture.

Jacob Van Ruisdael painted the landscapes of Holland, the country every Dutchman loved because he had fought for it. He was a profoundly serious and hard-working observer of nature, but the Dutch buyers, somehow, did not care for his dark, dramatic mountain torrents and cemeteries, and he

Jacob Van Ruisdael. *The Cemetery. Detroit Institute of Arts. One of the most poetic of landscapes, with a dramatic burst of light in a storm—made in a cemetery.*

Hobbema. *Avenue at Middelharnis. National Gallery, London. A popular picture everywhere, and a triumph of geometrical perspective of a road leading into a long reach of light and space.*

Vermeer. *View of Delft. Mauritshuis, The Hague. Vermeer's one outdoor canvas—his native town in lucid tones, the touches of blue in the trees predicting Impressionism.*

died in the poorhouse. He was a gloomy soul, alone most of his days; it was his habit to make careful drawings of the countryside, and in the privacy of his workshop, to build them into paintings which should stir anyone to admiration. His rendition of the *Jewish Cemetery* is one of the most somber and awesome and poetic landscapes ever painted.

The hardheaded Dutchmen, unlike the Italians, wanted nothing heroic in their art. Heroism was for the defenders of the country; art was an instrument to brighten the corner of the kitchen and a little corner of the heart. It was permissible to put a little drama into the paintings—but not too much, for drama, too, was for men of action.

Pieter De Hooch, son of a butcher, was a footman in the house of a rich merchant; he married a big-hipped girl from Delft, and died in Amsterdam without a penny to his name. To say more about his life would be to spin fictions, but his paintings tell us much. His ideas were as simple as arithmetic, as clean as a Dutch casement. He presents his people in courtyards, scrubbed and spotless—both the people and the yards—beautifully assembled; everything is observed in an atmosphere just

De Hooch. *Interior of a Dutch House. National Gallery, London. Everything rendered with ease and precision—a completely satisfying glimpse of the decorative cleanliness of Dutch life.*

rinsed by a rainstorm, everything lucid, spotless, and decorative, and set down with a craftsmanship that serves but one purpose, to record a typical view of Dutch life with lucidity and good sense.

Meindert Hobbema lived and labored in a damp corner of the Dutch countryside. Day after day, in all seasons and weathers, he inspected the trees and polders, the clouds and mists, the stagnant waters and reflected lights; and after storing his impressions neatly in his mind, he drew them out, one by one, and painted them, with changes to suit his sense of design, from the depths of his wonderful memory. His *Avenue at Middelharnis*—seen from the front, center, and offering a perspective problem professionals like to avoid—is one of the most popular landscapes on record, possibly because of its dense, poetic, and peaceful loneliness.

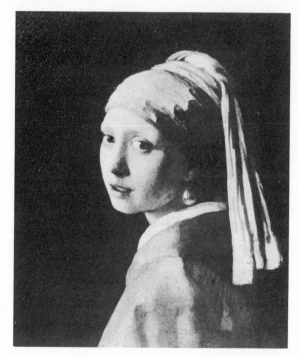

Vermeer. *Head of a Young Girl. Mauritshuis, The Hague. With a green background, green shadows, a blue turban, and a yellow dress, it is clean and pure in color and tone—a girl's head converted into a technical masterpiece.*

Vermeer. *The Artist in His Studio. Kunsthistorisches Museum, Vienna. Sole surviving self-portrait and a back view at that—the artist working from a model in exotic costume.*

Few things on this earth are so valuable as a painting by Jan Vermeer, not diamonds, not uranium, not the voice of Crosby. A few years ago a Dutch painter, soured by failures and longing for money, took vengeance on the collectors who had rejected his work. After fifteen years of the most painstaking preparations, he forged a number of Vermeer pictures—forged them so convincingly that before he was jailed he had sold the canvases for more than $2,000,000!

I do not know why a Vermeer is worth so much money, but I do know that no other canvases are quite like them—quite so perfect in their way. Jan Vermeer came from Delft, famous for its blue china. He went in for painting, married early—before he knew what he was in for—and had eight children, painted a few pictures, and died in his early forties, a bankrupt. The secret of his fame—and it is

PLATE 17. VELÁSQUEZ. *The Maids of Honor*. PRADO, MADRID

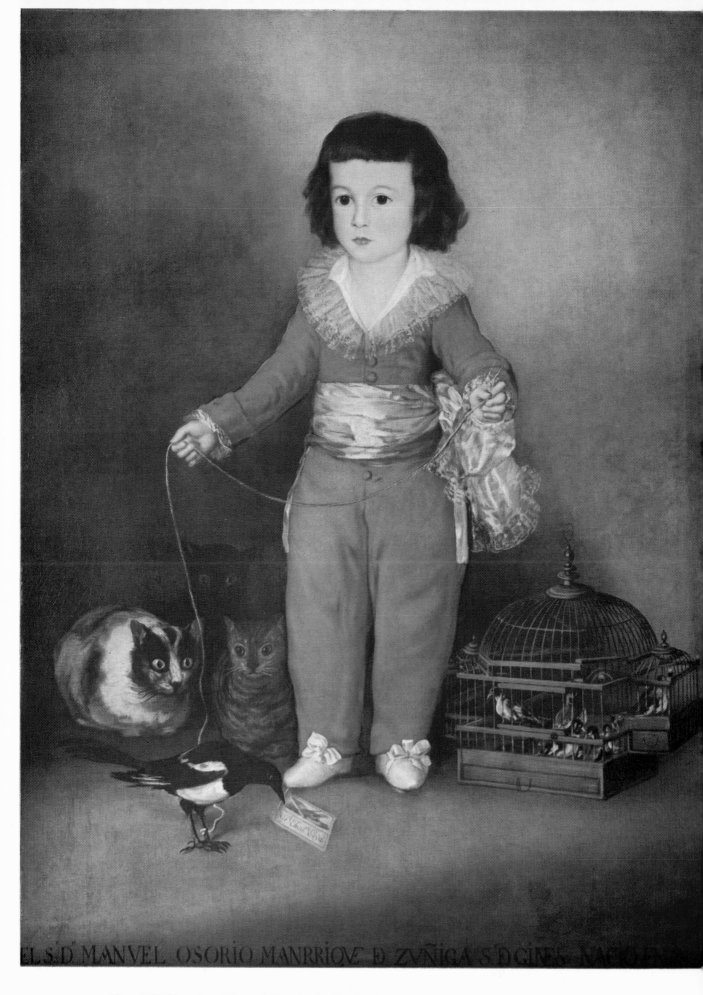

PLATE 18.   GOYA. *Don Manuel Osorio de Zuñiga*. METROPOLITAN MUSEUM OF ART, NEW YORK

hardly a secret—may be found in a remark by Michelangelo who said that little things, or trifles, done to perfection, build up into great things, or art.

Jan Vermeer knew exactly what he could do, and how to do it. He did not look on art as some vast philosophical system, like Michelangelo, but as one small job done beautifully. As a rule, he preferred one-room interiors: a small nook with a tiled floor, a wall hung with

Steen. *The Tooth Extractor. Mauritshuis, The Hague. Steen loved to paint doctors and dentists and to concoct little dramas of suffering patients.*

Vermeer. *The Letter. Rijks Museum, Amsterdam. The maid delivers a letter, possibly a love letter, but maybe a note from a suspecting spouse, or a sheriff's warning—a flawless interior seen through a vestibule.*

maps, and to the left, a window admitting the light on a single figure, usually a woman (see Plate 13). His favorite colors were blues and yellows, which he set down faultlessly in surfaces as smooth as old ivory. He worked for months on end on his small pictures, weaving his colors into transparent tones that suggest blue skies and amber, and observing his figures reflected in mirrors in order to see them from every angle.

Rubens. *Abduction of the Daughters of Leucippus. Haus Der Kunst, Munich. One of the most beautifully composed pictures in the world—complicated rhythms with animation throughout. An interpretation of the Greek myth of Castor and Pollux making off with two brides.*

13

The Prince of Painters

For a long time the Rubens family, of Antwerp, had been dealers in drugs, hides, and sundries—and with a spotless reputation until one of them suddenly dragged the good name of the family into the dirt. He was John Rubens, father of the artist, a doctor of laws stuffed with Latin like the scholars of his day, and a blunderer and coward. At the worst possible moment, when the Spaniards had let loose the Duke of Alba, or the hound of hell, on the Low Countries, he chose to change his religion to Calvinism and, to escape the cruelty of the invaders, scurried to Cologne, in Germany. Here he got into more trouble, with a princess involved, and was thrown into jail for a couple of years. His loyal wife stuck by him, and on his release she moved with her four children and her weak-willed husband, to a country town near Cologne. On June 28, 1577, her fifth and last child was born, and named Peter Paul after the two apostles on whose feast day he was baptized.

The Spaniards made a desert of the rich Flemish country, once the most prosperous in Europe. Half the population fled; villages were abandoned; the weavers found employment in England; skinny horses cropped at tufts of grass in the streets; and convents sprang up here and there to comfort the old and homeless.

When the boy, Peter Paul, returned with his valiant mother to Antwerp, the Spanish tyranny had lifted; and as the city recovered its wealth, through him the name of the Rubens family was not only made honorable again but raised to the highest eminence. The boy was an excellent Latinist, thanks to his father's tutoring; he had learned German in Cologne, and before he was in business as an independent artist, had mastered seven languages.

He was never idle, and was always quiet and agreeable, without a trace of the vanity that often affects those of exceptional talents. At the age of thirteen, while serving as a foot page to a princess, he learned French and the folderol of the highborn, but court life did not corrupt him. "They are always dressing and undressing," he said to his mother, "putting on too much, taking off too much. I had rather be an artist than a king."

His mother encouraged him, and he studied with three teachers, each a follower of the Italians; and with his natural gifts and his capacity for work, he was, at twenty-one, licensed to practice painting in the Guild of St. Luke, and pronounced the most promising artist of Flanders. At twenty-three, healthy and confident, he traveled from Antwerp to Venice on horseback.

Rubens. *The Painter's Sons. Liechtenstein Gallery, Vienna. Princely sons of handsome parents in these portraits done in full-blooded style with beautiful textures.*

The gods had been good to Peter Paul Rubens. He was the prince of painters: tall and handsome, with ruddy complexion, mild brown eyes, long auburn hair carefully parted and brushed back, a trimmed beard, and curled mustachios, and in keeping with his good looks, a flair for the finest clothing. So greatly favored by nature, in appearance and the ability to paint, he found the doors of the most influential Venetians opened wide to him.

The great artists of the Renaissance were

gone, but Rubens was equipped to equal their distinction. He was attached to the court of the Duke of Mantua as official painter, which meant that he was called upon for portraits now and then, and for large compositions of the Duke and his family engaged in religious observances. As the Duke's envoy, he supervised a cargo of presents to Philip III of Spain and the court: a coach and seven horses, a rock-crystal vase filled with perfumes, copies of paintings, a chest of silver, crucifixes, candlesticks, fashionable clothing, and expensive gewgaws. Some of the paintings were damaged by moisture on the voyage, and Rubens swiftly restored them, substituting his own for those completely ruined. On his return to Italy, he found time, in addition to his paint-

Rubens. *Elevation of the Cross, detail of central panel. Cathedral, Antwerp. Marking the formation of the artist's own style after eight years of study in Italy, and testifying to his religious convictions.*

ing, to study science, architecture, and antiquities, and to correspond in Latin with the learned men of Europe. During his ninth year in Italy, he received bad news of his mother's health, and he rode back over the Alps as fast as possible, only to discover, when he arrived in Antwerp, that she had died before he had set out from Venice.

In the homeland again, Rubens said, "I never painted anything entirely my own until I had warmed my blood at the Flemish hearth"—that is, until he returned from Italy to live with his own people.

Already famous, he was welcomed by the people of Antwerp and named court painter to the Viceroy. His country was at peace again, prosperity just around the corner, and the churches, denuded by Protestants, ready to be filled with pictures. In a few strenuous years, his productivity and ability made him the monarch of European painting.

He married Isabella Brant, seventeen years old, large, handsome, and Flemish, and to celebrate the happy union, painted himself and his bride (see Plate 12) holding hands in a bower of honeysuckle, splendidly dressed. He wore a doublet of yellow brown, black velvet breeches, orange stockings, and Henri Quatre hat, and showed Isabella in a black jacket, blue satin bodice embroidered in gold, violet skirt, and yellow petticoat.

Many artists are tragic figures, unable to cope with cruel realities and practical matters. Not so with Rubens. He was on good terms with the world, and in possession, as a French writer put it, of "the most remarkable balance that ever existed in a human brain." He was able to create living forms of every sort, not only single figures, nudes, and portraits, but many figures swirling in complicated rhythms, abounding with vitality and color and movement, and executed with technical brilliance. He was the most marvelous of painters, if not the greatest. He was also a shining example of modesty and good breeding, though he lived in princely style.

His house in Antwerp was a remodeled pal-

ace, with galleries for his pictures and carvings, and a studio in keeping with his large-scale operations, 46 by 35 feet, and 30 feet from floor to ceiling, with adjoining quarters for his assistants. Outside were broad lawns and formal gardens through which white peacocks and hunting dogs roamed at will, and, beyond the gardens, stables for his Spanish horses. Over one of the doorways was a quotation from Juvenal, *Mens sana in corpore sano*, etc., "a sound mind in a sound body," if you remember your Latin, "and a brave heart innocent of fear and avarice and unacquainted with the terrors of death."

From all parts of Europe came painters, scholars, and politicians to the Rubens palace, and he entertained them with the courtliness and unaffected hospitality of his expansive soul. Yet he—the most celebrated painter in Europe—lived temperately. At four in the morning, the year round, he was up, and after hearing Mass went to his studio. As long as there was daylight, he painted; late in the afternoon, he went out to relax and exercise his blooded horses. He ate and drank sparingly, and at night, in the company of visiting

Rubens. *Garden of Love. Prado, Madrid. To the left, Rubens and his young wife embracing in the company of richly dressed ladies and gallant gentlemen who are assembled in a baroque garden.*

Rubens. *Francesco Gonzaga IV. Kunsthistorisches Museum, Vienna. Portrait of one of the younger members of the Gonzaga family to whom Rubens was attached as court painter in his Italian period.*

vases were dispatched to European consumers.

Rubens observed to the letter certain rules for his studio. If the order were urgent, he executed it entirely by his own hand, since none could compete with him in skill and speed. If not, he designed the work himself, made the preliminary sketches from models, and left the actual paintings to specialists in his employ. In the selling of pictures, he was scrupulously honest, describing in detail the extent of his own labors and those of his assistants, and regulating the price according to his own participation in the job. His wholesale methods increased the demand for paintings and gave employment to trained men, but they also left

dignitaries and friends, discussed his collections and affairs of state.

With his *Descent from the Cross,* his leadership was assured, and young artists, instead of going to Italy to study, flocked to Rubens—that is, as many as he could accommodate, for he was obliged to turn away hundreds of applicants. So great was the demand for his pictures, that he organized a wholesale-production workshop equipped to manufacture gigantic decorations, religious and mythological pieces, portraits, landscapes, and designs for the tapestry weavers. He employed a staff of assistants, the most valuable being Van Dyck, a boy of nineteen and a dazzling artist who ran off to England later on. Under the direction of the master, some three thousand can-

Rubens. *A Woman's Head. Drawing, Haus Der Kunst, Munich. In the assured style of the artist at the age of forty, the modeling is a plastic triumph, the likeness superb.*

Rubens. *Flemish Kermis. Louvre, Paris. The riotous peasants, with color and physical abandon, create a swinging dance of life.*

the world many pictures now catalogued as the work of Rubens but, in truth, the work of "Rubens and Company."

For fifteen years Rubens kept his machinery in high gear. There seemed to be no limit to his energies. Besides filling the onrush of orders from Church, state, and wealthy laity, he found time to write a book on architecture and another on old gems, and to visit Holland on a diplomatic errand. The bigger the commission the better. "I confess," he wrote to King James of England, "better fitted to do works on a very large scale than to paint little curiosities. No undertaking, however vast in size and diversity of subjects, has daunted my courage." Michelangelo would have approved those words.

Shortly after this declaration, he was chosen for a task demanding the use of all his talents. Maria de' Medici, sister-in-law of his Italian patron, the Duke of Mantua, was now Queen

Rubens. *The Emperor's Palace. Pierpont Morgan Library, New York. A rare example of the artist's use of water colors—a simple sketch, or layout, of a palace and grounds.*

of France. A crafty, shameless woman, she built herself, in Paris, an ornate Italian palace, and appointed Rubens to decorate one of the galleries with episodes from her shady life. The French artists howled their disappoint-

Rubens. *The Coronation of Maria de' Medici. Louvre, Paris. The twelfth of the thirty-six murals designed for the Luxembourg Palace to celebrate the shady career of Maria de' Medici, who ordered the paintings.*

ment, but the fat Queen knew what she was doing. "There is only one Rubens," she said, "and all the painters of France and Italy would not accomplish in ten years what Rubens would do in four."

The commission asked for eighteen panels each 13 by 10 feet; three canvases 13 by 24 feet, and a number of 8-foot portraits. Rubens designed all the pictures and revised them, once in his studio, and again in the palace, galloping from Antwerp to Paris and home again, constantly bothered by the interruptions of the bossy Queen. Eventually, he told her where to get off—politely, of course—and permitted no one to view the paintings before the last panel was installed. At the end of three years, at the official opening, Maria gushed and raved and so did her son, Louis XIII, though he was much confused about the allegories; and all the royal parasites shouted that nothing so gay and resplendent and remarkable had ever before been seen on this earth.

The paintings are now in the Louvre, and in none of the panels did Rubens adhere to the facts. Instead of trying to disguise the sensational incidents in the life of the Queen, he relied on his imagination, and on mythological subjects which, in his time, were fresh and popular. The Queen became a heroine of a glittering carnival, attended by goddesses, nude Fates, muses, and nymphs, and was honored at her wedding by Jupiter and Juno.

The murals for Queen Maria were delayed by ventures into international politics. As an ambassador, Rubens was sent to Holland and Paris; and when his wife died, "to ease the sorrows of the heart," he wrote, he "plunged once more into politics," and rode over the mountains to Spain. He spent a year in Madrid, in conferences with the King, painting royal portraits, and counseling a young artist named Velásquez. From Spain he went to England, and then to Antwerp again.

Rubens was fifty-three now, a lonely widower. When advised to choose a lady from the court, he answered, "I have observed the arrogance which accompanies nobility, and I have in mind a young middle-class woman." Young indeed! She was just sixteen and the most beautiful girl in Antwerp—"a triple combination of wife, mother, and model," he said later, "and perfect in each role." You may see the face and figure of this blonde Flemish goddess in many of his pictures, in groups with her six children, as Mary Magdalene and the Virgin, as a pagan nymph, and as Venus in the *Judgment of Paris.*

Sick of politics and social life, Rubens bought a country home where he painted some of the most original and sweeping and powerful landscapes ever conceived. Inspired by his young wife, he kept his creative fires constantly aglow. He delivered 112 canvases in one consignment to the King of Spain. But his unparalleled labors were soon ended. After ten years of second-marriage happiness, his old enemy the gout, an undeserved affliction, caused him acute suffering, then paralysis of the arms, and finally heart failure. He died in his sixty-third year, and the religious orders of Antwerp celebrated seven hundred masses for the repose of his soul.

To satisfy his boundless interest, Rubens needed the whole wide world of art and life: saints and angels; the pomp of mythology and the drama of history; the realism of portraiture and the Homeric beauty of landscapes; the sturdy huntsman and little children; fields, harvesters, and rollicking peasants; and the opulence of life, the superb health and lushness of blonde Flemish women whom he transformed into strapping goddesses. He needed warmth and color and action; rich vermilions, golden browns, and the greens of springtime, and many figures woven together in deep space, in spirals and counter-spirals, to express his own version of the endless dance of life.

Rubens. *Wolf and Fox Hunt. Metropolitan Museum of Art, New York. An imaginary hunting scene organized by Rubens in his most spirited style and executed with the help of his assistants.*

Rembrandt. *Self-portrait with Saskia. Dresden Gallery. Painted shortly after the artist's marriage, it is a tribute to the bride, and one of his few happy pictures.*

14

The Last of the Giants

All of us know how Rembrandt van Rijn looked. From youth to death he painted his portrait, not to advertise his broad Dutch face, but to show how the gladness of life, and the stings and sorrows, are written in one's changing countenance, if the artist has the wit to read them and the talent to express them in paint. The young Rembrandt was brusque and even cocky. The popular, successful Rembrandt of early manhood wore silk shirts and velvet jackets and picturesque berets. In the last portraits—after he had gone through the mill, loving God, the memory of his frail and gentle wife, his blessed housekeeper, gin—the face is deeply seamed and coarsened, but direct and monumental, the face of a lordly man who in the end kept himself humble and lived by choice among the lowly. In the words of Joseph Conrad, "Rembrandt has the face and soul of a man who, by his great works, binds together all troubled, struggling mortals."

Rembrandt was born at Leyden, in 1606, into a family comfortably situated. His father owned several houses and a windmill that ground malt for the brewers. His mother was the daughter of a baker; and his four brothers, all older than himself, were happy to string along as shoemakers or grinders of malt. There was one sister—whom he painted over and over again, generally in costume as a fine lady and looking very scared. From the time that he cut his first teeth, it was clear that the youngest son would never be a humdrum Dutchman. The artist was imprisoned within him. Instead of examining the working machinery of his father's windmill, the boy was fascinated by the shadows; instead of sitting by the fireplace and guzzling ale, he was busy making sketches of the family. When he went out to the ramparts of the Rhine, he watched the colored sails and the salty faces of the bargemen, and stocked his head with impressions.

His mother worried about him—her favorite son—praying every night that he might be a preacher, or scholar, or, coming down a little, a surgeon, as the Dutch were the "sawbones" of Europe. In the long evenings she read the Scriptures to him—the only book in his whole life that interested him. When he was fourteen, she entered him in the Latin school of the University of Leyden, but it was a mistaken venture. He cut his classes, spent his study hours at the local zoo drawing animals or on the dikes sketching laborers. When finally brought to book, he rose up and said, with a boy's decision, "I am going to be an artist."

His first teacher, no great shakes as an

139

Rembrandt. *Hendrickje Stoffels. Collection of Duveen Brothers, Inc. The artist's faithful housekeeper and companion portrayed as the artist loved and esteemed her.*

is taken from a set dealing with tramps and paupers, little black-and-white pictures which some years ago were low-priced because of their subjects, but which are in high favor today.

At twenty-one, Rembrandt was on the way to popular fame, and his art was now his whole life. At twenty-five he painted a number of small Biblical dramas which do not suffer by comparison with the majesty of his later masterpieces. He moved to Amsterdam in his twenty-sixth year. Amsterdam, unscathed by the horrors of war, was thriving, the merchants growing rich and arrogant, and willing to buy pictures from artists capable of flattering their parvenu tastes. Fashionable painters, who aped the Italians with trumped-up scenes of Jupiter chasing plump Dutch nymphs, pocketed most of the guilders, while honest artists starved, or lived from hand to mouth.

artist, had enough intelligence to encourage him. Three years later, he was sent to Amsterdam to the studio of the famous Lastman, who paraded a style picked up in Rome, but who was practical enough to show his pupil the latest methods of lighting, and to teach him the craft of etching.

At Leyden again, Rembrandt worked like a trooper for seven years, learning most by observing his own people, but profiting by the Italian paintings in local collections. His art, first and last, began at home. The maimed and unlucky absorbed him. Swarms of beggars and cripples, the ugly backwash of the wars, roamed over Holland, pleading for a new crutch or a crust of bread, and he drew them on copper—etching them—sometimes with a lusty abandon that soldiers understand very well. I have on my walls a Rembrandt etching, done when he was twenty-one, of a crippled soldier haggling with a greedy girl. The print

Rembrandt. *Doctor Faustus. Etching, Metropolitan Museum of Art, New York. The old necromancer communicated with the spirits by means of the magic disk.*

Rembrandt defied the phonies, but by sheer ability and the technical superiority of his portraits he made plenty of money. His name circulated throughout Holland. The Dutch loved portraiture and Rembrandt was a dead shot at likenesses; but after setting down their unsmiling faces, he returned to his studio, and to the Bible for inspiration.

At one stroke, by a single canvas, he found himself head and shoulders above his competitors. The canvas was the *Anatomy Lesson,* now at The Hague. In reproductions, it hangs in the offices of doctors everywhere, a work of genius and a little ghastly, but hard to ignore as you squirm in a doctor's reception room. Professor Tulp, in a big hat, is giving a surgical demonstration to a group of bareheaded doctors, some of whom are staring, not at the corpse, but into space like bearded actors before a camera. It is a "group portrait," with the doctors faithfully presented for the pleasure of friends and patients. But the corpse, carefully painted from life—or death—gives it a dramatic center of interest.

Rembrandt's fame did not turn his head; nor did his growing income prevent his rise to a kind of art the unimaginative Dutch could not tolerate. He kept a hide-out in a warehouse on a canal which served as a refuge for the broken-down delinquents he loved to paint, and for himself when he wished to be alone with his visions. Here he depicted a naked scarecrow of a woman whom he called *Diana in the Bath,* a slap at the imitators of the Italians.

One day his dealer brought a cousin to the studio, a girl of twenty named Saskia, blonde, sweet-faced, soft of speech, and every inch a lady. She was an orphan from a patrician family and jealously guarded by a poor relation. Rembrandt wooed her impetuously and won her, sending her as a token a portrait sketch bearing the words, "Saskia, at the age of twenty-one, the third day after our engagement." Rugged and formidable, the artist was also tender and romantic. Her relatives were violently opposed to the marriage. Everybody

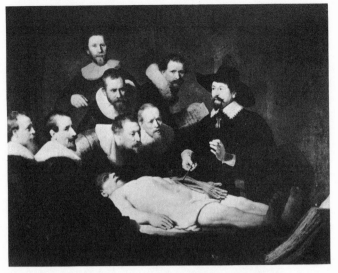

Rembrandt. *The Anatomy Lesson. Mauritshuis, The Hague. A Dutch professor in a clinical demonstration—a memorial painting for the surgeon's guild of Amsterdam.*

admitted that he had a reputation, and that he could keep a wife in fine style—but after all, he was only a painter and the son of a maltgrinder!

Rembrandt loved children and the joys of the home; and those domestic irritations which sometimes drive an artist to drink, or divorce, never got under his skin. After his marriage, to please his wife, he painted a nuptial scene: himself in regal dress, a sword at his belt, fondling the lovely Saskia on his knee. He laughs as he raises an exceedingly tall glass, and his bride is radiant. Underneath, however, he was far from lighthearted. He had captured the girl he loved, but the strange and sorrowful ferments that made him great were driving him away from his clients into a world they did not understand.

Saskia was a gentle girl, not jealous of her husband's real love, his art; not resentful of his solitary habits as he sat alone, always painting. She made no effort to reform him or drag him into high society; and if he put out money extravagantly for works of art, he indulged her with equal expenditures for jewels

Rembrandt. *Lady with a Fan. Widener Collection, National Gallery of Art, Washington, D.C. In the artist's final style and one of the great portraits of the world in depth of feeling and the living reality of the subject.*

To escape the busybodies of Amsterdam, and to observe the unfortunates who were the human material of his pictures, he moved into the heart of the ghetto—to a house large enough for his collections, his assistants, and a suitable studio. It was a blow to Saskia, whose health was none too robust, but she did not whine. Around him were Jewish refugees from Portugal, the children of an ancient people, patriarchs with long beards, scholarly rabbis, physicians, and the poorest of the poor in colored rags. They were not strange to him. Since childhood and the nights his mother had read to him, his imagination had been busy with the drama and mystery of the Old Testament stories, and now he put his brush to work with characters who seemed to come

and clothes. Her penny-pinching relations were less considerate and tattled of Saskia's "large pear-shaped pearls, her necklaces, diamond earrings, and finger rings set with stones bigger than stars." To shut them up, Rembrandt brought suit for slander and won the case. He was a man of wealth, but his passion for collecting old and contemporary pictures, and all brands of antiquities as well, eventually ruined him.

He worked in solitude; but his house was open to artists, scholars, rabbis, and connoisseurs appreciative of his greatness. He seldom talked about his art—and there was no need to talk about it. The pictures told the whole story. To the end of time, his pictures will proclaim the magic of his brush, the depth of his imagination, and his humanity, regardless of written words, or the absence of words.

Rembrandt. *The Slaughtered Ox. Louvre, Paris. One of the greatest of still lifes—a slaughtered ox made radiant and beautiful by the magic of Rembrandt's brush.*

straight from those stories. His religious pictures have the strange clarity of things seen in a dream, and the reality of events he had studied with his own eyes.

He painted twenty portraits of Saskia, often as a heroine from the Bible or classical mythology, and more often to preserve her loveliness before sickness took her away. Three children were born, and one by one they died in infancy, and his wife began to droop. His mother died and the hurt was deep. He derived no satisfaction now from painting wealthy merchants.

Then, at one fell swoop, he lost his public. The captain of a unit of Civic Guards, and sixteen of his men, ordered a picture for their armory, each chipping in for the privilege of having his portrait in the group. They counted on Rembrandt to make them exemplary specimens of military bearing—and they got the shock of their lives. Rembrandt flouted all the accepted rules of Dutch portraiture. In the first place, he showed the company in a state of confusion and obscurity, the captain and his aide in a blaze of light, the rest in thick shadows where no one could recognize them. That was the major insult. Furthermore, he had no reverence for regulation uniforms and clothed some of the men in red and gold. Worst of all, he added ten reservists, not one of whom had paid a penny toward the picture, and the odd figure of a dwarfish girl. The soldiers raised the devil—and we must admit they had the right to howl. The artist refused to make changes. He had no interest in the faces or the vanity of troopers. His whole concern was with a group of men in a clash of lights and shadows—something that would be worth looking at long after the soldiers were forgotten. The picture was called the *Night Watch* by the offended guards and squeezed into an anteroom, after three figures had been amputated with a saw, and two more cut in half.

The *Night Watch* provoked a scandal, and the Dutch buyers began to boycott the defiant painter. But the painter did not seem to mind.

Thereafter he would work from the purity of his imagination—from the golden substance of his soul.

A fourth child was born, a boy, who lived—to the great joy of the father; but while the Civic Guards were assailing the father, Saskia died. Rembrandt has left us a drawing of a forlorn old man trying to poke food into an angry baby; the sketch is called the *Lonely Widower*. He found diversion in landscapes, painting mountains he had never seen, old castles and windmills that rise from living shadows to gather the winds of heaven in their wheeling wings. He turned to the Scriptures and gave us the *Supper at Emmaus*, a miracle in paint, the atmosphere glowing with supernatural light the instant the Lord's identity is revealed to His disciples.

At night, with eyes swollen from peering into fine lines scratched on copper, he made etchings. In this field, no man, however gifted, can be compared with him. His *Christ With the Sick*, showing the Saviour between two groups of afflicted humanity—men, women, and children dug up from the ghetto—by

Rembrandt. *The Night Watch. Rijks Museum, Amsterdam. The picture that cost Rembrandt his popular fame. His clients complained that he had slighted their faces and had left the company in confusion.*

some technical and spiritual mystery, shines with the glory of the Lord's presence.

His market for portraits dwindled and died, but he was still in the money, thanks to his etchings and a legacy from his deceased wife. The role of lonely widower did not become him and, by the best of luck, he found a young woman to keep house for him. The young housekeeper, Hendrickje Stoffels, comes to us personally in the portraits Rembrandt painted. She was a wonderful woman, loyal and capable and companionable; and she gave her life to the artist so that he in turn might give all that was left of him to the world. She named their child Cornelia after Rembrandt's mother, and was a second mother to Titus, the child of Saskia. Rembrandt's careless habits did not disturb her. So long as he could work, he was at peace—and she was at peace—and the world could go hang.

The end was at hand. He dressed like a tramp, not because he preferred to live in rags as some Bohemian artists do, but because all his genius was overwhelmingly concentrated

Rembrandt. *The Supper at Emmaus. Louvre, Paris. By his miraculous command of light, the artist portrayed his characters in a supernatural atmosphere.*

Rembrandt. *Christ with the Sick Around Him, Receiving Little Children. Etching, Metropolitan Museum of Art, New York. Also called "The Hundred Guilder Print" from its record price at a sale. A section of humanity invested with spiritual glory.*

on his final masterpieces. Generally speaking, when a man forgets to bathe and lives in shabby disorder, the work he tries to do correspondingly suffers and becomes shabby and unclean. But the last of the giants had so disciplined himself that, in dirt and adversity, his spirit was clean and beautiful, like liquid gold from an old black crucible. He was engaged in some of his mightiest portraits: the old artist himself—if you could see those pictures of him!—so strong and resigned and scarred by life, but still the king of pigment—and his housekeeper and all those who had not deserted him. They were not exactly the faces you might have seen in Amsterdam—they were scooped out of radiance and shadow, somehow reborn and transfigured. There were no pretty faces in the whole lot—and no happy faces. He painted men and women after time and trouble had left their signature.

Careless of living, he was even more careless of his finances. His creditors pounced upon him and he was thrown into bankruptcy.

PLATE 19. WILLIAM HOGARTH. *The Graham Children*. NATIONAL GALLERY, LONDON

PLATE 20. JOHN CONSTABLE. *The Haywain*. NATIONAL GALLERY, LONDON

All that he possessed, his own paintings and collections and his household goods, were auctioned off at heartbreaking prices—and his home passed into the hands of a gloating shoemaker.

Rembrandt took his little family to a neighboring inn and reviewed the predicament without bitterness. He had done what he thought best, he said, and he would take the consequences. And to prove that he had no hard feelings, he invited the auctioneer and his party into the bar for a round of schnapps —and gave them an etching as well. His salvation lay in his work, but he could not paint in a Dutch tavern. His housekeeper snagged a place in the most squalid corner of the town and the family moved in.

The battered giant was asked to decorate the Town Hall. He did but the governors refused to pay him for his labors. Through the influence of a wealthy dyer, Rembrandt obtained his last big commission, the *Syndics of the Drapers' Guild*—solid Dutch officials, shining in a strange light that is not sunlight or candlelight, but the light created by Rembrandt as he molded heads out of dark masses shot through by sharp illumination.

The ship was foundering, but the old captain was on the bridge at his art; the skipper was a free man—perhaps the most completely free man since the death and resurrection of the Lord he worshiped—no resentments, no vengeance, and no servility before his accusers. His Hendrickje fell ill and went to the grave, and he was dependent on his feckless son.

In the last stage, Rembrandt lived as one dedicated to immortality. He was heavy and tired, but his wants were few and his pride, or conviction, was clear and firm. Sitting on his haunches all day long and nipping gin to keep going had made him slow-moving and overweight. Pestered by debts and toothless, he sat in his room over a smelly canal and painted.

He painted a portrait of his pale son and his son's bride—two pictures that will never die. The son died, and as he followed the body to the grave in his best rags, a fur-lined coat stiff with paint, he kept his head in the air, and men and women babbled at his composure. He had time for another portrait of himself, the last, a mask of plastic mud, laughing at the world that had conspired to best him.

He died in 1669, and in the funeral procession were his daughter Cornelia and a string of idlers who muttered, one to the other, "They say the old boy was once a famous man in Amsterdam. And who might he have been? I hear tell that he might have been an artist, God rest his soul."

Rembrandt. *The Syndics of the Drapers' Guild. Rijks Museum, Amsterdam. Solid, bourgeois governors of the drapers' guild—massive portraits painted with the depth and insight of Rembrandt in his final period.*

Dürer. *Saint Jerome in His Study. Engraving, Metropolitan Museum of Art, New York. The old saint, with his dog and pet lion, in his study, an interior displaying the artist's amazing skill in the engraving of lights, surfaces, and objects.*

I5

In the Rhine Valley

The great Goethe, whose knowledge of art and life far exceeded that of ordinary mortals, looked deep into the hearts of his people and came up with a comment: "The clue to the German character is before me. I can write it down in three words—*Gefühl ist alles*," which means, "Feeling is everything." Without true feeling there can be no art, a cry repeated from time to time by artists everywhere, and uttered in despair, in modern times, by Vincent Van Gogh. The Germans are famous for their feelings, or sentiments, in the arts.

In the beginning, the twelfth and thirteenth centuries, German art was limited to the adornment of religious manuscripts. During the fourteenth and fifteenth centuries, under the influence of the Flemish craftsmen and the Van Eyck brothers, schools of painting and wood carving appeared in the Rhine Valley, and when Gutenberg invented printing with movable type the Germans went in for book illustration. Because of their natural-born thoroughness, they were soon in the forefront as the most finished and proficient engravers in Europe, offering woodcuts and copperplates which, in the reign of the modern machine, we cannot hope to imitate.

Late in the fifteenth century and continuing into the next, German painting came forward with a strong native flavor, unmistakably Gothic, rooted in the emotions and simple vigorous feelings of the common people. Two masters of the first rank appeared, Dürer and Holbein, and a few lesser figures. But after a term of glory, the native German school died away and gave over to ridiculous imitations of the late Italians. The creative power of the Germans was reborn in the eighteenth and nineteenth centuries, notably in music.

First and last, German art showed a deep examination into the character of people, seen in outbursts of sentiment and pictures of human faces tormented by religious upheavals. It had lots of details, with little things exquisitely painted or engraved or carved, but often with too many of them. Hobgoblins and witches and bedtime horrors going back into the Middle Ages were popular subjects. In portraiture the Germans were masters, using only the finest materials and sparing no pains to achieve pictures of unequaled durability and perfection.

When the old Germans did good work; that is, when they were themselves, with no hankering after Italian graces, they were unbeatable. They examined men and women closely, and perhaps too literally at times, always searching for the hidden springs that made them behave as they did. Their Madonnas are harsh and over-large and homely of figure, but genuine mothers of children, and capable of infinite tenderness and noble feelings, and endless love for the Son of Man.

Matthias Grünewald was German to the core, but he rises above all his countrymen in depicting the agonies and exaltations of the

147

Grünewald. *The Crucifixion. Colmar, Alsace. Profoundly moving illustration of the most tragic subject in western art. The strained postures, dramatic intensity, and physical torture are overpowering.*

human spirit. He was virtually a one-picture artist, his fame resting on an altarpiece now in the Colmar Museum, in Alsace. This work, on eleven panels, shows episodes from the life of St. Anthony, the Annunciation, and the Resurrection, when unfolded; and when closed, one single, overwhelming scene of terror, the Crucifixion.

Grünewald claimed mystic senses, the power to understand feelings and tragedies he could never have experienced. He painted Saint Anthony tormented by a hippopotamus with wings, by poisonous turtles and fire-spouting devils. In another panel, the Virgin holds the newborn Child, filled with unearthly joy. The red rose blooms behind her; the shepherds guard their flocks on far-off hilltops; and the heavens part in a burst of rainbow colors. The *Crucifixion* stands out as the most terrible ever painted. On a rocky plateau hangs the body of the Lord, skinned alive, beaten and bruised, and bleeding in every pore. On one side is John the Baptist; the Virgin, on the other, all in white and reeling into the arms of St. John, robed in scarlet; and between them, the kneeling Magdalene lifting her hands toward the cross.

After this it is a relief to have a look at the pictures of Lucas Cranach, a busy and successful artist with a sense of humor not unlike the elfin fancies of the German legends and fairy tales. As for the Italians, he knew little about them and cared less, but he loved to burlesque the Roman deities, and to cut them down to Gothic size. His Mars is a grotesque little creature, a sort of washed-up night watchman in heavy armor, and his Venuses are thin, high-waisted girls, with bulging brows, slanting eyes, tiny mouths, and pointed chins. Cranach's portraits of children have nearly as much charm as those of Rubens, and his hunting pictures are carefully observed and lively, but sometimes fantastic in the German manner. His paintings of stags, if we may believe one of his friends, "were so natural that hounds barked when they saw them."

The medieval town of Nuremberg, which was bombed off its base in World War II, was the birthplace, in 1471, of Albrecht Dürer, who for centuries has lived in the hearts and minds of the Germans, as much loved as Goethe or Beethoven. He was the third of eighteen children. "My dear father," Albrecht entered in his diary, "passed his life in great toil and arduous labor, having only what he earned by the sweat of his body to support his family. He experienced many troubles, but he was patient and gentle—at peace with the world and grateful to his Maker."

Following his father's trade, the boy was trained as a goldsmith, but he was a graphic artist by instinct and was soon apprenticed to a local painter. Before he was thirteen he had made a drawing of himself which is so mature and professional that you wouldn't believe any twelve-year-old on earth could have done it; only Leonardo da Vinci did such things in his boyhood. His apprenticeship over, at nineteen, he embarked on his travels; but before leaving home he made a portrait of his father holding a rosary on which is lettered, for the first time, the most famous monogram in art, a capital "D" within a large, flat-topped "A."

After four years of wandering, Dürer returned to Nuremberg to marry, like an obedient German, a girl selected by his father. She was a good-looking, kitchen-minded *Fräulein* named Agnes Frey. "Any girl of nineteen is not bad to look at if she is not deformed," the artist said—and she brought him a dowry. But she turned out to be a nickel-nurser and a scold, like the wife of Socrates. Here is what a close friend of the artist said:

"He kissed her and petted her and called her 'Mein Agnes,' and made many beautiful drawings of her, and even took her to the Netherlands with him, where she made all the men sit up and whistle, for she was something for sore eyes in her fine clothes. But to say the truth, this sweet-sour Agnes worried poor Albrecht into his grave. She was virtuous and pious. I would prefer a kittenish little woman who was loving and forgiving to a nagging sourface."

Dürer, at twenty-seven, completed sixteen wood engravings of the Apocalypse, from the

Cranach. *A Prince of Saxony. Ralph and Mary Booth Collection, National Gallery of Art, Washington, D.C.*

last book of the Bible. His *Four Horsemen of the Apocalypse* have caught the popular imagination; some years ago they came into the headlines when the backfield of an unconquerable Notre Dame football team, under the name of the Four Horsemen, confessed that it was the woodcuts of Dürer that had inspired the title. These four "cowboys" of the Revelation came down at the blast of the trumpet, riding herd over monks, popes, emperors, and all who stood in their way, dealing out vengeance to sinners, and punishment to cowards, while the winged angels descended brandishing their swords to slay and kill and spare nothing.

Though married to a nagging woman, Dürer continued to work steadily and without damage to the quality of his art. He felt, perhaps, more at ease in his engravings than in his oil studies of religious subjects. Like Rembrandt, he painted many portraits of himself, but he was far-famed for his handsome features in contrast to the burly Dutchman's spreading face. In a study of himself at the age of thirty, still hanging in the museum at Munich—I hope—he holds together a fur-trimmed mantle with his right hand; the long, slender fingers are so artfully modeled as to confirm the opinion of his countrymen that "nothing more beautiful than Dürer's hands could be imagined." This portrait, as well as others of himself, strongly resembles the conception of Christ, as painted by the Italians, but the resemblance was not blasphemy, or coincidence, on the part of the artist. He painted his portrait as he saw himself, as close to the features as he could draw them, but there crept into the picture an ideal he used as a guiding light. It was his conviction that the life of a man is reflected in his features, and that an artist concerned with Christian beliefs should live as the pure in spirit. And certainly, he lived according to his faith.

Dürer had a magnificent brain and was continually experimenting with the theoretical, or scientific, side of art—in this he was the northern counterpart of Leonardo da Vinci.

He was forever searching for the laws of structure, proportion, and design, and at night, lay awake and worried, while his Agnes snored, lest his own canvases should lack the grace and beauty of Italian art. So he went down to Venice to see for himself.

At first the Italians were jealous of his reputation, but he won them all. Raphael, always a generous soul, wrote from Rome, saying it would be an honor to exchange drawings with him. And old Giovanni Bellini, fully aware of Dürer's skill with a paint brush, praised the German to the skies and became his sponsor.

At Bellini's invitation, Dürer came to the Italian's workshop.

"I should like to ask a favor of you," Bellini said.

"You have only to name it."

Cranach. *The Judgment of Paris. Metropolitan Museum of Art, New York. A classic myth revived in a comic mood—the goddess of love in a red hat and golden chains, her rivals in gold necklaces and without hats.*

Dürer. *Portrait of the Artist as a Young Man. Prado, Madrid. The finest of the early self-portraits. Famous for his manly beauty, Dürer painted himself, not with vanity, but as he aspired to be.*

"Those brushes you use in painting hair," the Italian explained, "could you spare one of them?"

Dürer quickly bundled together a fistful of brushes and begged the Italian to help himself.

"No, no!" Bellini objected. "I don't mean those ordinary brushes. I mean the brush that draws several hairs of a woman's tresses, or a man's beard, at a single stroke, for it is not possible to separate each hair at one stroke, in a perfect curve, with our brushes."

"I have no others," Dürer answered, "but perhaps this will answer your request."

He picked up one of the brushes, and with a single perfectly regulated, sweeping stroke of the arm, painted a lock of hair, very long and wavy like a woman's, but with each separate hair precisely indicated. The old Italian was flabbergasted, and went about Venice telling people of the wonders he had seen with his own eyes.

The warm-hearted Italians offered him a pension if he would remain among them, but he declined, and returned to Nuremberg. "I shall freeze here," he confessed, "after the sunshine of Italy, but I belong where I began."

He worked slowly and with infinite pains, and accumulated only fifty paintings in a whole lifetime. To keep out of debt, he returned to his engravings and, about 1513, finished three plates which represented the highest reaches of his skill in black and white.

Dürer. *Melancholia. Engraving, Metropolitan Museum of Art, New York. The best-known print by the greatest of engravers—the spirit of inquiry brooding over the fate of man, with depressing symbols everywhere.*

Dürer. *Knight, Death, and the Devil. Engraving, Metropolitan Museum of Art, New York. Death holds up an hourglass to warn the Knight; the Devil lurks behind. In the corner is the artist's famous monogram.*

One shows Saint Jerome in his cell pondering the salvation of man; another is *Knight, Death, and the Devil,* in which a lone warrior emerges from the shadows of a mountain road with Death pursuing him, and the wickedest devil you ever saw. And the third is called *Melancholia,* a print known far and wide. A winged female figure, crowned with laurel, broods over the destiny of man. The symbols around her interpret her thoughts: the compass she holds, the globe on the floor, the hourglass and bell, and the word printed in the arch in the background.

We know the thin, tired face of his mother from the drawing he made in 1514, before her death, and his written words tell us of his sorrow. "She kept us, my brothers and myself, with great care from all sin, and when I came home, or went away, it was her habit to say, 'Christ bless thee.'"

Dürer's position at Nuremberg was similar to Raphael's supremacy among the people of Rome or, later on, to that of Rubens at Antwerp. When he traveled into the Netherlands, he was welcomed by kings and artists. On the way, he stopped to sketch everything that interested him—people, landscapes, barns, animals, and flowers—and he never forgot to write in his diary, day by day.

He published several books that make dry and tough reading, works on perspective and human proportion; and while laboring on one of these, he died suddenly from some strange illness. In great pain he made a drawing of himself, with one hand pointing to a spot on his body, and beneath the drawing these words: "Where my finger points is the yellow spot, the seat of my sickness." He was fifty-seven years old.

Two years before his death, Dürer wrote

Dürer. *John and Peter, a detail from the Four Apostles. Haus Der Kunst, Munich. Perhaps the highest attainment of Germanic art. The Apostles, in two panels, were presented by the artist to Nuremberg, his home, "as something worthy of the giver."*

to the city council of Nuremberg: "For a long time, I have intended to present to you, as a humble remembrance, some picture of mine, but the imperfection of my works has prevented me. Now I have finished a picture on which I have bestowed more trouble than on any of the others, and I consider it a worthy tribute to my native town."

The picture was the *Four Apostles,* a work in two panels, John and Peter on one side, Paul and Mark, on the other. Referring to this painting, Goethe wrote: "In truth and nobility, and even in beauty and grace, Dürer, if one really knows him in heart and mind, is equaled only by the very greatest of the Italian masters."

Holbein was a German of different kidney. You may find it hard to connect his paintings with his cold-blooded ambitions and his attitude toward his family. But he was an artist, one of the best, and he is proof that the creative spirit, or the genius of art, is given to all sorts of men, some of them, at first glance, not easy to admire. You may not love Holbein's paintings, but you cannot help admiring and enjoying them, and marveling at their super-excellence. And one of them I'm sure you will love—the full-length portrait of little *Christina of Denmark,* in the long cloak— so delicately and beautifully rendered that every square inch of canvas is finished to perfection, and with style, and faultless taste, a quality uncommon to the Germans.

Holbein was determined, at anybody's expense, to be the leader of his profession. He had no love for his wife; he made friends apparently only to use them, and the quaint and tender customs of his people never touched his heart. It did not occur to him to decorate a Christmas tree—he never had a Christmas tree—he never lifted a stein or yodeled with sentimental cronies, or believed in Santa Claus. On the other hand, he had inflexible self-control, the resolution of Bismarck, and an unconcealed contempt for second-rate performances. He learned his business, step by step, from the ground up, in a stern and precise and unwavering devotion to drawing, always developing his extraordinary talents to their limit. And not once in his career—not for honors or money—did he produce a slipshod, cheap, or second-rate picture. That is the acid test of the true artist.

Hans Holbein, the Younger, was born in 1497, at Augsburg, a Bavarian town on one of the trade routes to Italy. He was the son of Hans Holbein, the Elder, a painter of distinction, and he was born, one might say, with a brush in his hand, his brother being a painter and his uncle, too. Painting was his business, and in learning it he followed the Rhine schools, which meant that he was severely trained as a craftsman in engraving and painting and taught to observe the smallest differences between faces.

At seventeen, Young Hans was a better artist than his father, but there were too many artists in the family and the next year, Hans, the Younger, went to the Swiss town of Basel looking for work. He found it immediately with a publisher who employed him to make the illustrations for a book, *In Praise of Folly,* written by the renowned Dutch scholar, Erasmus. During the friendship that developed between the two, Holbein painted several portraits of Erasmus, including the masterpiece now in the Louvre (see Plate 15). On the strength of this connection, Holbein wormed his way into the patronage of Burgomaster Jacob Meyer and his wife Dorothea, and painted their portraits. These portraits, done when he was only nineteen years old, have been described time and again as miracles of workmanship.

Holbein became a citizen of Basel and married a widow, to whom he was neither faithful nor attentive. He was on the way up, and accepted only those commissions which would bring him money or increase his reputation. If anything, he was a Lutheran, but he did not hesitate to paint for the Roman Church. His picture called the *Madonna of Burgomaster Meyer* is strange and unbelievable—a religious group, so plain and Ger-

Dürer. *Paul and Mark, a detail from the Four Apostles. Haus Der Kunst, Munich. Characterization of monumental grandeur, worthy to stand by the Prophets of the Sistine Chapel.*

manic, and yet so beautifully done that it remains a religious masterpiece. A versatile artist, Holbein made book illustrations, designs for stained glass, and a series of forty-five woodcuts called the *Dance of Death,* a subject that had haunted the Germans since the Middle Ages and has been used over and over again down to our own times, in painting and the theater. Death, personified in one form or another, tails every human being, rich or poor, young or old; Death slays the warrior, steals the rich man's money, lures the sailor to a watery grave, drinks the last health of the king, and inveigles the little child from the protecting home into the waste land of eternity. Unlike Dürer's wood engravings, which are woven together with innumerable lines and shadows, those of Holbein are simply executed and as powerful as paintings. The hero of the series and the most "living" of the characters is Death himself, depicted as a skeleton. Such is the power of art. To give his symbol of Death more freedom of movement and simplicity, Holbein created a skeleton with many of the less conspicuous bones deleted. Few observers have noticed the difference, the skeleton being so fearsome and dynamic.

Despite his fame and success, Holbein's markets began to decline. The followers of Martin Luther opposed and sabotaged religious pictures, and the civil wars had impoverished the wealthy portrait buyers. With an eye to the main chance, the artist went to England as the guest of Sir Thomas More, the Chancellor of Henry VIII. His portrait of Sir Thomas hangs in the Frick Collection, New York, one of the great portraits of the world

Dürer. *The Kneeling Donor. Pierpont Morgan Library, New York. Sketch for a painting, done to emphasize the intense piety of the subject and to fold the classic drapery into a new design.*

Dürer. *Christ on the Mount of Olives. Engraving, Metropolitan Museum of Art, New York. One of the many engravings of the Passion, a subject which deeply affected the artist.*

in character drawing and technical mastery combined.

Having sampled British money, Holbein decided to remain in London. To wind up his affairs, he hurried back to Switzerland, where he painted his wife and two children, a sad and bitterly faithful picture of a mother with eyes reddened from weeping over her loneliness, and of his confused children with their unhappy faces. When the art-smashing reformers destroyed in one day most of the paintings of the town, Holbein made it for England as fast as he could travel. No record exists to show that he ever intended, or ever promised, to send for his family.

The Lord Chancellor, his friend and patron, was no longer available, having lost his head by order of the king. The bloody business did not restrain the cold and prodigious German, who planned a new attack on the purses of potential clients. From an organization of rich German merchants in London, he selected a handsome fellow and painted him in silks and finery; and to show his amazing skill he included all sorts of objects, such as flowers, keys, letters, books, and what not. In other words, he made a prince out of a trader. The merchants fell for the picture, precisely as Holbein had figured, and ordered one portrait after another.

His fame spread into royal circles, and by fawning on the right people, he eventually won the job he desired most—court painter to Henry VIII, a title he clung to for the rest of his life, and never endangered by voicing political opinions, or commenting on the caprices of the King, or taking any part in the exciting events of his time. In the realm of painting he was as absolute a monarch as Henry was in the kingship. As court painter, he made portraits of the beefy ruler and three of his wives, and of a long line of courtiers— lords, ladies, knights, chamberlains, understudies, and all the imperial set. He did not flatter them, or lie about them, or make them angels or devils. The truth is that Holbein created for us the whole royal setup of his age and, whenever we think of Henry VIII and his women and his attendants, we think of them in the portraits of the German artist. He left us a history in pictures.

Ordered by the King, the artist went to the Netherlands to make a likeness of Princess Christina, of Denmark, on whom Henry had cast a roving eye. When the King saw Holbein's portrait of the girl—surely one of the loveliest portraits in the world—he immediately wanted her for his next Queen. This wish, put into diplomatic language, was conveyed to the girl who said, in reply, "I should

Holbein, the Younger. *King Henry VIII. Corsini Gallery, Rome. The most splendid of the portraits of Henry VIII and offering no concession to the size and cruelty of the burly monarch's face.*

gladly consent to be the Queen of Henry VIII, of England, if the Lord had given me two heads, one for the King to chop off, and one to wear home again."

The queen-crazy monarch sent his German artist on a second errand as matrimonial agent, and with more fruitful consequences. Here again we may see the authority and persuasiveness of art. Holbein went to Brussels, where he painted one of his most popular pictures, *Anne of Cleves,* known as the "playing-card queen" because of her superficial resemblance to the queen of the pack. The artist did not magnify the charms of Anne of Cleves— she was rather plain—but it is a magnificent work with velvet robes of brilliant red, with gold and jewels, and eye-catching details. Henry VIII was trapped by the beauty of the artist's workmanship, not by the subject, and he notified the woman that she was duly

Holbein, the Younger. *Christina of Den-mark. National Gallery, London. A lovelier portrait cannot be found. Painted from a drawing, it is a single study made in three hours! The child-princess refused a proposal from Henry VIII, saying she had only one head for him to chop off.*

Holbein, the Younger. *Anne of Cleves. Louvre, Paris. Known as the "playing card queen." Painted by order of Henry VIII, who was snared by the beauty of the artist's work-manship into marrying the woman sight un-seen. She was dull and not very glamorous and the marriage was annulled.*

named to be his fourth wife and queen. When Anne arrived at a British port, Henry found her so dull and homely and dumb—she knew not a word of English—that he forgot to hand her the gift he had brought. But the wedding arrangements had been made, and he took her to wife—and later on had the marriage annulled. He gave her an estate and an in-come, and she "lived happily in England, wearing a new frock every day—which no one saw but herself"—so an old historian tells us.

On the Continent, Holbein paid his wife a hurried call, appearing at Basel in silks and satins and royal furbelows, and offending everyone by his pretentious elegance. Again he said good-bye to his family, without a qualm, and returned to the court of Henry VIII. But the patron saints of plague and justice caught up with him; four years later, when he was only forty, he was stricken unto death, in the midst of painting another portrait of Henry.

He is a puzzling great man. He left his sitters as he found them, never using them, as Rubens did to express the dance of life, or as Rembrandt did to outline its tragedies. He presented their characters to the world without adding his own feelings. He was satisfied to give his sitters the individuality they brought to him. But one and all, like the artist who painted them, they are assured and self-possessed. None of them has a smiling face—none of them is excited. The artist was like a doctor or scientist in his ability to diagnose a patient.

Holbein examined a head with a marvel-

Holbein, the Younger. *The Artist's Wife. Tinted silverpoint, Louvre, Paris. The artist was twenty-five when he made this drawing of his wife, before he deserted her.*

Holbein, the Younger. *The Ambassadors. National Gallery, London. The French ambassador and his friend, the bishop, depicted with surpassing dexterity, as a showpiece. The foreshortened skull on the floor is a pictograph of the word "Holbein."*

ous eye. He observed everything significant—the profile of the face, all the little curves and lines, the structure of the lips, the depth and turn of the eye socket—with a degree of penetration unequaled by any other painter. When he took up his brushes, he constructed a speaking image of the sitter, done with taste, with the skill of a magician, with firm modeling and solidity. His oil portraits were developed from drawings in pencil and colored chalk, many of which are valued today beyond precious stones, and which may be seen in copies everywhere. Holbein's art is as finished and faultless as any art can be—assured and free from half-realized intentions. It may not raise your blood pressure, but it will leave you with the conviction that it could not, conceivably, have been better done.

El Greco. *Burial of Count Orgaz. S. Tomé, Toledo. The artist's masterpiece, show-ing the celestial excitement as St. Augustine and St. Stephen come down to earth to bury their devotee, the Count of Orgaz.*

16

The Soul of Spain

For more than three centuries, Spain has continued to fascinate the western world, casting a spell upon travelers like the incantations of her *brujas,* or witches. Since Cervantes told the story of the one and only Don Quixote, wanderers have gone into Spain, always uninvited, and have returned to write books about "the Spanish soul." I suspect that other nations also have souls, but the Spanish people, by their unchanging culture, their fierceness and color, their honor and picturesque slothfulness, their pride and strange dignity, form a collective personality, or unique national character.

In our romantic moods we build our "castles in Spain." We think of Don Juan and of gypsies; of pale, powdered, thin-waisted, small-footed *señoritas,* smouldering with romantic passions; of the grandees and hidalgos; of Carmen, the dancers, and toreadors; of pride and blood and the mysteries of religion.

The fine arts of Spain are another story. The arts of living and dying have been cultivated far more intensely by the Spaniards than the so-called creative arts. The best architecture was Moorish, which was combined with the Gothic to come out as the plateresque, because of its fantastic ornamentation borrowed from the silversmiths. The interior of the Roxy Theatre in New York is an example of this style. The plateresque style was a baroque development ending in orgies of ingenuity—of plastering the fronts of buildings and cramming the insides with a crazy profusion of trumpery. In this wilderness of odds and ends stuck together, you may discover some excellent pieces of sculpture, usually in wood and shockingly realistic, to exhibit the agonies of the Crucifixion and the sorrows of the Virgin, with the Spanish emphasis on blood and suffering. Popular Spanish sculpture, old or modern—those wax effigies in big and little churches and those wooden images carried in processions—are things to freeze one's blood.

Spain has not been particularly rich in painters, producing but three of the first rank —one an expatriate Greek, another a Portuguese aristocrat, and the third a lawless peasant—and three men of somewhat less importance. First, a few words about the second team.

José de Ribera, born about 1588 near Valencia, matured swiftly and went off to Italy where he spent the rest of his life under the nickname *Lo Spagnoletto,* or the little Spaniard. In Naples he captured the daughter of a new type of double-dealer, the picture merchant, and thenceforth always had work to do, and always was well paid, thanks to the father-in-law. Ribera was an upsetting combination of the mildest piety and volcanic impulses and was embroiled in many escapades, most of them probable, if not proved. He became

Ribera. *Saint Augustine. Prado, Madrid. Character study of a saint constructed in a spotlighting borrowed from Caravaggio.*

lean and racked, is fastened to a yardarm and ready to be twisted into insensibility before being flayed alive. This canvas, and others such as the *Dead Christ,* in the Louvre, with their ghastly lights thrown against the densest shadows prompted Lord Byron's comment: "Lo Spagnoletto soaked his brush in the blood of all the saints." In his final efforts, the *Adoration of the Shepherds,* for instance, he is less powerful, but more reverent and less inclined to dwell on blood and suffering.

While Ribera was working in Italy, a young painter named Francisco de Zurbarán was on his way up the ladder in Spain. Of humble origin, he was much occupied with religion and painted a masterpiece of a kneeling monk gazing upward from the hollow of his cowl. Zurbarán has the harsh monastic fervor of the Spaniards, as well as the tenderest moments of

Ribera. *Adoration of the Shepherds. Louvre, Paris. The shepherds are homely and reverent, the Virgin a wistful beauty.*

a professional highwayman and was captured and sold into the slavery of the galleys; he secretly persecuted his rivals by mixing dirt with their pigments and by sending them poison-pen letters. What is true beyond conjecture is his mysterious disappearance. When his second daughter ran away with Don Juan of Austria, who refused to marry her, the artist-father, grief-stricken and unable to avenge the crime, took ship for some undisclosed destination and passed out of sight forever.

Ribera was a painter of enormous strength, truly dramatic at his best, and brutal and theatrical at his worst. He recruited his models from the dregs of society, painting hardened beggars and sneak thieves as saints and philosophers. His *Martydom of St. Bartholomew,* when first exhibited on the balcony of his father-in-law's house, incited a riot. The saint,

PLATE 21. JOSEPH MALLORD WILLIAM TURNER. *The Fighting Téméraire*. NATIONAL GALLERY, LONDON

PLATE 22.   JEAN AUGUSTE DOMINIQUE INGRES. *Madame Rivière*. LOUVRE, PARIS

Murillo. *The Immaculate Conception. Louvre, Paris. The Madonna is graceful and statuesque with rosy cherubs around her.*

standing—and sometimes too softly—but they are honest jobs. Murillo is known throughout Christendom for his pictures of the *Immaculate Conception.* He painted fifteen of them, and they are reproduced year after year, in every land and clime: the Virgin Mary, floating into the stratosphere in a glory of cotton-wool clouds, surrounded by exultant angels and cherubs in vaporous colors. The Virgin is a very young *señorita,* wide-eyed and innocent and posed to no disadvantage of her physical charms. There is an element of softness and sentimental flimsiness in many of the pictures, but even so it is permissible to paint a Madonna who is an appealing Spanish maiden.

worship. He often posed his solidly drawn figures in effective silhouettes. He painted women saints with Spanish precision—in full and splendid dress like princesses, but sweet and chaste as a lady saint should be.

The most popular of Spanish artists is Bartolomé Esteban Murillo, born in Seville on New Year's Day, 1618. The fire and ecstasy and flesh-cutting tortures of his people did not tempt him. He cultivated a milder field, a more ingratiating form of art; for he was a successful, untroubled soul with little experience in suffering. He was also, at his best, very much of an artist, though inclined to be slipshod when relaxed and not too sharp in his draftsmanship. He painted beggar boys and waifs, with genuine sympathy and under-

El Greco. *Cardinal Niño de Guevara. Metropolitan Museum of Art, New York. The Cardinal in all his ecclesiastical pomp.*

Murillo. *Young Beggar. Louvre, Paris. Young waif at rest in the shade—painted with unaffected sentiment and fine technical skill.*

Of the three great Spanish painters, the first was El Greco. In the lower right-hand corner of his picture *Toledo in a Storm* (see Plate 16), if you look closely, you will see the artist's signature in Greek letters, Domingo Theotocopuli, which is the Spanish version of the original name. It is a hard name to remember and there is no need to keep it in mind. I bring it up only to point out that the painter was a Greek, born in Crete about 1542; and, while he happens to be numbered among the illustrious artists of Spain, he always thought of himself as the descendant of the greatest of the ancient races.

In his youth, he left his native island to join a colony of Greeks in Venice where he was mentioned as a pupil of Titian, but his early paintings indicate that his masters were Veronese and the thunderbolt, Tintoretto. The next time we hear of him he is in Rome, to see for himself if the Sistine Chapel was as wonderful as reported. He was a critical Greek and not

given to words. After looking over the Chapel, he said, "Michelangelo was an extraordinary man and a great sculptor, but he had no idea of painting. He tried to carve figures in paint and he did not understand color." So much for the opinion of one artist on another of different aims.

The next time we have record of him, he was in Spain, about thirty years old, and settled permanently in the gloomy old sword-making, fanatical town of Toledo. Apparently he found in the soul of Spain what his own curious soul required, for he wandered no more. We know little about his life. He was unusually sharp and sane, a good business man, and not afraid to say what he thought. The Castilians called him bizarre which, in

El Greco. *Saint Andrew and Saint Francis. Prado, Madrid.*

El Greco. *Portrait of a Man. Metropolitan Museum of Art, New York. Probably the artist, and similar to many of his heroes.*

that he lived like an aristocrat in a house of twenty-four rooms, and that he imported musicians from Venice to entertain him while dining. His tastes were scholarly; his library was large and he wrote treatises on architecture and painting. Like Leonardo and Tintoretto, he painted from clay models, and when a subject fascinated him, he painted it again and again. He was obsessed by figures in attitudes of strain and agitation, and evolved a style of composition in which the human models are stretched beyond their normal length to conform to his ideas of rhythm and movement.

The Greek created a world of his own—like all original artists—a world inspired by his Spanish environment but expressing the ferment of his own spirit like a fiery furnace; a world in which the bodies of men and women are pulled out of joint, like elongated specters, with eyes staring heavenward and arms upraised in a struggle to escape the flesh and leap to salvation in tongues of flame. He painted *Christ Embracing the Cross,* the *Baptism,* and sixteen versions of the *Agony in the Garden;* and he painted *St. Francis,* who conquered the flesh, in twenty different versions. He depicted

Spanish, meant brave and high-spirited, and he was both. He often went to court to sue delinquent clients.

Again and again he wounded the pride of the Spaniards, and they repaid him in kind—taking care to remind him that he was only a stepchild of Spain. They nicknamed him El Greco, or the Greek, not because of his classic origin but to remind him that he was a foreigner. He said, in retaliation, that the Spaniards were inferior to the Italians who, in turn, were below his own people, and signed his canvases in Greek characters.

As El Greco, the artist breathed the hysterical, religious air of Spain as freely as a native, and devoted most of his energies to the Church. In addition he painted portraits and landscapes seething with thunder and lightning and zigzag terrors. Never a popular artist, he was backed by a group of choice admirers, and his prices were high. It is recorded

El Greco. *Descent of the Holy Spirit. Prado, Madrid. Painted in the artist's last period, when the body was stretched beyond life-size to express agitation of the spirit, and with flares, instead of halos.*

Velásquez. *The Idiot of Coria. Prado, Madrid. Pathetic rendering of a court jester.*

figures with jets of flame spurting above their heads instead of halos; figures turned upside down or flying through the air against backgrounds overhung with greenish clouds and streaked with lemon-yellow lights.

In his masterpiece the *Burial of Count Orgaz,* a nobleman's interment, he was concerned with the separation of soul and body, or flesh and spirit, a concept forever burning in the minds of the Spaniards who tortured their bodies to release or purify the spirit. Two saints bend over the lifeless count, with a row of cavaliers behind them, each a portrait; and in the upper part of the canvas a lot of heavenly business is going on: an angel carries aloft the count's soul in the shape of an infant; musicians are folded in a cloud, with St. Peter near by, holding his keys; the Virgin is there, too, amid saints and apostles; and high in the vault is the figure of Christ in a white robe.

Out of respect for his friends, not for

money, El Greco painted a few portraits, though he seldom portrayed a woman. His portraits are noble works, Spanish in feeling. The cheeks of his sitters are hollow; the skin is stretched tight over the skull; the eyes deepset in bony sockets and burning with strange fires. They are men whom the pleasures of life have not tempted, creatures in the thrall of a mystical vision.

When the flame of El Greco's genius burns clean and pure, it lights up a region of the spirit in which he remains a master, a strange, supernatural province into which most of us have only flickering glimpses. When he falters into ghastliness, his cockeyed saints and gruesome symbols affect us like a bad dream.

The Spaniards, as I have said, did not take to him, notwithstanding his religious ecstasies and his insight into their souls. His daring technique offended them, and conventional painters branded him an exhibitionist "who painted in cruel slashes with great blobs of unblended colors." In consequence El Greco was forgotten after his death, but late in the nineteenth century, he "rose from the dead" and became a celebrated Old Master.

The Portuguese member of the Spanish "big three" was born in Seville, in 1599, and a greater contrast to El Greco, in temperament and technique, could hardly be imagined. Velásquez (whose full name was Diego Rodríguez de Silva y Velásquez) was reserved, compliant, always in command of his sober talents, and totally unconcerned about the state of the Spanish nation. He was the King's private property and obedient servant. He did what he was told to do, one face as well or as beautifully as another, and if the royal family bored him, he raised no protests.

Velásquez was apprenticed in his thirteenth year to a half-cracked painter, but soon left him for the amiable and scholarly Pacheco with whom he remained for five years. At the age of nineteen he made love to Juana, Pacheco's daughter, and married her, being fully grown and the best painter in Spain, except the Greek. He married the girl, he said, "be-

El Greco. *The Adoration of the Shepherds. Metropolitan Museum of Art, New York. The great Cretan-Spaniard animates an old theme with flashes of light, outstretched arms and hands in prayer, ecstatic faces, and tumbling cherubs.*

cause of her virtue, beauty, and good qualities, and by his own faith in his natural genius."

The young man suffered none of the hardships and years of struggle befalling so many artists. He was not an idealist and was as happy to paint the negroid faces of peasants whom the high-toned Spaniards affectionately called "pumpkins," as the face of a princess. His aims were clear and he never altered them: he would look at things sharply as nature offered them to the eye, and he would record them with his brush as beautifully as possible. He paid little attention to the great

Italians, and his religious pictures are no more than experiments—wonderfully painted but with no depth of feeling. In his still-life studies, however, his phenomenal powers of observation proved the value of his straightforward beliefs; and his pictures of low-life—countrymen eating or cooking a stew, water boys, and vagabonds—are, in their way, almost flawless. Imagination, as Rembrandt or El Greco had it, he did not possess. He painted what was before him.

At twenty-two, he moved to Madrid, and on the strength of an equestrian portrait and a little politics, was officially named the court painter to Philip IV, a knock-kneed sovereign of eighteen whom he served for thirty years. The honors were many; the pay was small. He was classified with the dwarfs and idiots—the royal playthings—and paid about as much as the cooks and clowns. He was obliged time and again to paint Philip, with his yellow hair, protruding jaw, and dead-fish eyes; and the anemic Infantas, with their green-sick faces and their little bodies inserted in preposterous band-box skirts. With a few exceptions, the women of Spain were portrayed as if they had no legs.

Velásquez. *The Surrender of Breda. Prado, Madrid. The conquered Dutch commander offers the keys of Breda to the Spanish leader.*

There were extras, of course, in his official capacity. The artist was provided with a studio in the royal palace and allowed to wear the King's cast-off clothing—and that was an honor indeed—and the royal cooks sent baskets of food and wine and garlic to Velásquez's wife who remained at home, as Spanish women did. As the painter's fame increased, more honors were bestowed on him. He was made Valet to the King's Bedchamber; twice he traveled to Italy on the King's expense account; and after a lifetime of painting and flunkeying, he received the crowning reward of Marshal of the Palace, with authority over fiestas and weddings. But the burdens were too heavy and, while preparing a nuptial fete for the Infanta Maria Teresa in 1660, he died from a heart attack.

In Rome, Velásquez astounded the Italians with his portrait of Pope Innocent X, composed with so little pigment and in thin spots

Velásquez. *Infanta Maria Theresa. Metropolitan Museum of Art, New York. The Princess at fifteen, with the heavy Hapsburg features, the unbelievable hair.*

Velásquez. *Don Balthasar Carlos as a Hunter. Prado, Madrid. The little Prince, in the role of a hunter on a barrel-shaped pony, as he gallops forth to uphold the dignity of a tottering regime.*

of color all fused together somehow, so light and living and unlabored. "It is made of nothing!" they cried, "But there it is, the Pope himself!" And in Italy, his notes on a painting by Tintoretto might be a definition of his intentions when he painted the *Maids of Honor* (see Plate 17), one of his best-known canvases. "It is hard to believe," he wrote of Tintoretto, "that one is looking at a painting. Everything is so truthfully and exactly done that you seem to be in a room occupied by real figures, with atmosphere between the figures." In *Maids of Honor,* he represented his studio as seen by himself in a mirror placed in the background. The effect is much the same as looking into an actual room, instead of a picture—and such was the effect Velásquez intended.

It is not possible for an artist to divorce himself from his subject. Unconsciously, he projects into the picture more or less of his own temperament, whatever that may be.

Velásquez brought to his pictures the marvelous accuracy of his seeing eye, some of the stiffness and much of the dignity of his imperturbable disposition. There is no movement in his canvases, no drama, no excitement. He painted a dwarf or a buffoon, or a couple of dead fish, with as much affection, or as little, as he instilled into his portraits of the King or the Infantas. He regarded them as models, or objects surrounded by light and air. His infallible eye could detect the high lights and cross lights and reflected lights, the darks and deeper shadows playing on the human head, and he molded them into beautiful, speaking images with a brush, as Whistler said, "dipped in light and air," in delicate tones of silver and grey and rose. Technically, he had few, if any, superiors, using oil with the lightness of water color.

The Dutchmen also painted interiors and objects in light and shadow, but they were captivated by little things and often dragged too many of them into their compositions. Velásquez knew what to leave out of the picture, and out of the faces of his models. He painted what he saw but not all that he saw. His faces and costumes are grandly simplified —he removed everything that might distract the eye from grasping the object as a single unit. He gave substance and completeness to the scattered stuff of nature, and made commonplace people and things beautiful—King Philip, for example—by the magic of his craft and his colors.

Francisco José de Goya y Lucientes was a character, a most conspicuous actor, in one of the most turbulent eras of modern life. Goya was born in 1746, a century after Velásquez's death, and as artist-historian of the violence of Spain, he recorded in paint and in his etchings, a complete history of his period. "One of his sketches," declared a French writer, "consisting of a few lines and shadows, tells us more about the manners of his country than the longest description." He lived in a world of upheavals, with all Europe battling for freedom, torn apart by the French Revolution and forced together again by Napoleon.

Spain was bankrupt in mind and body; such painters as she employed officially were cheap Italians or imitators of the French. The Hapsburgs yielded the crown to the Bourbons who were exceptionally vicious. Charles IV was a brawny gambler and sportsman; his Queen, Maria Luisa, who had the real power, was doubly notorious—one of the ugliest women ever to squat on a throne, and one of the wickedest. When Ferdinand VII took the crown, after Napoleon had collapsed, the country ran red with the blood of martyrs. "Every heretic," the rabid new king decreed, "shall have his tongue bored through with a red hot iron, and his body drained white on the rack."

Goya, too, had he been less rugged and less famous, would have died with a hot poker in his throat. He ransacked the soul of Spain for its mysteries and terrors, turning his experi-

Velásquez. *Philip IV. Frick Collection, New York. A luxuriously costumed monarch.*

Goya. *Self-portrait. Academy of Fine Arts, Madrid. The artist at seventy, deaf and in poor health, but powerful and truculent.*

ences into works of art; he explored every level of society from the bull ring to the battle-field, from the superstitions of the starving poor to the debauchery of the court. He was immensely energetic, afraid of no one, incap-able of lying or flattery.

In the mountain village of Fuendetodos, his birthplace, he worked in the fields with his two brothers and his sister, but a talent for draw-ing put an end to his misery. At the age of twelve he painted an altar curtain for the vil-lage church, and when he was fourteen, a man of means sent him to Saragossa, a few miles away, to study with a court painter. Here, in the capital of Aragon, foot-loose and fancy free, he began his picaresque journey through a violent world. Confident and gifted, he plunged headlong into a life of excesses. He had a good singing voice, knew how to use a sword and his fists, danced lightly on small

feet, as a Spaniard should, and was a gang leader of parts.

According to a plausible story, he fled to Madrid after a battle between his own and rival gangsters. In the capital he associated with bullfighters and gypsies, and one morn-ing was found in the gutter with a dagger in his back. Spirited away by a company of bull-fighters, he went to Rome to see the world. How he managed to live in Italy is not clear, but it is known that his pictures of Spanish scenes found purchasers among the French residents. Goya had no particular reverence for Italian art, but the gay and dangerous underworld of Rome was a challenge to his spirits. Among the daredevil escapades at-tributed to him, two may be named, both possible, but open to suspicion. It is said that he climbed the dome of St. Peter's and carved his name in the lantern, or topmost ornament, and that he broke into a nunnery at night and abducted a novice. Two years later, a Span-iard at heart, with strong family affections, he was home again, seeking work to relieve the poverty of his father and mother.

He was commissioned to decorate a church at Saragossa, and finished the job in six months, but not very impressively for two reasons: Goya was not a religious painter and his training had been fitful and insufficient. At twenty-nine he married the sister of a well-known painter. He left his wife at home while he reveled with the Bohemians—the gypsies, dancing girls, and matadors. She bore a sickly brood of twenty children, only one living to maturity—and the father loved them all, but not at the same time. He was a man of plain tastes, hating display even when he made large sums of money, avoiding art fanciers, and collecting no pictures. He ate too much and worked too hard, and as early as his thirty-fifth year he was subject to ill health and dark moods.

Fame came to him not early but suddenly. Attached to the royal tapestry factory, he made thirty designs (cartoons) for the King's weavers, and in these his true genius, heretofore undisciplined, came to light brilliantly. Instead of mythological subjects, the stock-in-trade of tapestry designers, he turned to things snatched out of his experiences, such as stilt-walkers, boys climbing trees or playing ball, and gallants and their girls picnicking. Done with the utmost rapidity, the decorations shone out with the electrical vitality he is famous for.

He was besieged with orders for portraits, altarpieces, and murals; and being a man of insulting candor and no tact whatever, as well as famous, he made enemies who peddled scandal about him to the court and did their best to besmirch him. But his masterful personality refused to be put down. He moved to Madrid and in his fortieth year was made President of the Academy; on the accession of Charles IV he was made one of the King's painters. His appointment to the court was followed by ten years of incessant activity in which one masterpiece after the other issued from his studio, despite intervals of bad health. At forty-two he survived a terrible attack of indigestion and, unheedful, went right ahead with his intemperate habits.

Women pursued him, and great ladies came, unattended, to his studio—in Spain a sign of sin. Duchesses fought over him, and the Duchess of Alba (his favorite, in all probability) posed for two of his most celebrated canvases, the *Majas,* or gay ladies. In one the gay lady is nude; in the other she is posed in the same reclining posture but clad in skin-tight breeches. The Spaniards, strongly objecting to the nude in art, denounced the paintings, both of them, but the painter let them rave, and added to the scandal by giving one of the canvases, not a phony classical name like *Venus,* but an unvarnished shocker. He called it *La Maja Desnuda,* or "the hussy undressed."

Brazenly careless of her conduct, the Duchess, at the Queen's suggestion, retired for a while to her estate in Andalusia; and Goya, with a leave of absence from the King, accompanied her to her exile. Legend has it that on a rough mountain road the carriage broke down, and that the painter forged the axle into shape again. The heat and exertion induced a chill which affected his ears and eventually led to total deafness. Life in Madrid was unexciting without the ungovernable artist; the King needed him and the guilty pair was soon recalled.

Goya's deafness aggravated his bad temper, and in a dark frame of mind he executed the first of his wonderful groups of etchings, *Los Caprichos,* in which the throne, the church, the law, and the army were ridiculed with contemptuous ferocity. He exposed the weakness of women he had known and men he had hated; one plate depicting a hideous figure, presumably the Queen, bears the words, "She says yes to anyone." The etchings were sold to wealthy buyers, some of them the subjects of his ridicule. When it was rumored that the artist, because of his attacks on the church, was to be taken care of by the Inquisition, the King called in the plates with the explanation that "the artist had worked at his command."

In return for the favor, Goya decorated the Church of San Antonio de la Florida, on royal

Goya. *Family of Charles IV. Prado, Madrid. "The butcher and his family, who have just won the grand lottery prize,"* wrote Gautier.

property near Madrid, with a hundred figures, all larger than life and done in three months! The decorations are dazzling sketches of a blasphemous nature, the kind of tour de force only Goya could have had the nerve and the skill to carry out. The angels are the wanton ladies of the court—his Duchess among them—rouged and made up; naked children clamber over railings, and ballet dancers and shameless beauties flirt with young rakes.

The King was delighted with the gay and daring murals, and rewarded Goya with the post of first court painter and gave him a seat in the royal coach; he even tried to converse with the deaf painter in sign language. The Queen added her approval by sending him a picture by Velásquez—the only picture, save his own, that he possessed. As the century ended, he was painting his best portraits (see Plate 18), many of them requiring only a day or two of hard labor. His large group picture, the *Family of Charles IV,* was characterized once for all by Gautier as "the grocer's family who have won the big lottery prize." They are a beastly lot—the heavy King and his odious Queen and the rest of the royal household, a dozen all told, in gaudy trappings, leering and peering and unsightly, but beautifully rendered in broken colors.

Goya. *Majas on a Balcony. Metropolitan Museum of Art, New York. Two charmers on display, painted four times by Goya.*

Goya. *The Execution, May 2, 1808. Prado, Madrid. The French invaders slaughtering the loyal populace at the gates of Madrid.*

The Duchess of Alba died in 1802—"before her beauty had faded," he said; his wife died in 1804; his son was a weakling. Goya lived on, alone most of the time, painting better with the years. On the second of May, 1808, the French marched into Madrid and slaughtered the populace at the city gate while the nobility cringed indoors. Goya painted the massacre—with a spoon it is said—and bequeathed to mankind a frightening curse against the horrors of war. Ragged people stand frozen with fears of death—men with their hands sticking up; hiding their faces, clenching their fists; dead bodies in pools of blood; helpless civilians before a firing squad.

Goya welcomed the French, but when the

Bourbons were restored, took the oath of allegiance to the new King. "You deserve to be hanged," Ferdinand told him, "but you are an artist, and all is forgiven."

Goya withdrew to his home, called the Deaf Man's Villa, on the outskirts of the city, and decorated his dining room with gigantic fancies, one of Saturn eating up his own children. Here he made etchings of the bull ring and painted many portraits. In his seventy-eighth year, in the burning Spanish summer, he traveled for two weeks in a stagecoach to Paris, but he was too old and rheumatic to enjoy the French capital and went to Bordeaux. He continued to work, drawing on stone, painting with rags and brooms. "My eyes are bad and I'm deaf as a post," he said, "but I shall live to be ninety-nine, like Titian." He died in Bordeaux in his eighty-third year.

Goya was a man of action, but he was also a man of intellect who pondered deeply over the problems of art when ill health forced him

Goya. *Unhappy Mother, detail from Disasters of War. Etching, Metropolitan Museum of Art, New York. Not death on the battlefield, but the suffering of women and children.*

Goya. *There Is No Remedy. Aquatint, Metropolitan Museum of Art, New York. "Death is the only remedy!" screamed the French invaders as they shot down the Spanish patriots.*

to curb his activities. He said that an artist gave out only so much as he took in, but the whole gamut of Spanish life entered his blood and nourished his work. He painted every type of Spaniard and every kind of face, making the ugly more repulsive and the attractive more alluring. His children, pint-size moppets with wise little faces and firm bodies and tiny feet, are among the world's finest. In his etchings of the horrors of war he displays a mastery of form and action, with tragic gestures and bloodcurdling effects of lights and shadows. The body of a man dangles from a tree —lynched. A woman, clasping a naked baby to her hip, drives a lance into a soldier. Another woman offers water to a group of dying soldiers; and the legend of the etching says, "What good is a single cup?" They might be dying soldiers of any war asking the same question.

Reynolds. *Doctor Johnson. Tate Gallery, London. Reynolds painted the ponderous bulk of his friend, the Doctor, with palpable dignity and assurance.*

17

Oh, To Be in England–!

This royal throne of kings, this scepter'd isle,
This happy breed of men, this little world,
This precious stone set in the silver sea—
This blessed plot, this earth, this realm, this
*   England,*
This nurse, this teeming womb of royal kings,
Feared by their breed and famous by their
*   birth—*
This land of such dear souls, this dear dear
*   land,*
Dear for her reputation through the world.

In his play, *Richard II*, Shakespeare thus paid his respects to his homeland. This "dear land," even today, though no longer "feared by their breed," is still dear for her reputation. Mark Twain, who loved England and loathed her snobbery, summed it up: "Even the angels speak with an English accent."

England has produced more poets of the first water probably than the other nations combined, and more than her share of great novelists, too, but we are inclined to forget her painters. In the last century and a half, so widespread has been the prestige of French art that the valid men of Great Britain have been neglected. In Paris, in the days of my first visit, if you admired an English painter, no matter who, you were an oaf and a yokel or, more likely, just an American. But to many Americans—the throngs that elbowed their way into the Metropolitan Mu-

seum of New York, about ten years ago, to view an exhibition of the works of Hogarth, Constable, and Turner—the glory and loveliness of British painting were nothing less than a revelation.

In the earlier centuries, a noble Christian art flourished in England and Ireland in the form of decorated manuscripts, needlework, wall paintings, and miniature portraits; in the thirteenth and fourteenth centuries the Gothic cathedrals ranked with those of France; and later on, the Renaissance architecture of Jones and Wren was carried far and wide—and across the seas into New England. Under the patronage of kings, beginning with Henry VIII, portraiture came into fashion, and in the eighteenth century landscapes began to be shown. In these two departments the British achieved worldwide distinction. The first portrait painters were imported from the Continent: Holbein, Rubens and Van Dyck, Lely the Dutchman, and a pompous German named Kneller.

The long reign of George III (1738–1820) contains the great names of British art. Despite her wars and her crackpot king, England grew rich and in need of culture. As wealth poured in, the upper-class Englishmen began to travel, to make the Grand Tour into Italy before settling down to the serious business of living like lords and gentlemen. In Venice they collected pictures glorifying the

Reynolds. *Miss Bowles. Wallace Collection, London. Little Miss Bowles embraces her dog. Reynolds at his best captured the freshness and roguish charm of childhood.*

the place of the modern camera, but with a radical difference. The purpose of the Georgian "face painters," as they were called, was not a close likeness, but to make the Englishman, his wife, and his children the most enviable and charming people on earth.

Prices were comparatively low, Reynolds and Gainsborough charging two to five guineas a head before their great popularity and from seventy-five to one hundred at the summit of their fame. Sir Thomas Lawrence almost went out of his mind in his efforts to paint a woman's blushes and Hoppner, who would stop at nothing, frequently remarked that "in portraying a lady, he would make as beautiful a face as he could, and then alter it cautiously until a slight resemblance to the sitter came forth." With the King and the court and all the lords and ladies to be served, and every family of means clamoring for por-

merchants of the Adriatic. The next steps followed naturally: a British school of artists developed who could be depended on to paint the gentry in the refined and charming style of the Venetians. The Royal Academy was founded, giving painters official sanction with obligations to the Crown and society, and all the rest. Scholarships and prizes sent young students to Italy to prepare themselves for the grand manner, and painting began to boom.

In fifty years England boasted of more portraits than the continent of Europe had produced in three centuries! Sir Joshua Reynolds, the first President of the Royal Academy, painted more than two thousand; Gainsborough at least one thousand; and Romney listed nine thousand sittings in twenty years, the items of his agenda reading: "Mr. Pitt at 12; Lady Betty Compton at ¼ to 2; Lady Hamilton at 4," and so on. The brush took

Gainsborough. *A Child with a Cat. Metropolitan Museum of Art, New York. The artist was unexcelled in combining the wonder of childhood with a poetic landscape.*

traits, a condition arose in art which painters of today would find hard to believe—the demand was greater than the supply.

The most famous of the portrait painters was Reynolds, by virtue of his position as head of the Academy and by his large and undeniable talents. His *Discourses,* or lectures, to his pupils testify to the breadth of his scholarship, his veneration of the Italians, and his ambition to found a superior British art—on principles derived from Michelangelo, Raphael, and the Venetians. The notion of taking the best from this man and that and rubbing it together did not turn out too happily—but it was the spark plug of some excellent painting.

In his desire to be impressive and classical, Reynolds displayed in his reception rooms layouts or "fancy poses" for his sitters to choose from, when they wished to be preserved not as healthy British folk, but as something they obviously were not—muses, goddesses, and heroes. When he discarded his pretentious paraphernalia for the best that was in him, he painted with largeness of style and fine, compact characterizations, as in his *Dr. Johnson,* bringing out the strength of his men and the true refinement of his women. His portraits of children, who tumbled him from his high horse, are among the best of their kind, truly British, but at the same time glowing with the freshness and roguish glee of all children.

The most lustrous ornament of the face-painting school was Thomas Gainsborough, whose heart was not in the fashionable role he played. "I'm a landscape painter," he pleaded, "and yet they keep coming to me for portraits. I can't paint portraits. Look at that damned arm! I've been at it all morning and I can't get it right!" But he was not altogether just in his outcry. Generous and lighthearted, fond of music and tramp fiddlers, he had a fascinating personality that endeared him to the aristocrats and social leaders; and in his gay and passionate nature flowed a spring of delicacy and charm which rubbed off, as we say, on his portraits. He was best with women on

Gainsborough. *Duchess of Devonshire. Morgan Collection, London. Women, like this one, fluttered Gainsborough's heart, and he painted them with irresistible lightness and ease.*

whom he lavished his own magnetic charm in a painting style that was feathery, buoyant, and irresistible. His popularity, needless to say, was a source of pain to his rival, Sir Joshua.

But nature was Gainsborough's first and greatest love; though sidetracked into the fashionable art of portraiture, thereby gaining wealth and renown, he remained faithful to the countryside of Suffolk, where he had spent his first fifteen years. Faces and costumes he handled lightly, enveloping them in his sparkling style, but his whole soul went into his landscapes. There was, he said of his Suffolk home, "no picturesque clump of trees, nor even a single tree of any beauty, nor hedgerow, stem or stump," that he did not know by heart. He was one of the founders of the British school of landscape—the men who took painting into the open air, under God's

Constable. *The Cornfield. National Gallery, London. A wheatfield to an American—a British view of coolness and deep peace.*

great blue sky, and revealed the moods and blessings of nature. One of the first to appreciate Gainsborough was Constable, who wrote: "His landscapes are soothing, tender, and affecting. The stillness of noon, the depths of twilight, and the dews and pearls of the morning, are all to be found in his canvases. The lovely haunts of the solitary shepherd—the return of the rustic with his bundle of wood; the darksome lane or dell, the sweet little cottage girl at the spring with her pitcher —these were the things he delighted to paint and which he painted with exquisite refinement."

My affection for Constable's pictures goes back into the first years of my childhood. In the hall of our house a large steel engraving of the *Cornfield* was hung, and often, in the hot dry summers of the West, I used to look into this English landscape with its blessed coolness, dampness, and deep peace. To me the scene was more beautiful than a dream:

the boy, flat on the ground drinking from a running brook; the sheep dog waiting patiently with turned head; the ambling flock; the old silent trees; and the fat clouds reeking moisture. But the title puzzled me. The grain was a field of wheat, or maybe rye, but not the corn that I knew. I did not understand that the word "corn," to an Englishman, meant the most important cereal crop, which was wheat. Years afterward, in London, I saw the painting of the *Cornfield*, which expresses the peace and contentment which came from a companionship with nature.

John Constable, born in 1776, was a miller's son, like Rembrandt, but he had nothing in common with the Dutchman except patience, faith, and self-discipline. His road to fame was long but his patience was unflagging, and his wife was sympathetic and intelligent. In his forty-eighth year, in the famous Salon of 1824, in Paris, his pictures were a sensation. They stole the show and the artist was greeted by Delacroix as "the father of modern landscape." The praise did not turn his head and he went back to the country.

Constable's aim was to plan, or compose, his pictures as carefully as Rubens had created

Constable. *Stoke-by-Nayland, Suffolk. W.W. Kimball Collection, Art Institute of Chicago. Painted in the open air, in divided tones recorded side by side, heralding the Impressionist method.*

PLATE 23. EUGÈNE DELACROIX. *Oriental Lion Hunt*. ART INSTITUTE OF CHICAGO

PLATE 24.   HONORÉ DAUMIER. *The Washerwoman*. METROPOLITAN MUSEUM OF ART, NEW YOR

landscapes, but to make them more vivid and truthful by closer observation of trees, clouds, and light. He was the first artist to paint, to any extent, in the open air; to examine the light that streaks among the leaves, and the colors that change with the position of the sun. When he painted water he made it really wet and soaking. He put on canvas the freshness and dewy sparkle of the out-of-doors, and his sky is not a backdrop but a covering of atmosphere and color. (See Plate 20.)

His method of painting influenced all the French romantics of the nineteenth century and heralded the movement known as Impressionism. He flooded his landscapes with light and air and used very bright colors—many of which, I am sorry to say, have lost their brilliancy. He divided his tones: what appears, for example, at a distance to be a patch of green, if seen closely, is a collection of different shades of green, each stroked by the side of the other. This method, in his own day, was almost revolutionary; in the last quarter of the nineteenth century it was employed by a whole school of French painters from Monet to Renoir.

While the portrait painters were plying their fashionable trade, a solitary man of genius, unlike any other artist before or since and belonging to no group or school, was laboring day and night in London. His name was William Blake; he died, as he had lived, in obscurity, and was buried in a pauper's grave. He asked for no public attention and had little. He said, in his last illness:

"I should be sorry if I had any earthly fame, for that kind of popular glory is so much taken away from a man's spiritual glory. I have done nothing for the sake of money. I have lived for art and I am quite happy."

Since his death in 1827, however, his fame on this earth has steadily increased, and today he is recognized as one of the most original artists of recent centuries and a designer of terrific power. He created his pictures, not from living models or from nature, but from the depths of his uncanny imagination.

Rossetti. *Lady Lilith. Metropolitan Museum of Art, New York. Adam's first wife, according to an old legend, "the witch he loved before Eve," in Victorian form and intended as the personification of female loveliness.*

Blake was a born visionary—that is, he communicated with spirits and supernatural "presences," as he called them. At the age of four he was frightened out of his wits when he saw God's face against the window; and while still a child he surprised a flock of angels sitting among the boughs of an oak tree and came upon Ezekiel in an open field. His father, a poor hosier and a man who believed in spirits and spooks, too, on dark nights, encouraged the boy and had him apprenticed to an engraver so that he might learn to draw and, at the same time, make a living.

At twenty-five, after long years of grinding toil, Blake had mastered his craft, and had married the girl of his dreams, Catherine Boucher, daughter of a gardener. She could neither read nor write, but he taught her to do both, and to color his manuscripts and to see visions. Catherine has gone down in history as the perfect wife; she is known to have remained cheerful and uncomplaining, though sorely tried by the strange behavior of her remarkable husband.

Except for three years in the country, Blake's whole life—he lived to be seventy—was passed in London; and one thing taken with another, it was a noble and satisfactory, if not exactly a happy, life. He wrote some of the most imaginative lyrics in the rich treasury of English verse; he engraved, decorated, and bound his own books; he composed vast prophecies that few read and nobody understood, seven epics as long as the *Iliad*, and twenty tragedies the length of *Macbeth*. To eke out a livelihood, he worked for publishers, illustrating the Book of Job, Dante, Milton, and other English poets. It was a pretty thin living

Blake. *Queen Katherine's Dream. Rosenwald Collection, National Gallery of Art, Washington, D.C. Illustration in water color for a scene in Shakespeare's "Henry VIII."*

Blake. *The Morning Stars, from the "Book of Job." Engraving, Metropolitan Museum of Art, New York. Blake heard the voices of the morning stars and pictured the stars in rhythmical designs of spectacular originality.*

he got from his ceaseless toil in a two-room flat in Leicester Square—at times only ten shillings a week; but with his sweet and patient wife, a few devoted friends, and his "creative business," he asked no more of the world.

Blake has frequently been called a madman, and many of his writings might be urged against his sanity, since his prophecies and verbal symbols make no sense to the average reader. But his drawings and water colors are the work of a man in full possession of all his faculties, the clear-cut, precisely designed imaginings of a profound and lucid mind.

It is true that he invented fantastic situations; that he worked by inspiration alone, picking up old figures and poses wherever he might find them and using them in his visions. And it is true that the angels and saints and devils of his imagination were more vivid and real to him than actual persons, and he used them as spiritual models as they trooped before his eyes.

It is hard to talk about Blake's spiritualism, or his philosophy, without lapsing into a language which makes no sense to those unable to see visions or to talk with the departed dead. But his drawings and water colors will not leave you either cold or confused. He gives us heaven and hell, fiends and angels. Along with hundreds of little scenes connecting man with God or the devil, he portrays the *Soul Hovering Over the Body, Macbeth and the Witches, Elijah and the Chariot of Fire,* and *Queen Katherine's Dream,* an illustration for a passage in Shakespeare's Henry VIII. He is the only man who has made a convincing picture of the morning stars singing together—he heard them as you and I hear the voices of our friends.

Blake's best designs are perfectly put together—nothing wasted, nothing unnecessary. He groups or aligns his figures in long flowing friezes and swishing rhythms, and balances his leaping forms with giant trees, a vast ocean, or screaming gods. His pictures are never static or dead; the figures glide and whirl in a region of monsters with flying arms and squads of angels, or they swoop over a darkened moor where a shepherd is dreaming. It is a strange world—a visionary world of joy and tenderness and wrath, of freezing terrors and mirth —"the real world," he said, "of the spirit."

Two other great Englishmen of this period, Hogarth and Turner, are reserved for another chapter. Then this display of national genius in painting came to an end. In the latter half of the nineteenth century we have the Pre-Raphaelites, a brotherhood of sensitive and intelligent men, some of them very gifted. But they were, as a group, ineffectual as painters, often trying to translate poems into pictures, and their honest and admirable attempt to re-

vive religious painting died as it was born. Holman Hunt's *Light of the World,* a modern conception of Christ, is still widely circulated in color prints; and Millais was a first-rate craftsman, but the genius and mainspring of the movement was Dante Gabriel Rossetti, half Italian, a poet second only to the great men, and a painter of remarkable originality. He was truly devotional and truly imaginative, as witnessed by his water color of the Virgin done at the age of twenty.

Rossetti's painting of *Dante's Dream*—he was a profound student and translator of Dante—and his sumptuous portraits of women are put together with a curiously lyrical flow of lines, despite the fact that he was not much of a draftsman. He looked upon beautiful women with a sort of Latin adoration that was part mystical, part sensual, and pictured them as stunning Madonnas, thus unsettling the Victorians.

At the close of the nineteenth century the most successful British painters were members of the Royal Academy, and most of them were pedantic and uninspired. A belligerent enemy of the old Academy crowd is Augustus John, a painter of technical brilliance and integrity and with many of the qualities of the lords of portraiture.

Augustus John. *Tallulah Bankhead. Tallulah Bankhead Collection, New York.*

Hogarth. *The Shrimp Girl. National Gallery, London. The madonna of the fish market, a plate of shrimps on her head, a bravura piece of authentic beauty, and technically, an object of adoration to this day.*

18

Hogarth and Turner

British painting, as a national movement, began with William Hogarth, who remains to this day the first of his countrymen in versatility, intelligence, and downright technical skill —the ability to use a brush with the strength and confidence of, let us say, a painter like Rubens. For the British painters of his own generation he had nothing but contempt, calling them frauds and imitators of the Old Masters. He was so disgusted with the nonsense uttered about the Italians by dealers and collectors that he labeled the Renaissance painters the "Black Masters," and made burlesque copies of their famous canvases. He was as independent as a man can be and get his work done, and always ready to fight for his rights.

Hogarth was born in London in 1697, the son of a poor schoolmaster, and his education was so scant and irregular that he might be termed self-taught. He was suspicious of the schemes for improving the young mind, and had no interest in the dull studies shoved at him by the pedagogues. He had a large stock of good humor, a sharp tongue, and a capacity for work. "Genius," he said, "is only labor and diligence. I cut a poor figure at school. Blockheads with better memories could surpass me. I was fond of shows of all sorts. I had a good eye, and I was always drawing."

He was apprenticed to an engraver, and at the age of twenty, on the death of his father, opened his own studio as a commercial artist, designing coats of arms, shopkeepers' signs and cards, and invitations to banquets and funerals. He pursued his trade for ten years, at the same time training himself with the labor and diligence he said were the basis of genius —and sure enough, in his early thirties, his genius as a painter burst upon London.

The London of his time was a rough-and-tumble town. The upper classes went in for frivolous pastimes imported from France and Italy, the lower orders for more beastly recreations; and popular with both classes were cock-fighting, bear-baiting, dueling, and gambling. At night nobody was safe as the oil lamps flickered dimly in the fogs. Irish thugs and drunken stevedores, like New York muggers, lurked in the shadows to hold up stragglers or beat them to death. Art was in the hands of crooked auctioneers and pirates, and gin was the national beverage. But in this rowdy town, there were groups of appreciative and intelligent men —hard drinkers and hard fighters— most of them writers whose books are classics of English prose. One of them, a stocky, blue-eyed man with the keenest wit and the tenderest heart of the entire company, was Hogarth, painter and engraver.

Hogarth knew his London and loved it, and no form of life, high or low, escaped his atten-

181

Hogarth. *Laughing Audience. Etching, Metropolitan Museum of Art, New York. The rabble at the theater, caricatures made from the sharpest memory in Anglo-Saxon art.*

tion. He loved the fresh-complexioned, rosy-cheeked loveliness of the English girls and the beef-eating men whom he painted with the bulk of sculpture. He frequented the taverns and side shows, watched the redcoats on parade, and followed the crowds to the hangings which they enjoyed as people today cheer and scream at a prize fight.

He formed the habit of observing the faces and attitudes of people so minutely that he could draw them from memory. He could not remember what he had read, but what he had seen he never forgot, and his visual memory was staggering. He drew from models, but he was not a slave to his models; he referred to them from time to time, to correct his impressions. When he enrolled in the classes of a well-known artist to draw from the nude, he found exactly what his natural suspicions had warned him to expect. "Drawing," he said, "with my teacher was only a species of copying—and copying is like pouring water out of one vessel into another."

The venture in life-drawing ended very happily. His teacher had a daughter named Jane —twenty and a British beauty—whom Hogarth persuaded to elope with him. Neither had any reason to regret it, nor did the father —after the impetuous young rascal had come into enormous popularity on the strength of his first important work. The work was begun soon after his marriage, to test his ideas "of composing pictures on canvas similar to representations on the stage"; and the subject was far from uncommon in the London of 1730.

The subject was *A Harlot's Progress,* a social drama unfolded in a sequence of paintings, each treating a significant circumstance in the wayward path of Moll Hackabout, a pretty country girl who came up to London and went to the bad. She falls into loose company; she quarrels with a rich admirer; she is brought before a judge; she beats hemp in prison; she dies; she is buried. And at the funeral, her little son is perched on the coffin winding his top, "the only person," according to Charles Lamb, "in that assembly who is not a hypocrite."

The picture-drama was a "smash hit," as our reviews say of an immensely successful play; and Hogarth, after a custom followed thereafter, reproduced the work in the form of engravings which netted him £1260, a tidy fortune in those days. The plates were immediately pirated (copied and sold without permission) and Hogarth appealed to Parliament for the protection of artists and writers. A copyright law was passed and piracy in pictures and books slowly disappeared. Highbrow painters and dealers tried to convince the public that the pictures were not really works of art, but the public did not listen. They loved the painter's honest realism and his knowledge of their own frailties. Hogarth had revived the oldest and most appealing form of art, that of story telling, which he used as a connected series of pictures, and the British drank it in like children at a circus.

His next story in paint was the *Rake's*

Progress, eight episodes in the career of a young heir, Tom Rakewell, as he gambles, falls into low company, marries an old maid for her money, and dies in Bedlam, or the lunatic asylum. Though superior to the story of poor Moll, the second work was not so sensational. The idea had lost its novelty—and the artist was now exposing the dissipations of a higher social level where sinning was taken for granted, and even envied.

The artist was not distressed by the fickleness of public tastes. He had many things to do before he was ready to sign off, among them the building of the first Foundling Hospital in England. On his father-in-law's death,

Hogarth. *Lord Lovat. Etching, Metropolitan Museum of Art, New York. A famous criminal who was hanged. At the execution the artist sold prints among the crowds that gathered to enjoy the show.*

he took control of an art school where, he said, he would see that "talent is developed freely and not shaped to copy the dead for dealers"; he had the highest respect for the dead, but he was opposed to those who used the Old Masters for personal gain or to stifle native talent. If he were in need of ready cash he could always turn a potboiler into a masterpiece, as in his *Lord Lovat,* a portrait etching from his painting of a famous criminal who was hanged, and one of the consummate drawings of northern art. On the day of the execution, Hogarth sold copies of the etching at Tyburn, or the hanging grounds—sold them like hot cakes at high prices.

Hogarth disliked the French almost as strongly as he opposed the snobs and idlers of England; and in one of the scenes of the *Rake's Progress* he gives the center of the stage to a half-pint French ballet master, a conceited little fop, dainty and exquisite and half-woman, the type who then strutted about English drawing rooms. The *Gate of Calais,* one of his masterpieces, was a private blast at the French for arresting him unjustly at the gates of the town where he was caught sketching. It is a beautiful piece of painting, but it contains some starving soldiers, a libel in the eyes of the French. The Englishman pitched into the French with more prejudice than judgment, but at the same time he was much more vehement in attacking the follies of his own people.

Hogarth's third dramatic performance *Marriage à la Mode,* the high-water mark in his social narratives, was a flop in the buying market, probably because it brought before the public the scandals in the life of an earl and a countess. In his last decade, his health was poor and he was involved in controversies over his art. "After a good quarrel," he said, "I always felt restored." In his final years, he wrote *The Analysis of Beauty,* the first book on esthetics in English—and plain English at that. He died at the age of sixty-six from hardening of the arteries and was buried, in the words of a clergyman, "in

Hogarth. *Marriage à la Mode. Tate Gallery, London. "My picture is my stage," the artist said, "the men and women my players." Engraved from a picture-drama of high life.*

a neat mausoleum, with an elegant inscription by Davy Garrick."

The whole of England fills Hogarth's art to overflowing—the bitter and the sweet, the coarse and cruel, the rollicking and the tender. His engravings of *Beer Street* and *Gin Lane* show us the guzzling lower classes making love in public and the horrors of drunkenness. His paintings of men and women are the flowers of portraiture in England: his sister *Ann;* his *Servants*—you can almost hear their accent they are so unmistakably British; the actor *Garrick,* for which he was paid £200, at that time the highest price ever paid for a British portrait; *Peg Woffington,* the *Graham Children* (see Plate 19), and many others. They have all the ingredients of fine painting: exquisite color, a draftsmanship Rubens would have admired, and beautiful execution. His women have health, intelligence, and sweetness of character; his men are rugged and unbending, but noble and decorative, "feared by their breed and famous by their birth." And the *Shrimp Girl,* his most popular canvas, is so dazzling and skillful, so charming and delicate and lightly painted, as

to fetch shrieks of admiration from the French who love stylish painting. "My picture is my stage," the artist wrote, "my men and women my players." He created an art for men, in a man's country. On the honor roll of the great Englishmen of the eighteenth century, you will find Fielding, the novelist; Swift, the satirist; Newton, the scientist; Dr. Johnson, critic and essayist; and not least, Hogarth, painter and engraver.

Joseph Mallord William Turner sold himself to art, body and soul, with the unconditional surrender of a religious martyr, on the one hand, and the dark, mysterious, secretive energy of a creature of genius on the other. He was gifted as only the great are gifted: he was a professional artist at ten; at fourteen he had studied with seven teachers and was admitted to the classes of Reynolds, earning his way from the sale of drawings exhibited in his father's shop; at fifteen his paintings were shown at the Royal Academy; at eighteen he was an independent artist with his own studio; he was famous at twenty-five and a member of the Royal Academy at twenty-seven. And during his three-score years of in-

Hogarth. *Hogarth's Servants. National Gallery, London. British types, so articulately defined that you can hear their accents, portrayed with the intelligence of a master.*

Hogarth. *Self-portrait with His Dog. Tate Gallery, London. The solid, fighting Britisher who beat the high-toned painters at their own game. On the palette is the famous double curve, his "line of beauty."*

his son educated in art, but for the sole purpose of making money. The boy had the constitution of an ox, but he was far from good-looking, and suffered alike from pride and humiliation. He was sensitive to everything noble and poetic, but in a country where birth counted for so much, his low inheritance shamed him into seclusion. Nobody ever saw him paint; nobody knew where he lived. As his fame and wealth increased, he ceased to live decently, hoarded his money like a miser, and his pictures, too. He dedicated his powers to the art of landscape which he carried from the most painstaking studies of nature to fabulous visions of sunlight and color.

Turner had little schooling and the little he had was wasted on him. He learned to read and write and to add pounds, shillings, and pence; and the classics, which he struggled through in translation, filled him with grandiose projects. As time went on, and he withdrew from human associations and learned to express himself in paint, his English slipped away, and his attempts to write it were a ludicrous muddle.

cessant artistry he traveled, mostly on foot, twenty-five miles a day, over a large part of the British Isles and Western Europe exploring the face of the earth—the atmosphere above it, the mountains, the vegetation, the structure of the sea, and the architecture of the clouds with the same sustained observation that Leonardo da Vinci summoned when he studied human anatomy. He toiled while others slept, and left a fortune of £140,000, more than two thousand finished pictures and nineteen thousand water colors and drawings!

He was born in London, in 1775, the son of a barber. The ugliness of his childhood clung to him like a disease. His mother was vicious and subject to spells of insanity, and he never mentioned her to anyone. His father was a windy, greedy cockney who was eager to have

Turner. *Grand Canal, Venice. Metropolitan Museum of Art, New York. The magnificence of Venice in the old days—the shimmering mists, the gondolas, and the palace architecture.*

Turner. *Calais Pier. National Gallery, London. The sculptural sea, the heaving boats, and the huddled fishermen in a marine drama of marvelous observation and execution.*

Three minutes from his father's shop ran the Thames. "The Great River," he called it and he was always near or upon it, among the ships and fishmongers, observing the light effects in the fogs swollen by smoke and steam. He went to sea, got the hang of ships, and made himself a sailor. Ruskin, describing his facility in water color, tells how he painted from memory in three hours a most complicated picture of a man-of-war taking in stores; the ship was drawn in detail, with guns, rigging, portholes, and anchors, with two other ships in the distance, and with smaller craft, dancing waves, and a cloudy sky.

From his fifteenth to his twenty-fifth year, he earned a living by washing in backgrounds for architectural plans, and by drawing accurate portraits of estates, cathedrals, castles, and manor houses for the portfolios and walls of country gentlemen. During this period, he was on the go continually, walking and sketching rural life as eagerly as he had studied the sea. A born tramp, he held his luggage in a handkerchief at the end of a stick, and took to the open road. He could eat anything put before him and sleep outdoors or in. If

there were no water handy for mixing his colors, he spat into the mess and converted it into beautiful pictures. At the turn of the century he was a celebrity in London, at an age when most artists are wondering which way to go.

Turner knew exactly which way to go, but he never told anybody, and our knowledge of his middle years is full of uncertainties. He was always wandering but his routes were kept to himself, as well as his headquarters in London. His art, however, was an open book, and he had no hesitation in telling the public how great an artist he was. From his knowledge of nature, which no other artist has seriously contested, he would "construct" landscapes—not copy what he had seen—as complete and moving as Michelangelo's constructions of the human body. He was also a student of the Dutch artists, whose pictures of the sea provoked both his envy and his scorn, and of the classical Frenchmen, Poussin and Claude, who tormented his ego and urged him into his most ambitious undertakings.

At the age of twenty-eight he had surpassed the Dutch in a series of dark, realistic masterpieces such as *Calais Pier,* in which the waves of the sea pile up like masonry—a sculptural sea as only Turner could paint it. At the same time he was wrestling with mythological pictures in an effort to be classical. After a visit to Italy, the darkness went out of his pictures; and upon the solid foundation of the world as he had observed it, he composed scenes of light and color, such as his famous *Ulysses Deriding Polyphemus* where land and sea, ships and sky are bound together in a fiery atmosphere of gold and blue.

During this period he was also occupied with his *Liber Studiorum,* a collection of one hundred drawings, etchings, and mezzotints assembled to show his range as a landscape artist, and to contrast the beauty of woods and streams with the devastations and ugly buildings of man.

Turner longed for friends and affection but

was at a loss to obtain them. At twenty-five he employed a girl of sixteen as his housekeeper and the girl remained till his death, loved or unloved. He left her in charge of his affairs while he traveled in the Alps or sailed up and down the North Sea with fishing fleets. He purchased a couple of houses in London, which he remodeled into a home and a picture gallery where the public was welcome, free of charge. His bad habits got the better of him, and he drank heavily after working for days with feverish concentration.

During the last ten years of his life Turner was an old hermit buried in paint. He was now absorbed in the problems of light and color, and after another visit to Venice, he produced his last masterpieces: the *Fighting Téméraire* (see Plate 21), the *Sun of Venice*, the *Slave Ship*, and *Rain, Steam, and Speed*. Because of his studies of the effects of light and atmosphere on the color of natural forms, Turner was called after his death, by a group of distinguished French artists, "the father of Impressionism."

He pottered about his old house which was dying, like himself. The rain beat in; the furniture fell to pieces; the paintings moldered in the dampness, and water colors and drawings—more than 30,000—lay in piles upon the floor. He was away most of the time, nobody knew where, and his housekeeper, old and rheumatic, was under orders to touch nothing and answered no questions. When the master did not return, she traced him to a den by the river where he was guarded by a cancerous old woman. He was called the Admiral, in the neighborhood, from his habit of observing the skies and weather. He died as he had lived, in dirt, the western sun shining upon his face.

No one was more deeply moved by nature than Turner, or more responsive to the variety of growing things. He expressed, first, the good earth and the dangers of the sea, and next, the desolation of the country by the work of man and the industrial revolution. At the same time, in *Rain, Steam, and Speed* he made an express train beautiful by immersing it in an atmosphere of tones. In his last stage, he was a slave to sunlight. He said that the sun was God, and painted the Thames as a river of light. He had dissolved the foundations of nature and ended by painting magic veils of light and bursts of color.

Turner. *Ulysses Deriding Polyphemus. National Gallery, London. The Cyclops myth in a world where ships and sky are bound together in an atmosphere of gold and blue.*

Corot. *Gypsy Girl at Fountain. George W. Elkins Collection, Philadelphia Museum of Art. Corot was at his best in carefully drawn studies of rugged young girls whom he placed in outdoor settings.*

19

The Capital of Art

After the creative glories of the Italian Renaissance had dwindled away, the center of culture passed into France, and in France, or more exactly Paris, it has remained to this very moment. For three centuries, or from the time the French had the fine arts nicely organized, Paris has been the international home of everything gracious and civilized and refined. The British, of course, have not been dispossessed as the arbiters of social etiquette, formal behavior, and home life; but the French have retained priority in the arts, proclaiming the freedom of the creative spirit over all rules and conventions. In other words, the French have guided the direction of painting and sculpture for a long time, and today, with their country at low ebb economically and politically, they continue to attract artists of all the world to their capital.

More than eight centuries ago, Paris was the seat of learning for all Europe; and Paris owes her supremacy in modern times, as the center of culture, to her old tradition, and to her Bohemia—that quarter of the city which caters to the cravings, romantic fevers, and artistic ambitions of talented men and women the world over.

At the opening of the twelfth century, Peter Abélard, philosopher and teacher (better known for his love affair with Héloïse, the learned nun) was holding forth in the cloisters of Notre Dame, and young students from all parts of Europe traveled to Paris to listen to his eloquence. As the old city swarmed with students, the University of Paris was founded on the Left Bank of the Seine, in an area known historically as the Latin Quarter, since Latin was the common language of the students of various tongues.

The ancient quarters of the Left Bank, which seem so quaint and picturesque to modern artists, afforded no romantic charms to the original inhabitants. The streets were undrained and dark, the houses disreputable; and the half-starved students, to drown their hardships, ganged together in fierce rivalries, cutting up in the streets, drinking and dancing in the taverns when they had a franc or two to spare. In the infancy of Paris, the café appeared, one of the most popular of French institutions. From the time of Abélard, Paris provided cafés for all classes of people: for fashionable loafers, scholars and poets, cosmopolitans and fugitives, artists and authors, politicians, preying women, crooks, mechanics, jockeys, and garbage collectors. The cafés give color and atmosphere to the city, providing a jolly meeting ground for the exchange of ideas and, at the other extreme, a refuge for failures, idlers, and foreign pretenders with money to spend.

The middle of the nineteenth century marked the golden age of the Latin Quarter, a period celebrated by Murger's *La Vie de*

189

Arc de Triomphe. Paris. Erected during the Empire in honor of the Grand Army of Napoleon whose ashes passed through it after his death at St. Helena.

Bohème (Life in Bohemia), a novel larded with the most seductive aspects of the Quarter—and by no means truthful. The novel was followed by a play of the same name, and later, by an opera which is still one of the most popular. Thus we have the word "Bohemian," taken from the old word for gypsy, and meaning careless of money, dedicated to art, and unconventional.

By the end of the nineteenth century the Bohemian quarters of Paris (the Left Bank and a rival district in Montmartre, across the Seine) had lost much of their integrity—the spirit of companionship in poverty among young people of artistic ambitions—and had become pleasant places in which to drink and talk and, occasionally, work a little. The French, with their shrewdness in exploiting the arts, have systematically maintained their Bohemia as a prearranged background for artists of all nations—an artificial world in which life is so congenial that an artist never hates himself if he doesn't work, and every man would be a Michelangelo or a Rubens, if wishes were artists.

At the arrival of the seventeenth century, French art in all its departments—architecture, sculpture, and painting—was given over to imitations of the Italians, a sin and a shame after the wonderful cathedral building of the thirteenth and fourteenth centuries, the great Gothic sculpture, the stained glass, and the painters of miniatures and manuscripts. But in 1648, the French promoted their prestige by an official move, turning art into a patriotic industry under the control, first of kings, and afterward of politicians. They invented the Academy to guarantee high standards, uniformity of taste, and elegance; to support the artists by giving them state jobs to perform, and, as Napoleon put it, "to satisfy the French hunger for Glory."

The Academy was chartered and brought into state control by Louis XIV. To further its schemes for making France the successor of Italy, millions of francs were thrown into art, resulting in a riot of make-believe classical architecture—the palace of Versailles, for example—furniture and tapestries, sculpture and painting. France was imposing a bureaucracy, or state regulation, on the artists, from which it has never recovered; and during the nineteenth century, the best and most independent artists were united in their attacks, tooth and nail, on the Academy.

Throughout their history, the French have been great producers of sculpture. After the cathedral carvings, much of it was decorative sculpture, a sort of window dressing on the façade of Paris. From the Arc de Triomphe to the fountains of Versailles, the boulevards, courts, and official structures are enlivened by statues; the public monuments are cluttered with symbolical nudes; the fountains are profuse with nymphs and sea gods; and the glory of *La Patrie,* the one and only France, is embodied in figures somehow standing for "Liberty, Equality, and Fraternity," the motto of the Republic.

The first of the decorative sculptors, and the best, was Jean Goujon, born about 1510. All his important works were done for monu-

ments, and with a Frenchman's love for un-
dulating forms, he achieved a masterpiece
in the *Fountain of the Innocents*. The three
nymphs of this fountain, a French version of
the ideal figure, with their graceful poses and
exquisite drapery, have often been compared
with the figures of the later Greeks. The finest of the portrait sculptors was Jean Antoine
Houdon (1741–1828) whose characterizations
of Voltaire, in Paris, and Washington, in
Richmond, Virginia, have not been surpassed
since the old Italians. The greatest of modern sculptors of animals was Antoine Louis
Barye (1796–1875) who observed his beasts
in the zoo and then modeled them from his
imagination in death struggles, animal with
animal, or animal against man. Under the influence of the fleshly figures of Rubens, in the
Third Republic, Jules Dalou constructed me-
morials which, though given fancy allegorical

*Louvre. Paris. An old château, rebuilt by
Francis I, and converted by Napoleon into the
great art gallery.*

*Place de la Concorde. Paris. The famous
square with government buildings, obelisk,
fountains, and sculptures in the French refinement of the classical tradition.*

names, are realistic figures of large nudes,
some of them surrounding portrait statues of
famous men.

The most original and the most famous
French sculptor of the last quarter of the nineteenth century was Auguste Rodin, who has
sometimes been described as a modeler since
he fashioned his figures in clay sketches and
had them cut in marble or cast in bronze by
assistants. Rodin, with a mastery of anatomical science, created a kind of plastic poetry
in sculpture—in noble portraits and in fluid
and tender nude figures. The *Thinker* is a
giant cave man concentrating with all his
might to have one little thought. Of more recent sculptors, one man stands alone, Aristide
Maillol, whose figures are as solid as architecture, massive and rugged figures reminding
us of the strength and simplicity of the early
Greek statues.

Turning to the painters, we must burn a
candle for the repose of Nicolas Poussin, who
has been dwelling among the shades of the
pagan paradise for three hundred years. Poussin, a poor boy from Normandy, born in 1594,
went to Paris to study art, his head filled with
cold reverence for the Italians and the old
Greeks and Romans. He wanted to go to

Rome, an empty hope until he married the daughter of a wealthy chef. With his wife's money, he built a house on a hilltop near Rome, and there he lived all his days save for one visit to Paris, at the King's request, to decorate a gallery of the Louvre.

Poussin lived among old tombs and monuments, digging and measuring in the hope of discovering the secrets of ancient art, and he examined everything Raphael did, thinking to find therein a formula for the making of a classic style. He painted the heroes of antiquity, the gods, nymphs, and nudes of Homer and Virgil, and maybe an exciting incident from the Old Testament to please the Churchmen—and very remarkably, too, for he had a calculating mind, something between a surveyor and a poet, and a horror of commonplace details. There is no drama in his paintings and no action, but nothing is out of place or superfluous—not too much, not too little. Everything is exact, smooth, and sedate, like the seven hills of Rome in the sunsets of October. His skill as an organizer of pictures has made him a great favorite among artists concerned with the craft of putting the parts of a picture together smoothly.

Without doubt, Poussin had the cadences of the heroic French poets in his soul, but the

Barye. *Theseus Fighting the Minotaur. Brooklyn Museum, New York. The great sculptor observed his beasts in the zoo and modeled them in imaginary struggles.*

Façade, Château of Versailles. Versailles. A tribute, in Renaissance style, to the pomp and glory of Louis XIV.

titles of his pictures are not very helpful. In the *Arcadian Shepherds* an old man, attended by a couple of shepherds—and a girl to clinch the mood—is deciphering an inscription on an antique tomb, and muttering about it. *"Et in Arcadia Ego,"* the old man reads, suddenly conscious of the little time we have on earth; "I, Too, Have Lived in Arcadia" (the Eden of the Greeks) echoes the voice from the tomb. In the picture of Orpheus, and the rest of his antique paintings, it is best not to look for a specific story, but to enjoy the scholarly, beautifully proportioned world of a shrewd Frenchman in love with the art of the ancients.

Another Frenchman who went down to

PLATE 25. GEORGES SEURAT. *La Grande Jatte*. ART INSTITUTE OF CHICAGO

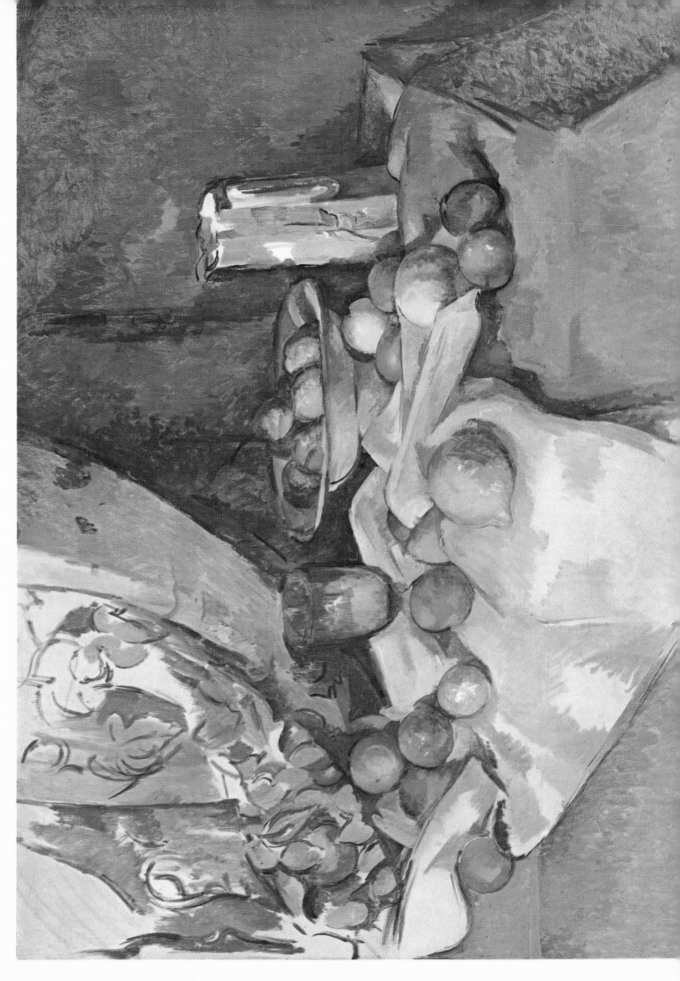

PLATE 26. PAUL CÉZANNE. *Still Life with Apples*. MUSEUM OF MODERN ART, NEW YORK

PLATE 27. VINCENT VAN GOGH. *L'Arlésienne*. LEWISOHN COLLECTION, NEW YORK

PLATE 28. PABLO PICASSO. *Gourmet.* CHESTER DALE COLLECTION, CHICAGO

Rome with a view to capturing the heroics of the dead was Claude Lorrain, a poorly educated pastry cook born in 1600. Unlike Poussin, his strivings after the grand style did not come off—his faked marble houses, his puny figures and idle waters—but when he looked directly into nature for his inspiration, he found what he was born to do beautifully. He loved nature as a man loves the girl of his heart, and he observed the landscape as an artist out to record the effects of light and atmosphere over trees, grass, and water. The figures he dragged into his pictures are not important, those in the *Ford,* for example, but the mood he created will never be worn-out.

African Fetish Figure, Ivory Coast, Baoule Tribe. African Art Sponsors Fund, Cleveland Museum of Art. Religious fetish of the Africans carved in wood with simplicity and fine craftsmanship. African sculpture has strongly influenced modern art.

Poussin. *Peter and John Healing the Lame Man. Metropolitan Museum of Art, New York. Everything is reasoned out, with every figure an old Roman placed in a New Testament story with scientific precision.*

It is a peaceful mood in a world lit by the golden rays of the setting sun, a world untouched by the dirt and toil of man, but happy in its pleasant shade and quiet sentiment.

While the pastry cook and Poussin were in Italy looking for subjects to paint, three half-mysterious brothers named Le Nain were producing small, familiar, peasant scenes of an appealing nature. Which of the brothers painted this canvas or that, and whether the pictures were co-operative affairs, are unanswered questions, but Louis Le Nain is known to be the sole author of at least one painting, the *Peasant Family,* of the Louvre. His sincerity makes the picture heart-warming, and also his insight into the subjects: the old man, bitter and foxy; the sad old woman resigned to her lot; the young woman eager for life, and the children too innocent to know what awaits them.

Georges de la Tour, born in 1593, and ignored for more than three centuries, has recently been singled out for extravagant praise because of the startling similarity of his pic-

Rodin. *Beside the Sea. Metropolitan Museum of Art, New York. The plastic poetry of Rodin as created in the polished form of a nude bather.*

and his children saying their prayers, as good things to have and good things to paint. He spent hours arranging his still-life models and painted them slowly, touch by touch, to build kitchen masterpieces which have the charm of minor poetry.

Antoine Watteau, born in Flanders in 1684, wandered to Paris in his youth, went through ten years of poverty and ten good years, marred by ill health and melancholy, and died of consumption at the age of thirty-seven. He was not blinded by visions of French glory, nor did he bother his frail soul about the grandeur of the ancients. He had but one idea: men and women dedicated to making love, and playing at the game as a form of art. They are dressed as gallants and ladies of quality, avoiding vulgar and uncultivated gestures and displaying the greatest delicacy in

tures—his sharply drawn, geometrical figures—to the works of the Cubists, led by Picasso. But his true fame as an artist is not wholly technical. He owed much to the late Italians for his spotlight effects, but his deep and mystical spirit, which is almost primitive in its simple faith, is his own. He uses a candle as a torch, or a flaming orchid, to illumine his pictures and to make them dramatic when the characters, like those portrayed in his *St. Sebastian,* are gentle and grave. His *Magdalene,* plain and penitent, holding a skull as a symbol of death, gazes past the flame into the world to come.

Jean Baptiste Siméon Chardin, born in 1699, when France was seething with the fashionable wickedness of the monarchy and getting ready for the Revolution, was a plain man, the son of a carpenter, and happy among ordinary people. As an artist he was faithful to kitchen utensils, loaves and bottles, and household occurrences, which he converted into a domestic art. He loved his fruits and pots and pans, his neighbors and servants,

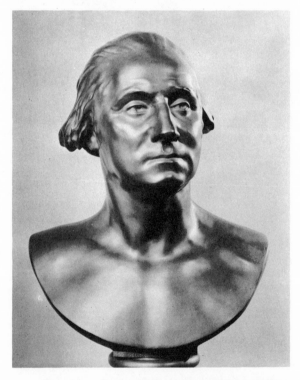

Houdon. *Bust of Washington. Metropolitan Museum of Art, New York. Modeled at Mt. Vernon on a visit by the French master. Not a needless furrow or wasted plane, the head smooth and elegant.*

Claude Lorrain. *The Ford. Metropolitan Museum of Art, New York. The figures are unimportant, the mood is everything. A pagan world untouched by the toil of man, and going back into peaceful distance.*

their preoccupations. The *Embarkation for Cythera* is typical of what he had to say: here the assembled couples prepare to sail away to the blessed isle where there is no death and where love-making goes on into eternity—the French idea of heaven! Watteau filled his albums with sketches of heads and figures, all done from life with the utmost grace in the manipulation of light and shade—and with everything coarse or plebeian excluded.

Typical of Parisian artists in the early eighteenth century was François Boucher, born in 1703, the favorite of Louis XV and all his court. Boucher had studied Watteau, but he was of a more worldly breed, frankly a decorator of the sensual side of fashionable life. He painted the royal ladies as goddesses or shepherdesses, draped or nude. Venus, his favorite deity, was only an excuse for a plump rosy figure amid clouds, trees, or draperies, attended by glowing nymphs wrapped in blue foliage. His paintings, or many of them, were designed for the panels of royal boudoirs, and he was the bedroom artist par excellence.

Boucher's assistant, Jean Honoré Fragonard, born in 1732, was also a boudoir painter but not exclusively. He could dash off

sketches and wash drawings with amazing rapidity and was perhaps the most dexterous painter of the French school, and an excellent artist indeed in his more serious undertakings. With the most subtle coloring he depicted the course of true love in the hearts of innocent young girls, his *Storming the Citadel* being one of the panels in love's journey. The innocence is only an attitude; the scene is a stage setting in the grand manner, and a brilliant interpretation of the frivolity preceding the Revolution.

Jean Baptiste Camille Corot, born in 1796, in the fury of the Revolution, was a generous, simple-hearted man who lived to be eighty years old, happy to the end and hopeful, he said, "of painting in heaven." He paid no attention to political matters or the squabbles of artists, and when he was not at work in the open air, with a song on his lips, he was in his studio painting bathing girls and pretty milliners. His popular fame rests on his landscapes, but his figure pieces are now in demand at enormous prices.

In early life he painted what the French call his "classical landscapes," so termed because

Poussin. *Orpheus Asking the Way to Hades. Metropolitan Museum of Art, New York. The story is not very clear—serving as a pretext for the beautifully measured, stately world of the painter.*

Maillol. *Female Torso. Metropolitan Museum of Art, New York. In the spirit of the primitive Greeks, the artist carved figures as strong and substantial as pieces of architecture.*

of their firmness of structure and their organized tranquillity. In his middle years he painted innumerable scenes in his silvery-gray style, many of them filmy, fuzzy, and sentimental, and turned out for money which he gave to artists and other friends in poor circumstances. It has been estimated that three thousand of these wistful landscapes (some undoubtedly spurious) veiled in shadows and often with a ring of tiny nymphs in the foreground, have found their way into America. His figure studies are clean and chaste, drawn from close study of the girls who posed for him—always girls—but without sacrificing their personalities.

Born in 1748, with a furious hatred of the bedroom art of the times, was Jacques Louis David. Like Poussin, he returned to the ancients for guidance, and he became, with the Revolution, the Caesar of French painting. He was famous for his *Oath of the Horatii,*

Louis Le Nain. *Women Making Soap. Private Collection, Paris. Probably by Louis Le Nain, one of three brothers who signed their pictures with the family name, and found dignity and human worth among the poor and humble.*

Rodin. *The Thinker. Metropolitan Museum of Art, New York. A giant cave man, concentrating with all his might on his first thought.*

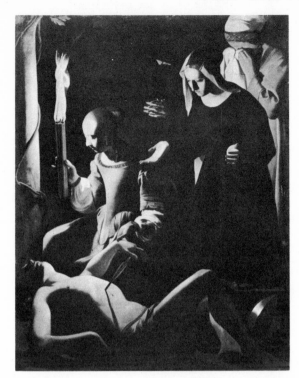

Georges de la Tour. *Saint Sebastian Mourned by Saint Irene. Kaiser Friedrich Museum, Berlin. A favorite subject by a neglected master now famous again because of his brilliantly illuminated, sharply defined forms.*

representing an incident in a mixed-up Roman legend about the feuding between the three sons of one mother against the three sons of her twin sister. David abolished the old Academy and founded his own. He designed Empire furniture and a classical evening gown, the "Empire," which any woman with a good figure would love to wear at a formal party. And he flattered the vanity of Napoleon by painting the Little Corsican and his henchman as descendants of Caesar.

But David had great ability. He had a hard, metallic style based on copies of ancient statues; and his historical pictures—all fanatically serious—are studies of old Romans and their nudes, converted into something as artificial as our modern plastics. In his portraits he was a different David, a cold-blooded master capable of lending a severe decency and even dig-

nity to anyone who sat for him. Mme. Récamier, a famous woman of the world, did not like her portrait—she said she looked like an uncomfortable woman unable to undress and relax—but the picture has been popular ever since it was finished.

Jean Auguste Dominique Ingres, the pupil of David, was also an academic painter of the first degree, with his eyes glued on the art of Leonardo and Raphael. He lived in Rome for a score of years, partly from scholarships and partly from the meager returns he earned by making pencil portraits of travelers—little sketches distinguished by exquisite taste, tact, and astounding craftsmanship, in fact, the best small-scale portraits the nineteenth century has to offer. Ingres lived to be eighty-seven, growing more intolerant with years, and inspired to his last gasp by his young French models.

His portraits, so sharply edged as to suggest the cuttings of a razor, are authentic likenesses, without warmth to be sure, but without anything spongy or cheap (see Plate 22). His historical pictures are as frigid as those of his master, David, and his nudes are sleek French grisettes. In recent years, Ingres has been admired for his skill in devising flat patterns and cunning arrangements of flowing lines.

While the French were waging a civil war in

Goujon. *Nymphs of the Fountain of the Innocents. Paris. Panels from the fountain of the nymphs in the square of the Innocents—figures carved in the late Greek style with consummate taste and skill.*

art—one faction, led by Ingres, shouting for the classical point of view in opposition to the embattled romantics under the leadership of Delacroix—a big, full-blooded fighting man appeared who all but slaughtered the warriors of both factions. He was Gustave Courbet, and if any one man deserves the title of founder of modern painting, he is the man. He was born in 1819, at Ornans, near the border of Switzerland, half-peasant, half-bourgeois, but wholly a painter. It is said that he began to paint before he could walk—an exaggeration perhaps, but it is true that he hated books and knew, or felt, in childhood that he would be a great artist.

After breaking down his father's resistance, he went to Paris where he worked like a horse and lived on crusts, never losing confidence in himself and never uncertain as to where he was going. He found his inspiration in France herself, and to the end of his days his finest pictures were those portraying the plain French people and the flowers and fruits of

Chardin. *Kitchen Still Life. Museum of Fine Arts, Boston. From his own tidy kitchen, the artist extracted the magical effects of plain things, creating little masterpieces with the sentiment of minor poetry.*

France—old men and women, husky young girls, landscapes, still life, and animals. He was a democratic soul, but bluff and outspoken, and called himself a "Realist." He said that he painted only what he could see, and that he would gladly paint an angel, if one could be produced. Unfortunately, his enormous egoism and braggadocio got him into trouble in left-wing politics, and he wound up in jail as a subversive. It is now known that he was always a loyal French patriot, but he was fined 300,000 francs just the same. He managed to escape into Switzerland where he died at the age of fifty-eight.

As an artist, Courbet was magnificent—and his masterpieces were turned out with incredible rapidity. His celebrated *Atelier* (Studio), a canvas twenty feet long by twelve, with more than a score of life-size figures—his favorite model and curious friends eager to take a peep at her—was the work of a couple of months during which he drank gallons and gallons of wine and beer. Out of his experiences—and he lived with gusto and huge animal joy—he created pictures of the greatest vigor and beauty: sometimes a forest glen with the wild

Georges de la Tour. *The Education of the Virgin. Frick Collection, New York. La Tour painted candles as bright as torches to bring the figures into dramatic focus and as symbols of revelation.*

deer watching, for he was a hunter, too; more often, peasants and the women he had known and loved. The *Beautiful Irishwoman* is a study, one of several, of a colleen who was not only a popular model but the girl friend of Whistler, a companion of Courbet.

Édouard Manet, born in 1832, was a Parisian of the old school, well-bred, well-dressed, a man of the world and a man who meant what he said when he painted. Few, if any, artists—not Velásquez even, or old Frans Hals— took painting with the routine ease of Manet. Every morning, at the same hour by the clock, he began to work, as a carpenter or bricklayer would begin; and late in the afternoon he laid aside his gear, changed his clothes, put on his top hat, and hurried off to the same table in the same café to chat with his friends and admire the girls. He was no Bohemian dabbler; he was in dead earnest about his work, but his work began and ended in his studio. He did not much care what people thought or what they did; one thing was as good as another when he lifted a brush. It was his job to select a subject—a soldier, bullfighter, blind musician, attractive woman, or a bouquet of flowers—and to put that subject in paint with

Watteau. *Heads from Album. Louvre, Paris. Sketched from life with the utmost grace in the use of light and shade, and with everything coarse excluded.*

all the skill he possessed—and he had enough skill for a regiment. As he grew older and a little weary of studio confinement, he turned to outdoor subjects such as horse races and sports, and worked from photographs as a short cut.

Sad to say, he paid a heavy penalty for his honesty and his brilliancy. Claiming the right to paint what he pleased, as the Venetians had done, he portrayed an outdoor scene in which two artists, dressed somewhat fancifully in Latin Quarter style, are lunching with a couple of woman models who liked to relax in the sunlight with nothing on. The French protested. The result of their indignation was that Manet, one of the most honorable and gifted painters of the nineteenth century, was persecuted and died a nervous wreck at the age of fifty.

Eugène Delacroix, born in 1798, is one of the heroes of modern painting, and painting to this man was no casual business, no soft job for nondescripts, but a profession asking for ideas, for intellect, energy, courage, and, of course, the talent necessary to prove that one was born to handle a brush.

The French artists were divided when he appeared. Delacroix was trained and ready

Watteau. *The Embarkation for Cythera. Louvre, Paris. A fantastic landscape, the point of departure for couples preparing to sail away to the sacred isle of Venus where love-making continues into eternity.*

Boucher. *Madame de Pompadour. National Gallery, Edinburgh. The brilliant Madame, indispensable to Louis XV, portrayed in a moment of privacy by the most gifted of boudoir painters.*

admired Goethe, Beethoven, and Balzac, was the first to go to bat for Goya and Daumier, and appreciated Rembrandt, Rubens, and Holbein, along with the Italians. He took his grand pictorial ideas from Scott, Shakespeare, Byron, and the Greek myths, and wore himself out in emulation of his idol, Rubens. As leader of the Romantic school, he journeyed to Spain and Africa for color and exotic subjects, forgetting the French who were on his neck. (See Plate 23.)

What a magnificent figure he was! He dreamed up and carried out a big program: his figures have size and power; he brought his ideas into being with color, energy, and action; and the elements of greatness lie in all his work, from the large canvases and murals down to the water colors and lithographs.

Delacroix was despised by the Academic politicians of his times, but he has become one of the wheel horses of the modern movement. It is not for his art alone that he is honored, but also because he remains a brilliant symbol and a guiding star, the one man, with Courbet, of the nineteenth century to invest painting with the glamor of the Renaissance masters. When the official artists were covering walls with cheesecloth goddesses labeled *Peace and War* or *Art and Nature,* he cleansed the atmosphere by a blaze of color and painted the only

for an assault on the old guard who turned to Italy for instruction. He threw a challenge, a red rag, into their faces, called the *Massacre of Chios,* a subject borrowed from the struggle of the Greeks against the Turks. His challenge drew blood. The academic crowd bawled themselves hoarse, calling him "a savage, a maniac, and an ignoramus in drawing," and asserting that he had "perpetrated the '*Massacre of Painting,*' with a drunken broom soaked in raw colors." Answering the insult, Delacroix said, "I am the most hated of artists. I am refused bread and water—but I am delighted with myself."

Instead of calling names, he answered his accusers with more pictures. A scholar and an intellectual, he read the classics, and the poems of Byron as they were published; he

Corot. *Souvenir of Mort Fontaine. Louvre, Paris. Corot in his most popular vein—a soft and vaguely sentimental piece of landscape.*

Delacroix. *Liberty Leading the People. Louvre, Paris. The spirit of France in her proudest moment, and the symbol of liberty in the art of Delacroix.*

murals in French art comparable to those of the Venetians.

There is something of Delacroix in all modern men. He was a great colorist, testing his theories in the laboratory with scientists and employing a full orchestra of tones in his canvases, rich and brilliant tones singing together. Inspired by the uprising of 1830, when the Bourbons were uprooted, he composed one of his masterpieces, *Liberty Leading the People.* When we look at the picture and think of France at her best and proudest, the symbol of Liberty in the world, we must also think of Delacroix as the spirit who led the art of

painting out of the bondage of the Academy to the people of France.

Daumier was born in Marseilles, in 1808, and was brought to Paris in childhood. His father, a glazier and a mediocre poet yearning for literary honors, succeeded at nothing, and the family was desperately poor. The boy Honoré, busy with his drawing from his seventh year, roamed the streets of Paris as a waif, and to keep warm while looking at works of art, sneaked past the guards into the Louvre. Nobody told him what to look at— nobody told him whom to admire. He turned to Rembrandt, attracted by the great Dutch-

David. *Madame Récamier. Louvre, Paris. A famous woman of the world in the days following the French Revolution. She insisted that she looked posed and uncomfortable—but the painting remains a popular favorite.*

man's sympathies with the underdog, and he was fascinated by the sculptures of Michelangelo. Later, when he had acquired a little fame, he made a lithograph of a schoolmaster en route through the Louvre with a company of teen-age students. As the troop enters a room the schoolmaster divides his youngsters into two sections, with this directive: "Those next to me take the right side of the room, the others take the left side, and that way we shall finish in short order."

He had no teachers, but he was always drawing and modeling little figures in clay or wax. It is recorded that the novelist, Balzac, on looking at Daumier's youthful caricatures, made this wise remark, "There is much of Michelangelo in this boy." For a while, he was an usher in the courts of law, which meant that he wore a black gown and led visitors to their seats—those who came to watch the lawyers perform. And it is recorded that Daumier, after he had drawn and painted and modeled the faces of all classes of people, made this comment: "There is nothing on earth more fascinating than the mouths of lawyers in operation."

Fragonard. *Storming the Citadel. Frick Collection, New York. A stage-setting in aristocratic style—the cultivated frivolity of the overlords before the Revolution.*

David. *The Oath of the Horatii. Louvre, Paris. The Horatii were triplet brothers, two of whom were slain in a feud by another set of triplets—here we see the surviving brother, fufilling his oath, about to put the killers to death, one by one.*

modeled them in clay, and drawing from the clay, made lithographs for his newspaper.

Daumier developed into the greatest draftsman of the nineteenth century. He drew like an Old Master, constructing heads as solid and massive as sculpture—not giving the effect of clay or crayon, but of living heads. There are no drawings of mouths, past or present, to compare with his. The mouths of drinkers, expanding into moving caverns; the mouths of lawyers opening and snapping shut like elastic traps, wheedling or condemning. No surgeon, or anatomist, if he had torn apart and rebuilt a thousand jaws, could make such drawings. Nor could an artist by studying all the painted mouths in the museums, or by observing all the lawyers in practice—unless he

Ingres. *Portrait of the Artist as a Young Man.* *Metropolitan Museum of Art, New York. A severe, competent, pseudoclassical job done under the influence of his mentor, David.*

For a while, in his youth, he was delivery boy for a bookseller, but he decided that it was better to starve as an artist than as a flunky. Before he was twenty he had mastered lithography, and at twenty-one he published in this medium some of the most original and powerful drawings ever done in France. His memory was almost superhuman. He hired no models to pose for him; the people of Paris in action, going about their daily business, he said, were his models. Once he had observed a situation—a windbag of a lawyer defending a guilty woman, or a washerwoman with a child tugging at her skirts (see Plate 24)—he forgot nothing of importance. He dug into the secrets of dirty, battered souls; noted the lines and planes of blubbering faces; noted huge violent mouths spouting the law, gulping beer, swilling soup; and after he had observed his models in action, he returned to his garret,

Ingres. *Portrait of a Lady Seated. Pencil drawing, Metropolitan Museum of Art, New York. One of many small pencil-portraits done for bread and butter, and done with exquisite taste and scrupulous craftsmanship.*

Courbet. *Hunting Dogs. Metropolitan Museum of Art, New York. Courbet, a mighty hunter, painted animals as he painted human beings—with vast enthusiasm, and the swift, sure hand of a master.*

were fired by Daumier's convictions about lawyers. His knowledge of the human head was not surgical nor scientific—it was knowledge built up by common observation intensified and sustained by his feelings of right and wrong. The lawyers did something to him and he did something to the lawyers, and the two, mutually active, produced the pictures. But another factor must be included in the process. You cannot make a work of art simply by loving or hating—by feelings alone. You must command the technique of your craft, and Daumier toiled like a slave to control his lines and shape his black-and-white masses into a murderous instrument.

By the time he was twenty-one, he was ready to make trouble. He joined the staff of a radical paper called *La Caricature,* and when his cartoons appeared, cabinet officers shook in their boots. He took a particularly hot shot at the King, Louis Philippe, representing him as a royal Gargantua swallowing moneybags stolen from the people. For this he was sent to prison, but he refused to mend his ways and, on his release, began all over again. His paper folded and he found work on another as social satirist. For more than forty

Courbet. *The Atelier (detail). Louvre, Paris. Detail from a panorama of the artist's studio, a canvas 20 by 12 feet, with a score of figures, and executed in two months. Here we have the central section, a small boy watching the master and his model.*

Courbet. *Portrait of Jo. Nelson-Atkins Gallery of Art, Kansas City, Missouri. Sometimes called "The Beautiful Irishwoman," a popular model in Paris, and the girl friend of Whistler.*

Manet. *Matador Saluting. Metropolitan Museum of Art, New York. A Frenchman's impression of the bull ring—the matador of one hundred years ago, after the kill.*

Manet. *The Old Musician. Chester Dale Collection, National Gallery of Art, Washington, D.C.*

Delacroix. *Self-portrait. Louvre, Paris. The Frenchman who was at home with duchesses and sailors, and an inspiration to modern painters.*

years he earned his bread by cartooning, but it was a poor living for his contributions—two each week to make a grand total of four thousand lithographs.

Daumier lived with his wife Marie, a dressmaker, on the top floor of an old house near the Seine, and about the time of his marriage, in 1848, began to paint in oils. His first canvases were received with enthusiasm by the best artists of Paris, but the collectors thought them crude, if not incompetent. Twice he competed for state decoration; twice he was rejected, and with stoical courage went back to his lithographs. At times he worked on eight stones simultaneously, hoping from the sale of prints to be free to paint. The strain was great and he was never free. The streets of Paris, his first art school, never lost their hold on him and at the end of the day, from a seat by the window, he observed the fishermen, the laundresses, and the habits of people as poor as

Manet. *Boy with Sword. Metropolitan Museum of Art, New York. The artist, after the example of Goya, painted youngsters in the role of grownups.*

Delacroix. *Massacre of Chios. Louvre, Paris. Called the "massacre of painting" by the artist's enemies—today an accepted masterpiece.*

Daumier. *The Legislative Paunch. Lithograph, Metropolitan Museum of Art, New York. The large-bellied windbags whom the artist observed in political assemblies.*

himself. "We have our art to comfort us," he said to his friends, "but what have these wretched folk?"

His friends were celebrities—Delacroix, Courbet, Baudelaire, Corot, Gautier, Barye—and they had incomes. They came to his quarters above the river, as comrades; sat on the floor by the stove and drank beer together, knowing well who was the great man among them. The stocky great man was always at work, always busy with his stones or his press. He was a poor talker and the dialogue on his drawings was written by his editors. One night, as Daumier was peering through the smoke at a drawing, his head very close for his sight was nearly gone, someone spoke. "Isn't it too bad," he asked the others, "that old Daumier has to work for a living?"

The old man heard the query, straightened up slowly, and turned around. He had the right words this time.

"It's not too bad that I have to work," he

replied, "but too bad I have to work so hard, and have so little time for painting. But let me tell you something. You have incomes, every one of you, but I have a public, and between the two I'll take the public."

He had to work for a living but the mass of his work, his lithographs, was circulated by the papers thus bringing him a sizable public, if not much money. His friends had no real public—only dealers and a few collectors who hoarded paintings for years, eventually releasing them, one by one, to rich Americans.

In his last years, as his eyes weakened, the burden was too much for him, and he would have starved but for the help of his friends. He retired to a little house in the country, a gift from Corot, alone most of the time and unable to work. When offered the ribbon of the Legion of Honor, he refused the decoration. In 1878, when a committee formed by Victor Hugo presented a large exhibition of his oils and water colors, the returns from sales were not enough to pay the expenses of the gallery. The following year, blind, paralyzed, and alone, he died, and was buried by the state.

Daumier depicted what he knew and understood: the men and women with whom he had toiled and suffered—sometimes the hypo-

Daumier. *Advice to a Young Artist. Gift of Duncan Phillips, National Gallery of Art, Washington, D.C. A wise old connoisseur shows a novice how to make salable pictures.*

Daumier. *Third-Class Carriage. Metropolitan Museum of Art, New York.*

crites who prey on society, sometimes the commonest aspects of French life, both in a style that could be heart-rending or terrifying. His washerwomen are noble figures; on the other hand, his politicians, as witnessed by the *Legislative Paunch,* are indecently fat, a gallery of foul representatives, half-asleep, ugly as sin, and thinking, if at all, with their bellies. The *Third-Class Carriage,* one of several paintings of the subject, is a direct view of the occupants of a compartment, the figures plain and bulky, but alive with the charity, the strength, and the compassion poured into them from the soul of a great artist. It tells not only the story of the dreariness of one aspect of French life, but the story of forlorn humanity everywhere.

Picasso. *Woman in White. Metropolitan Museum of Art, New York. The artist in a classical vein, the woman painted as an early Greek, large and undisturbed.*

20
The New Age

In 1874, a group of painters who had been cold-shouldered by the official Salons organized a stock company and exhibited their work independently in Paris. The group included men now prominent in modern French art—Renoir, Degas, Cézanne, Sisley, Pissarro, and Monet—but its first showing was greeted with jeers and laughter. One of Monet's pictures was listed in the catalogue as *Sunrise, an Impression,* and a smart reporter, picking up the title, jokingly referred to all the exhibitors as *Impressionists.* The word caught on, at first as a mark of ridicule, but as the men thus branded refused to be put down and gained in popularity, it became an honorable title for all painters united technically in recording sensations of light and color.

The Impressionists introduced a movement in painting which, to a public unacquainted with the experiments of Leonardo da Vinci and Titian, the study of light by the Dutch and Spanish, and above all the investigations of Constable and Turner, was almost revolutionary. They went mad with joy over sunlight and the analysis of the atmospheric phenomena, and from direct observation of the outdoors—of nature at twilight or in the blazing sun—they went to the laboratory to test the chemistry of pigments, the breaking up of white light by prisms into colors, and other experimental matters, some purely scientific.

They wanted to come to grips with nature—to look at the world with what they called "the innocent eye"—the eye that looks at life with a fresh vision, as if through a window suddenly opened; that looks at a hill or a sunset without the confusing memories of the mind; the eye that is not hampered by any knowledge of the way painters, dead and gone, have rendered the visual world. They desired the wide-open eyes of children, for the purpose of pure seeing, and they would translate what they saw into pictures by means of their immense knowledge of color and pigment.

The first thing to do was to get into the open air and go to work. They selected the strongest contrasts of light and shadow in order to use the brightest colors—the orange rays of the setting sun, trees and grass at high noon, flowers and snow in every degree of light. They were after the vivid, dancing colors of nature which they had never seen on canvas, the vibrating atmosphere as it settled upon the hills and turned the shadows blue, and the brilliancy of the growing world, like a garden blooming on canvas. They used pure, or primary colors and, to heighten the animation of a scene, began to shoot complementary tints into the shadows of their pictures. This needs a word of explanation.

When you take sunlight apart, or break it down, you find that it is composed of three

209

Monet. *Banks of the Seine, Vetheuil. Chester Dale Collection, National Gallery of Art, Washington, D.C. The French countryside in spring, recorded with the small strokes of Impressionism to show Nature's vibrancy.*

primary colors, red, yellow, and blue, and that the rest of the spectrum colors are combinations: red and yellow make orange, blue and yellow become green, red and blue blend into violet. A complementary color is one which, when mixed with its opposite, produces a blank, or neutral tone. Thus, the complementary of red is green; of blue, orange; of yellow, violet. In nature, if you look too long into the red ball of the sun and then close your tired eyes, you will see greenish disks everywhere. And if you are a painter and wish to bring out the fullest intensity of a color, you place the complementary next to it.

They applied the paint in small facets or streaks, or dashes and lozenges—each artist having his own pellets or ribbons of paint. For example, in painting grass, they did not squeeze a prepared green from a tube and brush it on the canvas, but instead, placed little touches of blue and yellow one next to the other; to the eye, the blues and yellows blend at a distance, and you see only green—the most vivid green imaginable. The Impressionists, you see, devised a method—or if you will, a scientifically tested formula—by which the light from the sun was recorded convincingly by their pigments, even though the colors are put up in tubes like toothpaste and contain no light.

Impressionist paintings, if you stand too close to them, look like crazy quilts or a riot of drunken colors, but seen at the proper distance are clean and refreshing views of nature. The artists went to infinite pains to create the illusion of the brilliancy, the vividness, and the vibrating atmosphere of the outdoor world—and in their best canvases you behold nature rejoicing, nature bathed in color and tone. When the opposition to the movement subsided and the school became an accepted fact, the Impressionists of France lived to find themselves the most popular painters of modern art.

Claude Monet is usually designated as the leader of the school; he was the first to finish his paintings in the sunlight. He had the satisfaction of seeing one of his canvases, as it passed through the hands of dealers, rise in price from ten to 100,000 francs—and in his day a franc was worth twenty cents. He was absorbed in the study of light with a priestly devotion, always working in the open air, and painting the same subjects every day, ten times a day, to show how things change in appearance with the position of the sun. He painted everything as seen through shimmering veils of atmosphere—the architecture of cathedrals, barnyard fowls, faces, his famous haystacks, and his beloved pond lilies, which he examined day after day like a botanist, and painted like an artist determined to make the lilies bloom and bloom again, and never with quite the same form or color.

Georges Seurat, partly because of his untimely death at thirty-two and partly because of his complicated, time-consuming style, left only a few pictures (see Plate 25): picnic parties, circuses, dancers, and models, any one of which today is worth as much as a Vermeer. He was an intellectual artist with a scientific rule for every move he made. From his practice of painting in minute dabs, or circular dots, he and his disciples were named Neo-Impressionists, Divisionists, or Pointillists—

take your pick. He covered large canvases with countless thousands of colored specks, every single one set down according to rule and with precise knowledge of its effect on other specks. His paintings are hard to see, and unless viewed at exactly the right distance, reveal nothing more than dim figures buried in a shower of confetti. His canvases are beautifully, one might say perfectly, designed, each part or piece taking its exact position in space; the figures, as a rule, are motionless, as if suddenly frozen by the artist, but in their over-all effect his pictures have the completeness of architectural structures.

Edgar Degas spurned the elaborate dot-and-dash method of the Impressionists, but he was one of their company in his efforts to record instantaneous views of nature. His ambition he said was "to observe his models through a keyhole," to catch them off guard in unconventional poses—in other words to present arresting impressions of life. A follower of photography, he painted horse races, ballet dancers, and women in bathtubs, with a camera eye—with the realism of a snapshot, or what the cameramen call angle shots. He was marvelously skillful with pastels (dry crayons),

Toulouse-Lautrec. *At the Moulin Rouge. Helen Birch Bartlett Memorial Collection, Art Institute of Chicago. The elite of Paris, enjoying a drink at a famous cabaret.*

Degas. *The Rehearsal. Frick Collection, New York. The artist specialized in ballet scenes, sketching the dancers at rehearsal, and developing the sketches into finished pastels and oils.*

making study after study of women. These pictures seem clean and decorative to us, but they offended French taste. Accused of depicting ugliness, Degas ceased to show his pictures and lived as a recluse for thirty years, avoided by all because of his rages and sarcasm.

Henri de Toulouse-Lautrec, son of a count and a descendant in direct line of one of the noblest French families, was born at Albi, in a southern province, in 1864. Afflicted from birth with a weakness of the bones, in his childhood he twice stumbled and fell, breaking both thighs. He was left a cripple for life. His torso developed normally but his legs shriveled into those of a midget, and he was a strange figure, indeed, when standing. He was greatly talented as an artist and before sixteen was painting horses and portraits with professional skill.

At twenty-three he went up to Paris. Impelled by some inborn craving for low life or by his deformity, or both, he deliberately cast his lot with the sinners and denizens of the underworld. He was at his peak from twenty-eight to thirty, during which time he produced his incomparable posters—he is the creator of the modern poster—oils and lithographs of jockeys, cancan dancers of the Moulin Rouge, cabaret entertainers, and the talented degenerates and daughters of evil haunting the slums of the Bohemian quarters.

Lautrec made a good living from his posters and illustrations, though he had no need to work for money. He was one of the most accomplished draftsmen of his time, and in his style of painting in broken colors and streaks of brilliant colors, he was influenced by the Impressionists. Hard and totally devoid of sentimentality, he interpreted the underworld of his day with invincible courage and honesty. He died at the age of thirty-six, weakened by heavy drinking and other excesses, and the splendor of the noblemen of Toulouse was buried with him.

Pierre Auguste Renoir, born in 1841, is one of the most enjoyable of modern painters. He was a man of sunny tastes and single-minded determination, but by no means wanting in guts and fighting courage. He was on good terms with life—free from inhibitions and anxiety—happy to be alive and to paint, and more than happy to send his responses, in the shape of pictures, into the more prosaic lives of others. He had his roots in the rich soil

Toulouse-Lautrec. *Troupe of Mlle Églantine. Lithograph, Gift of Carter H. Harrison, Art Institute of Chicago. Cancan dancers in a characteristic act—a lithograph by the man who originated the modern poster.*

of old France, in the fundamental, important, charming things which French artists tend to forget when they huddle together in the cafés of Paris. He did not pretend to be a sage or philosopher; he did not sour his radiant soul by brooding over the misery of man or the destiny of the human race—and he never bowed down, for money, to the second-rate, the eccentric, or the absurd.

Renoir painted trees and sunlight, fruits and flowers, the recreations of ordinary Frenchmen, children—and such chubby, drowsy, high-colored kids!—and the female nude. He loved to paint the nude, and said, with respect to his models, "I am not hard to please. I can get on very well with any sturdy girl who will sit still and let me look at the light on her flesh." He used the same model, a domestic servant, for years, and never failed to glorify "the old crock," as he called her. He faced the difficulties of his profession with sweetness and forbearance. In his last years, nearly eighty and a rheumatic cripple, he painted in a wheel chair with a brush strapped to his arthritic fingers. Renoir is included with the Impressionists, technically, and with no superiors. He wove together hundreds of

Degas. *Woman with Chrysanthemums. Metropolitan Museum of Art, New York. A tour de force testifying to the artist's powers of observation and his technical skill with flowers.*

brush strokes from which light comes forth in a web of glowing colors, to express his delight in the physical world.

Paul Cézanne arrived in Paris from a southern province in 1861, about a hundred years ago, as the Civil War in the United States was just beginning. Then a young man of twenty-two, he was an "odd one," ambitious to become a painter, but poorly equipped for life in Paris. He was not much to look at and his manners were uncouth; he had a funny accent and an ugly face, and when he spoke he used an unpleasant dialect. But he was no fool. He had patience, a belief in himself, a deep reverence for the Old Masters, and uncommonly good judgment of the men around him. Ab-

Renoir. *Le Moulin de la Galette. Louvre, Paris. A café at the old mill of Montmartre before the tourists arrived, the lights and animation rendered in broken colors.*

Renoir. *Girl with Watering Can. Chester Dale Collection, National Gallery of Art, Washington, D.C. The Impressionist style in full splendor, with figure and background, costume and colors, all woven into a brocade in paint.*

normally shy and touchy, he would suddenly blow his top to hide his timidity or put on a Bohemian swagger that did not become him. To those who did not understand him, he was just a misguided rustic; and to his sympathetic friends, he was a problem child—too humble at times and, again, entirely too free with his criticisms. He lived on an allowance from home and at no time had to please a single soul save himself—and he never pleased himself, his ideals being the highest. More than once, in a fit of despondency, he cried out that he was a failure—"only a beginner on a lonely road."

The official academies would have none of him, and he spent much of his time in the Louvre studying the Old Masters and seeming to go exactly nowhere at a snail's pace. But he was not wasting his time—he was never trivial and he was a colorist by God's grace. He tried to follow Delacroix but not for long, for he was a peasant without a background of scholarship and unable to paint anything he could not see. He loved Courbet's masculine strength, but he was technically miles behind the prodigious realist. He fell back on his own resources again, with staunch faith and a palpitating heart. When the official Salon turned him down, he was furious and howled like an angry child, not because his own work was so exceptional, but because the chosen canvases were so bloodless and stupid. Hurt and insulted by the bureaucrats of Paris, he returned every year to the South to lick his wounds and paint landscapes.

Cézanne was mortally afraid of women, always muttering that one of them "would get her hooks into him"—meaning that she would interfere with his painting. All his life he longed to do what Courbet found easy and so pleasurable—to paint an undressed model in the open air—but he was too shy to tackle the problem. In 1867, probably by some miscalculation, he married a plain and rather stupid woman from the country of his birth. She proved to be a good wife to him, never coming between him and his work, and sitting like Patience on a monument while he painted her, not once or twice, but as much as one hundred times for a single portrait! Encouraged by Renoir and Pissarro, he began to paint landscapes in sunlight and twice exhibited with the Impressionists, but his canvases were held up for an unmerciful drubbing. The other exhibitors were painters gone wrong, but accredited painters; he, Cézanne, was called a nincompoop, a clodhopper, a jackass painting with his tail. The French were tough critics in those days—and they still are rough on original talent.

At the death of his father, who had supported him for twenty-three years—not very willingly, however—Cézanne came into a big property and retired to his estate in the South, "sick of Paris," he said, "and the whole stinking art racket." In his last years he struggled alone in his studio or painted in the fields, more and more savage and bad-tempered—destroying his canvases, throwing them out the windows, abandoning them in the fields, or giving them to his son as material for jigsaw puzzles. "I am one," he said, "who has a piece of gold, and cannot use it." The peasants called him a crackpot—but always behind his back, for he was a man of property and they respect property. In 1906 he caught a fever while painting in the rain—and the fever killed him.

This uncouth and unattractive painter, for the first quarter of the twentieth century, reigned over art with the authority of an Old Master. Today, he is less discussed and less needed, but his canvases are worth their weight in gold. He remains a great and gifted painter who broke his heart trying to raise his art to the level once enjoyed by painting. He opened the art of painting to so many avenues of interest and provided the Modernists with so much ammunition for a new attack that his place in history would seem to be permanently fixed.

Cézanne's aims, in fact, were the noble and

Renoir. *By the Seashore. Metropolitan Museum of Art, New York. The seashore is vague, but the girl embodies the unmistakable charm of France as Renoir responded to it and revealed it glowingly.*

lofty aims of the greatest masters. First and last he strove to make things real and true: to paint portraits as rich and full-bodied as those of the Venetians; to construct strong and solid figures in dramatic situations, as the Old Masters had done and Daumier had done; as he repeatedly said, "to make out of Impressionism something as solid and durable as the masterpieces of the museums"—something easier hoped for than done.

Cézanne loved and worshiped the "museum artists," as he called the great masters, but he found that much of their work had been dimmed and dulled by centuries of fading, and that the glory of their achievements was obscured by darkness and pigments gone black, or neutral. He was, by allegiance to Renoir and Monet and Pissarro, an Impressionist, one who believed in brightness and sunlight, but he held a genuine and secret suspicion that much of the Impressionist work was a little flimsy and shallow, though joyous and bright. He would work out a formula—and it was very complicated—whereby his subjects would be monumental, but at the same time beautiful in color, resonant and gay.

What he did, or tried to do, was a technical problem, for the solution of which he gave attention to the structure of objects, their geometrical planes, cubes, and cylinders. This innovation had an important effect on the modern movement. Thus, when he painted an apple (see Plate 26) or a head, he painted the light as it fluttered in patches and planes over the object, and he recorded the patches in brilliant colors, doing his best to hold them together by blue outlines. It was a complex process and it nearly killed him. Often his figures seemed to be dislocated; his apples and oranges rolled out of the picture; his portraits were rigid masks of colored "cement"; and his landscapes looked like those seen on the moon through a telescope.

His nudes and portraits caused him the most trouble—he worked so slowly that his models could never sit long enough—but in

Cézanne. *Card Players. Stephen C. Clark Collection, New York. One of the artist's heroic struggles as he sought to realize solid forms in colors of high intensity.*

all his efforts, crude as they sometimes were, his beautiful color kept them alive. In his landscapes of southern France, a country he loved and knew by rote, he represents nature on a monumental scale; and in his still-lifes, which he could study closely without embarrassment, he has the stature of a great artist. His fruits, flowers, tablecloths, and crockery, have the dignity and grandeur—even the dramatic substance—which other artists extract from human beings.

Vincent Van Gogh, a preacher's son, was born in Holland in 1853 and would have entered the church himself, had he been of more pleasing appearance. One who knew him described his face as "something between a convict's and the pictures of Christ," and however truthful the assertion, he was not a man to inspire the companionship of little children. Not that they feared physical violence, for he was frank and holy and unselfish, but to look at his head—the orange-red hair crew-cut, the snapping-turtle mouth, the deep-sunken, green eyes staring at the cold world with a baby's innocence—to look at that head was to see a man who would die for his convictions. Such men are called martyrs and fanatics!

Cézanne. *Self-portrait. Bavarian State Gallery, Munich. The father of modernist art in one of several self-portraits—an obstinate, grotesque, and unpersonable man with the patience and originality of genius.*

At sixteen, he went to The Hague to work in the branch office of a Paris art gallery, and so admirably did he behave that he was soon promoted to the London office. He did well in England, too, wore a morning coat and a topper, smoked a Virginia mixture, and fell in love with the landlady's daughter. The girl answered his words of love with a mocking laughter that nearly killed him—and he was charitably transferred to the home office in Paris.

In Paris he talked religion, instead of pictures, to the gallery's sophisticated clientele, and made a ridiculous show of himself. Without a word of warning, he departed for London again to preach Christianity in the slums —and to renew his advances to the landlady's daughter. For the second time his love was refused, and he hurried across the North Sea into Belgium as a sort of lay-preacher among the coal miners, teaching children to read and taking care of the sick. He was also making pictures—or trying to—of the miners, and crying aloud in a voice still heard in the world of art—still heard with searing accents. "I am trying to save my soul," he wrote to his brother, Theo, "and I work in living flesh and blood, as Christ did, the greatest of artists."

He signed his pictures simply "Vincent," as a child volunteers identity by a Christian name, and Vincent we shall call him. He yearned for a woman's love, but no woman smiled on him and he wandered and worried and suffered—going to Antwerp, and back to Paris to his brother who managed the gallery, and then into Holland again. Only a few years of life remained to him, and he used them up like a man counting strokes of doom. In Paris, dependent on his brother for subsistence, he studied with the Impressionists—Pissarro, Lautrec, and Seurat—who recognized his genius and gave him a hand. His days were numbered and he hurried to the south of France—to a little house in Arles—"The House of Light" he called it, where he painted most of the canvases upon which his fame rests today. (See Plate 27.) "I must begin all over again," he said, "—get down to the earth, feel the warmth of the sun and smell the ploughed fields."

Hatless in the southern sun, Vincent painted like an intoxicated fanatic—hundreds of pictures, each at a single sitting! It was a dream come true, until Gauguin came to share the house—or, more likely, to dominate it—and Vincent had his first serious attack of madness. An old hand with the girls, Gauguin took him to a Christmas party where a thoughtless brunette jokingly suggested that Vincent send her one of his ears—and such big ears!—as a holiday greeting. Vincent thought about the girl, her pretended love, his big ears, until his mind wandered; he cut off his right ear with a razor and sent it to the brunette with his undying love.

There is not much left to tell. Theo, the long-suffering brother, put him into a private asylum near Paris. Sometimes off his rocker, sometimes more lucid than sunlight, he painted portraits of the doctors assigned to him and landscapes which crackled under his brush. The day came when everything was crystal clear. There was no hope. He saw himself permanently mad and calmly fired a bullet into his stomach. "I've been shooting," he said gently, and asked for his friendly old pipe. He was thirty-seven and they buried him in the cornfields he had loved to paint.

Vincent was as right about his own art as Shakespeare and Dickens and Mark Twain were right about their art. He wanted to make pictures "for women rocking cradles and lovers holding hands, and sailors on the high seas." He sold a half-dozen canvases, one for 400 francs—the top price. Not long ago, an American collector paid $85,000 for one of his canvases, and that is the way art often goes.

Vincent had many drawbacks—he was poorly trained, he died young, and he painted like one possessed—but his soul shines out today like a star. In the clutches of an overpowering mood, he worked with hectic rapidity. His subjects sent his soul skyrocketing into

Van Gogh. *Sunflowers. Metropolitan Museum of Art, New York. The sunflower to Van Gogh was the emblem of radiance leading to eternal splendor. Here is a frenzied study, with the flower fused into a golden dream.*

the blue: a pair of old shoes, a cluster of sunflowers, a cornfield with crows flying above it, or a simple postman who was one of Christ's messengers—to these things he applied paint in streaks like colored lava, yellow and blue. He painted babies in long dresses, old women with "faces like dusty blades of grass," and "young girls as fresh as the fields." His models were human beings and landscapes seen through his wild green eyes, and his blazing sunflowers, yellow against yellow, live with an unearthly light and animation.

Before the most familiar things of life—a bunch of flowers, a baby, or a row of cypress trees—he lost his head, and he would paint like a spiritual drunkard to transfer his feelings to canvas. He worked at white heat, in bright colors like the Impressionists, but extending their strokes into spaghetti lengths of whirling ribbons and contours. His backgrounds were yellows or blues; his trees, placed against them, were in convulsion; his houses shook and toppled over, all to express the agony of the man himself—the intense feelings, the faith, the suffering that went into the pictures of Vincent Van Gogh.

Paul Gauguin, born in 1848, the noble savage of modern art as he has been recently

Cézanne. *Mont Sainte-Victoire. George W. Elkins Collection, Philadelphia Museum of Art. A mountain summarized in structural planes, a landmark in modern painting and the herald of Cubism.*

called, was a remarkable figure any way you may take him. He boasted that he was descended from the Borgias of Aragon, and perhaps he was, but the bad blood in his veins was an infiltration in the Creole strain of his mother. She was of Peruvian stock, and the boy's childhood was spent in the color and luxury and some of the filth of Lima—and those first impressions remained with him. In adolescence he was a sailor and boxer, and in his twenties a successful stockbroker; but in the first flush of his business career he began to paint, and there was no turning back. As a Sunday painter, his extraordinary talents were soon apparent, as well as his brutal insolence and resolution. He was soon a figure in Paris and in Brittany, where he founded a school of art. During his prosperous years, he married a prim, conventional Danish woman whom he deserted but never divorced, always hoping—not too strongly, however—for a reunion with her and their five children.

As Gauguin's talents ripened and his sav-

Van Gogh. *Bedroom at Arles. Helen Birch Bartlett Memorial Collection, Art Institute of Chicago. The artist's bedroom—one of three celebrated pictures, each in pure color "to evoke the pulse of life," the artist said.*

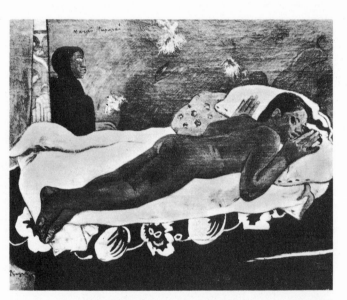

Gauguin. *Spirit of the Dead Watching. A. Conger Goodyear Collection, New York. A Tahitian picture—"the Spirit," Gauguin said, "an old woman—thinking of the girl and the girl of the Spirit, the living united to the dead."*

age instincts grew more assertive, he closed his office and sailed away to the island of Tahiti, where he took up with a dark-skinned girl and "went native"—or imagined he did. For a time he was contented with his tropical home and his island bride, but he was a Parisian artist—and an artist must exhibit his pictures. He returned to Paris, fantastically dressed, and hoped to take the capital of art by storm with his South Sea canvases. He was disappointed—and he did not take defeat lightly. He sailed away again to the South Pacific where he died in the Marquesas Islands, burnt out by disease and orgies of painting.

His pictures of the dark Polynesian women, of tribal customs and superstitions, and of luxuriant vegetation, attracted a host of artists fed up with too much civilization; and many drifted into far-off places in quest of a new Eden and a new type of Eve. One by one they came home again, to Paris or New York, disillusioned and ruined in health. Only Gauguin achieved anything worth saving. His escape from civilization supplied him with a world of new material which he composed into decorative patterns of rich and beautiful colors.

His pictures resemble gorgeous tapestries in which the dark or orange bodies of the island people are placed against backgrounds with large areas of vivid color.

Another Frenchman, Henri Rousseau, never grew up as an artist and never acquired the usual technique of a professional. In his youth he traveled in Mexico with a military band, and in his forty-first year, while employed in a customhouse, he began to make pictures with no thoughts of fame or money. At heart he was a true primitive (or as close to one as is possible in modern society), untrained, childlike, fanciful, and heedless of technical difficulties. He could not draw from nature, could not draw at all in the professional sense, but such deficiencies did not hinder the work he was fitted to do. He painted, from vague Mexican memories, jungle scenes with quaint nude princesses fondling snakes or hiding in huge flowers; strange animals with ferocious expressions; sleeping Arabs watched over by lions; and portraits that bring smiles of delight. Rousseau had a genuine flair for painting and did not spoil it by attempting more than his naïve imagination could handle. His paintings have the charming innocence and fascination of folk tales, and the effectiveness of a born designer. He died in 1910, at the age of sixty-six.

Amedeo Modigliani, born in Tuscany in 1884, began to draw when very young and, in his twenty-second year, threw himself into the Bohemianism of Paris. There he produced a fragile flower of art and died of tuberculosis, at thirty-six, in a charity ward. Everybody

Henri Rousseau. *The Sleeping Gypsy. Gift of Mrs. Simon Guggenheim, Museum of Modern Art, New York. Also called "La Bohémienne Endormie." A lion guarding a sleeping nomad—a "made-up" picture of fairy-tale forms and a nonprofessional masterpiece.*

loved him, and he hurried from bar to bar, and from girl to girl, painting excessively between times and, as his illness increased, resorting to drink and to dope. As you will see in all his work, he was influenced by African Negro sculpture, which Picasso had studied, and he developed his own style—usually a single figure with an egg-shaped head set on a long neck, with a very long body, and with arms and legs neglected. The *Gypsy Woman* was painted a year before his death, one of the last of his canvases and typical of all; it is a study in orange and green and white, tender and pathetic, with the neurotic charm of one of the wayward souls of modern art—an Italian with some of the fire of his ancestors.

Modigliani. *Gypsy Woman with Baby. Chester Dale Collection, National Gallery of Art, Washington, D.C. Painted shortly before the young artist's death—a study in orange, white, and green, with the sad, neurotic charm of the Italian's personality.*

Gauguin. *Ia Orana Maria. Metropolitan Museum of Art, New York. Polynesian title for Ave Maria. A tribal Mary in a gorgeous tropical background.*

Pierre Bonnard, born in 1867, was the last of the great Impressionists, those clean, honest, joyous Frenchmen who loved the fruitfulness of the countryside and painted it in warm, brilliant colors. The sensational movements of modern art did not disturb him; he was content, as in the *Breakfast Room,* with a little enclosure or framework for what he called his "table compositions," to emphasize his affection for the most enjoyable aspects of French civilization.

Georges Rouault, born in 1871, a religious

man, studied the designs of Gothic stained-glass windows and developed a style with strong reds and blues outlined, or edged, in heavy black lines. He painted clowns and unfortunates, and Biblical pictures, always with the fervor of a believer and with an ambition for the powerful and tragic.

When Henri Matisse died in 1954, at the age of eighty-five, he was known as "the grand old man" of modernist art. He was honored everywhere; his pictures were as much in demand as the museum pieces Cézanne talked about; and furthermore he was a modest man, of soft personality and not given to exaggerated claims for his particular brand of art. Yet this same unassuming Frenchman, in his early years, had been rasped by the wheels of pov-

Rouault. *Christ Mocked by Soldiers. Museum of Modern Art, New York. The artist, a religious zealot, formed his style on the colored segments and heavy outlines of medieval stained glass.*

erty and had experienced a most unbecoming notoriety. He was recognized as the leader of the *Fauves*, or Wild Beasts of Art, another name coined by a critic for those who were raising shocking new issues in art; but Matisse was too much an artist to favor wildness for its own sake.

Matisse came to Paris from the north of France in his early twenties to study pharmacy, but soon turned to painting—a decision that caused his parents much pain. To make a living he copied Old Masters in the Louvre and sold them to the Government for distribution among provincial museums—but he was no ordinary copyist. He held his wits close to him and studied the history of painting while at work, but felt that he was getting nowhere. He joined the Impressionists under the influence of Cézanne and Van Gogh, ex-

Bonnard. *The Breakfast Room. Museum of Modern Art, New York. Bonnard's gay and exquisitely painted table compositions are among the enduring joys of Impressionism.*

amined Negro sculpture, and by accident came across the manuscript decorations of the Persians. During his salad days he married a wonderful woman, the owner of a hat shop, and she kept the soup cooking while her husband rose to fame. After the first insults greeted his original style, his lot was easier, but his contributions to a New York show in 1913 were called childish and depraved. "Tell the American people," he wrote, "that I am a devoted husband and father; that I have three fine children, and a fine garden—like any man —that I am not a hoodlum."

Matisse loved the paintings of children, who use colors boldly for reasons of their own, and make patterns by instinct, putting perhaps a tree or a hill on one side and an enormous cat on the other to balance the design. Children do not try to copy a tree, a face, or a cat; they simply make a vivid little painting to express their experiences with objects—

Matisse. *The Purple Robe. Cone Collection, Baltimore Museum of Art. The figure, the flowers, and the background are freely proportioned in beautiful colors to build a joyous rhythm.*

Matisse. *The Moorish Screen. Philadelphia Museum of Art. A bright interior, with figures, walls, and objects blended into a decorative pattern.*

the way they feel about a tree or a cat. It was Matisse's ambition to create with the unhampered freedom of a child, but at the same time to create with the skill of a wise and scholarly artist who could not forget what he had learned. "My dream," he wrote, "is an art of balance, of purity and peace—something friendly and calming."

Of all the artists striving to proceed with the purity of a child's vision, and with the bright, fresh, sensuous splendor of an art not soggy with imitations of the dull, or dead, Matisse has won the laurels. But he was not a child— a more scholarly artist never worked in the Louvre. He gradually realized a style of picture making which the world has greeted with warmth and appreciation. He does not attempt to depict things realistically like Courbet, and he does not much care what he does to the shapes of objects. He will alter the proportions of a woman, expanding or reducing the curves and shapes to conform to his pattern of beauty. That is exactly what children would do if they knew enough.

Human beings, as Rembrandt drew them, or Daumier, do not flourish in Matisse's French garden, or his villa on the Mediterranean. He was a decorative painter devoted to the "joy of life"—he has a picture with that title—and he is one of the most splendid and original colorists of modern times. His half-draped figures, lolling like exotic flowers in full bloom, and his vivid patterns find their home, not only in the collections of museums and millionaires, but in the designs for wallpapers, chintzes, and other decorations.

Picasso. *Girl Before a Mirror. Gift of Mrs. Simon Guggenheim, Museum of Modern Art, New York. The girl is redistributed in a fantastic design of curved lines and bright colors.*

Braque. *Man with a Guitar. Lillie P. Bliss Bequest, Museum of Modern Art, New York. One of the first Cubist pictures, the man and the guitar disappearing in a design of geometrical fractions.*

The most famous of living artists, and in truth the most famous artist of the last generation, is Pablo Picasso, a Spaniard by birth, and the ruler of the modern school of Paris by the suffrage of countless disciples. He was born in Málaga in 1881, but after tasting the freedom of the French Latin Quarter, at nineteen, he knew that France was the place for him, and he has lived there since his twenty-first year. His first master, in subject matter and style alike, was Toulouse-Lautrec, but he had a way from the beginning of impressing his own individuality on his borrowings. In his early twenties he produced the canvases of his Blue Period, preferred by many of his admirers above his later works. His beautifully painted little *Gourmet* (see Plate 28), done before he was twenty-one, is one of the most attractive and popular of his early pictures, and indeed of all his pictures.

But Picasso, though he has favored a few subjects, such as bulls, Minotaurs, and fighting cocks, has not been primarily interested in his subjects—in what he paints. He has been constantly and fiercely concerned with the construction of pictures—in how they are put together. In this respect, he is unique among artists, deriving inspiration from all sorts of pictures and sculptures, and transforming the styles of others into his own baffling structures—the early Greeks, the Sumerians, Raphael, Ingres, El Greco, Cézanne, and Negro sculpture—to mention a few. He is endowed with marvelous skill and audacity, and the fertility of his inventiveness seems to be inexhaustible. It may be honestly argued, I think, that as a master of methods—of the hundred and one technical styles of art—and as an inventive genius, Picasso remains without a parallel.

As he concentrated on lines, planes, and masses with the logical mind of the inventor, he arrived at the inescapable conclusion of his experiments—he would abolish representation. In other words, instead of painting a figure recognizable as the human body, he would paint only the lines, planes, and masses composing the figure—the abstract basis, the scaffold of the figure. In arriving at this conclusion, he was spurred on by Cézanne and by Negro sculpture. Cézanne, in trying to make things solid with the bright colors of the Impressionists, had emphasized the surfaces or planes of objects—their geometrical make-up—and had said that all natural forms were composed of cubes, cylinders, and cones. And in the wooden images carved by the African Negroes as religious idols, the geometrical basis of the human figure was utilized with strange skill. Picasso put two and two together, and when he finished had founded a school of art now familiar to everyone as Cubism. In his experiments with abstract or nonrepresentational form, he was accompanied by Georges Braque who may have been the first to show a Cubist picture—the records are not clear—but it was the prestige of Picasso that made Cubism an international movement in art.

There have been many variations of Cubism, and many interpretations of its philosophy, but for these we have neither time nor space. It is enough to say that Picasso, in painting a head, for example, changed the nose to a cone, the eyes into triangles, the cheeks into bumps of many facets. This was the first step, the conversion of the subject into its geometrical equivalents. Going further, he sliced the head into sections and shuffled the sections together again, putting an eye here, the nose somewhere else, and the mouth round the corner. Finally, he forgot all about the head, and put all the fragments together in a flat pattern—and how it did raise the blood pressure of the old fogies!

Cubism spread far and wide like a contagion, embraced by young artists striving to increase their knowledge of structure and de-

Picasso. *Gertrude Stein. Metropolitan Museum of Art, New York. The friend and patron of the artist, after eighty sittings; the face is a mask and a haunting likeness.*

PLATE 29. WINSLOW HOMER. *The Gulf Stream*. METROPOLITAN MUSEUM OF ART, NEW YORK

PLATE 30.   JOHN JAMES AUDUBON.   *Snowy Heron or White Egret*

Picasso. *Guernica. On loan from the artist, Museum of Modern Art, New York. Inspired by the bombing of a Basque town in the Spanish Civil War. The horrors of war are symbolized in the distorted style of Oriental fabrics.*

sign and also giving birth to many absurdities, some honest, some merely rabble-rousing. Picasso, never much of a talker, left the wordy warfare to others, and carried the movement away from cubes and angles, into curves, blots, and circles, so far, indeed, that he was drafted by the Surrealists in their attempt to paint the nightmares and visions of the subconscious mind. Year after year, the Spaniard comes forward with something new, or inventive, or simply horrific. Years ago, he painted Gertrude Stein—in eighty sittings— and said, "It looks like her—the old Oriental priestess." He painted a serene Grecian head called *Woman in White,* which most people love. During the Spanish Civil War, he painted *Guernica,* based on the bombing of a Basque town by the Germans, and horrible, not because of the bombings, but in the way in

which the artist has torn his figures to pieces. Recently he has made designs for pottery; next year, he may design a thermonuclear explosion. As he says, *¿Quién sabe?*

The moral is very simple. Picasso, by his incredible ability which seems never to grow stale—his researches into the styles of others —and by his own pictures, which stand alone in a world of hideous trouble, has given the youth of the world a form of art, or a substitute for art, that will have to do until a better world is born. Whatever the moral issues— one thing stands out beyond denial. Everywhere in France, and everywhere in America, the young in art are busy with the making of designs, with the abstractions made popular by Picasso, and those who go to exhibitions find delight in the patterns and programs originating with the Spanish master.

Eakins. *Walt Whitman. Pennsylvania Academy of the Fine Arts, Philadelphia. The good gray poet faithfully presented in old age.*

21

This Side the Atlantic

Whenever I read or hear that America is "such a young nation," and therefore common, crude, and vulgar, I fall into one of my minor rages. True, we do not have the antiquity of Egypt or China, both of which spent thousands of years a-dying; and true, that my grandfather was born only fifty years after the signing of the Declaration of Independence. One fact stands out like a skyscraper in Oklahoma: America was not settled by savages or illiterates. Our founding fathers, Washington, Jefferson, Franklin, Madison, and the others, were men of superior breed and great men in statesmanship and in the arts, not surpassed or equaled by their successors. America moved on handsomely in the early days, laying the bottom stones for our civil liberties, erecting neat and nicely designed houses, and cultivating the art of painting with intelligence and foresight. In the Colonial days we did very well in the arts; but when we decided that our background was raw and unrefined and our culture too primitive to stand the higher European tests, we formed the habit of running off to London, Rome, or Paris for instruction, with the result that we lost faith in our own talents and our own civilization, and looked abroad for redemption. In the arts of painting and sculpture—but not in literature and music and architecture—we are still suffering from inhibitions and inferiority complexes.

Our first artists were portrait painters from England, with a few Germans horning in, and some Frenchmen among the Huguenots of the Carolinas. They were fairly well trained and they brought to New England the technical methods practiced in London and France, thus giving advice and guidance to the local Yankee artists, called "limners" from the old Latin word meaning "to illuminate." The limners traveled from town to town, painting the faces of Grandma Deborah, Auntie Prudence, brother Miles, and baby Abigail. In those days, the camera had not been invented, and the cost of a portrait was almost nominal—a couple of dollars for grandma and two bits for the baby. The old limners were excellent craftsmen, capable of making heads which, today, are treasured by collectors, but often leaving the rest of the body badly drawn, for who cared?

From this background of sturdy craftsmanship came John Singleton Copley (1737–1815), the first indisputable Colonial master and one of the best portraitists in American art. Copley was born in Boston of Irish stock and was largely self-educated, but he was familiar with British portraiture as well as with Rubens and the Italians in engraved copies. By demanding twenty-five sittings for a single picture and by the closest study of Yankee heads, he developed into a portrait master. He is the pictorial historian of the early Colonial period, his gallery of portraits numbering judges, preachers, merchants, politicians, and their sinewy wives; he immortalized the Winthrops, Pepperells,

227

Pickmans, Adamses, and Mayhews—the tight-lipped patriots who defied the mad English king. Copley portrayed his sitters in the cold clear light of New England and they are Puritans to a man, or woman—upstanding and a little stiff in their laces and velvets, but never wanting in backbone and not to be ignored anywhere.

The honor of painting the most famous picture in American art goes to Gilbert Stuart (1755–1828)—a portrait so generally accepted as the one and only, the genuine likeness of the first President of the United States as to arouse Mark Twain to this animadversion (his own word): "If Washington should rise from the dead, and not resemble the Stuart portrait, he would be denounced as an imposter." Stuart was born in Rhode Island, the son of a Scottish snuff-grinder, and after a juvenile-

Stuart. *George Washington. Athenaeum portrait, Museum of Fine Arts, Boston. The immortal portrait of Washington, the best of twenty studies, and a part of the American heritage.*

Copley. *John Hancock. Museum of Fine Arts, Boston. The first signer of the Declaration of Independence, a little stiff in his Sunday clothes and a living image of the old tight-lipped patriot.*

delinquent youth of painting and tramping, went to London to seek his fortune. He was soon recognized as a painter of brilliant gifts and attracted a wealthy clientele, but he lived in Bohemian recklessness, drank to excess, and returned to America with an empty purse.

"It was whispered about," he explained, "that I fixed on Washington because I needed the money. How true! I was as broke as last year's bird's nest, but that isn't all. I believed that Washington was the greatest man in history, and I'm not too modest to say that I was the only artist capable of doing him justice." His first attempt at General Washington was unsatisfactory, but at the second trial his portrait won its way into the hearts of his countrymen. All told, he executed twenty pictures of Washington, mostly copies of his own work, but the second version, known as the Athenaeum head, is as much a part of the

American heritage as Abraham Lincoln or Davy Crockett or Buffalo Bill.

The Colonial period, like its counterpart in England, produced thousands of portraits, some superlative, some fair, others not worth buying and falsely exploited at the roadside "shoppes" and in wayside galleries in New England and New York. The best Colonial painters, Copley and Stuart, are to be judged by the standards applicable to Goya or Hogarth, and the second-best, Trumbull, Waldo, the Peales, Sully, Greene, and Malbone, are part of our American culture.

While the Colonial portrait painters were wandering from place to place "taking faces," another man was also wandering in the interest of art, but with totally different aims. He was John James Audubon, born in Santo Domingo in 1785, the son of a French naval officer and a Creole mother. He was a romantic figure with an acute sense of the dramatic, and he has become a national hero and the somewhat legendary idol of wild-life cults and frontier zealots. He helped to create the picturesque legend of himself by carrying a dagger in

Bingham. *Stump Speaking. Boatmen's National Bank of St. Louis. A political candidate before a rural audience in the pioneer days of campaigning.*

Bingham. *Fur Traders Descending the Missouri. Metropolitan Museum of Art, New York. Tramp traders in the morning mist that hangs over the great river—a rare example of the artist's mastery of atmospheric effects.*

the wilderness, wearing long hair—like an American trapper or a Bohemian artist—and by passing in the literary circles of Europe as an esthetic Leatherstocking.

But he was a great man, every inch of him, and his romantic fripperies adorned his temperament. As a young zealot he voyaged down the Great River and explored the forests of Ohio, the swamps of Louisiana, and from there, the coasts of Carolina, with a burning conviction equal to that of the early French missionaries. He was drawn by a passion to immortalize the feathered life of America. From his paintings in water color was published in London *The Birds of America*, 435 hand-colored impressions from engravings, the most remarkable and beautiful book of its kind in existence.

As a painter of winged life, Audubon set a standard that makes his most devoted followers little better than dull bird stuffers. (See Plate 30.) Without departing from the truth, he treated birds as personalities, making them larger than life and more stately and imposing than American cabinet officers or French presidents. He portrayed smaller birds in

Audubon. *Woodpeckers. Water color, New-York Historical Society. A big family of busy little birds, true to life, each a personality.*

George Caleb Bingham was a true pioneer, hardy, self-reliant, respectful of the past but not enslaved by it, and as venturesome as Daniel Boone or old Thomas Hart Benton. He was born in Virginia in 1811, and migrated, in 1819, to Missouri with his parents, where he lived for the rest of his days—except for an occasional straying. In his extreme youth he read law and preached the gospel, and at nineteen earned his corn pone as a hitch-hiking portrait painter. He studied his craft in New York, Philadelphia, and Düsseldorf, and spent his last years at Columbia, Missouri, attached to the State University as professor of painting. My father, who was one of his pupils at the University of Missouri, used to tell me how the boys would steal Bingham's wig—the great painter was as bald as a doorknob—and then return it in shame. For they loved him and honored his genius; as my father asked se-

Durand. *Kindred Spirits. New York Public Library, Main Branch. A tribute to the American scene from one of the Hudson River school—the artist and his friend, the poet Bryant.*

death struggles with hawks and snakes, and by his originality as a designer made the battles as exciting as human conflict.

In the first half of the nineteenth century, as our home-bred painters began to invade Europe for counsel, we produced a group of landscape painters—the Hudson River school —who set out to do for our scenic background something as noble and epic as Cooper had done in his novels. One representative will suffice, Asher B. Durand (1796–1886), whose pictures are honest, strong, and poetic tributes to his native land. In his *Kindred Spirits* he painted a fellow Hudson Riverite, Thomas Cole, with his friend Bryant, the poet, "holding communion with the forms of nature"— as Bryant put it.

Ryder. *Death on a Pale Horse. J.H. Wade Collection, Cleveland Museum of Art. A parable in paint inspired by the death of a friend, a waiter who bet all of his savings on what turned out to be a slow, pale horse—and then killed himself.*

Whistler was a man of exquisite taste and the quality of his paintings and etchings lies in the skill and delicacy of his arrangements. He was influenced by the Japanese and by Velásquez. To invite attention to his genius as a composer he gave musical titles to his canvases, such as *Nocturnes* and *Symphonies*. But fate played a perverse trick on the exquisite master. He painted a portrait of his mother, to whom he was devoted. To keep his devotion a secret and make his enemies believe that he was hard-boiled even where his parents were concerned, he called the picture *Arrangement in Grey and Black,* warning the public to ignore the subject and admire the arrangement. But the world has refused to ignore the subject, and the painting, now enshrined in the Louvre, is no longer cherished as a perfectly silhouetted design, but as the most reverent embodiment of motherhood in modern art. It is the one painting circulated in every corner of America on Mother's Day.

John Singer Sargent was described as "an American, born in Italy in 1856, and educated in France; who looked like a German, spoke

dately, "What other university in America ever had a professor—a full professor of painting, or revered him justly?" Bingham made his pictures out of his own experiences: out of the jolly raftsmen he had seen on the Mississippi; out of the pioneers crossing the Cumberland Gap; and from the political scenes he had participated in as a candidate for Congress.

In the middle years of the nineteenth century, in the exodus of artists to European centers, America boasted of two cosmopolitans, Whistler and Sargent, who were at home everywhere except in the United States. James Abbott McNeill Whistler, born in Massachusetts in 1834, was expelled from the Military Academy at West Point and went to Paris, where he immediately attracted attention by his talents as an artist and his deadly sarcasms. Moving to London, he spent the rest of his life in poisonous disputes with British critics—but he was more than a verbal defender of his art. He worked long and hard and ceaselessly for the technical perfection required for his ideas of beauty.

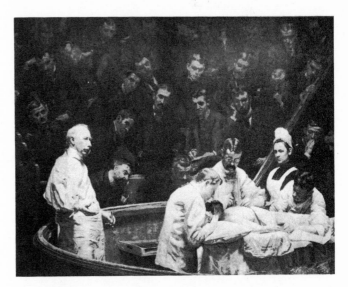

Eakins. *The Agnew Clinic. University of Pennsylvania, Philadelphia. In the exacting spirit of the old Dutch realists, Eakins composed an anatomy lesson in a modern clinic.*

Whistler. *Arrangement in Grey and Black, The Artist's Mother. Louvre, Paris. No longer remembered as an arrangement of tones, but as the most reverent conception of motherhood in modern art.*

Homer. *The Lookout—"All's Well." Museum of Fine Arts, Boston. The man on watch, an old-fashioned Yankee, pulls the bell rope and sings the ancient call.*

like an Englishman, and painted like a Spaniard." This goes to show that when America sets out to produce an international, she does a complete job of it. Sargent opened a studio in London in 1884, and for forty years was the historian of high life in Great Britain, or, as one critic expressed it, "by painting all the titled people of England, he gave them passports to posterity." So clamorous was the demand for his portraits that he is shown in a cartoon by Max Beerbohm as peeping dejectedly from his studio window into a queue of duchesses extending from his doorstep as far as eye could see—all waiting to be preserved by the American's brush.

Sargent had an amazing talent for likenesses and human proportions, a hand that worked with athletic fluency, never missing the actual size of a sitter, as a whole or in parts, by more than one-sixteenth of an inch. He was scrupulously upright, always revealing the social position or physical health of his clients and rendering them with a dexterity sel-

Sargent. *Robert Louis Stevenson. Taft Museum, Cincinnati. A remarkable characterization of the gallant Scot, thin from the ravages of consumption but indomitable.*

dom seen in art since Hals or Goya. His portrait of *Robert Louis Stevenson* is a masterpiece of characterization: the incomparable Scotsman, a prey to the ravages of consumption, a bag of bones with skeleton hands, but with the enchanting, unquenchable spirit of a dark, glowing, tough, Scottish saint in his face.

Let us turn from the cosmopolitans to the essentially native art of two Yankees, Winslow Homer (1836–1910) and Albert Pinkham Ryder (1847–1917). The first took the hard road to fame. Born in Boston, where he served a long apprenticeship in lithography, Homer acted as a correspondent and illustrator for *Harper's Weekly* during the Civil War. After that, to improve his painting, he went to Paris —filled with Yankee misgivings. Paris neither helped nor hindered him; he was a codfish out of water. But on a holiday among the fishermen of the British seacoast, the sea that was in his blood and the blood of his ancestors hammered at his heart. From that moment he painted nothing but marines. (See Plate 29.) At the age of fifty he built a cottage on a forlorn headland in Maine and, save for an occasional voyage into the West Indies, lived

Bellows. *Stag at Sharkey's. Hinman B. Hurlbut Collection, Cleveland Museum of Art. Terrific action of the squared circle by the champion artist of the modern prize fight.*

alone in his rockbound studio. He garnered an international fame he did not seek and sold everything he painted—he had no use for money but, Yankeewise, put it out at interest —and was extravagantly lauded by the French as the first typically American artist.

In all changes of weather, Homer studied the sea. At midnight under the moon, at noon under the sun, in fair weather or foul, he studied the sea, as the Englishman Turner had scrutinized it—the sharp contrasts of light between the northern and southern waters, and always the power of the waves over man. The sea was a New England problem, and he painted it graphically in connection with the lives of sailors and fishermen. His water colors of the West Indian seas have been imitated by present-day artists, American and French, but his best work is in oils, a medium he used to present the rugged grandeur of his people and the might of the sea as it worked against human elements, and the action of the sea, which Walt Whitman called "the cradle endlessly rocking."

The rarest of the Yankee solitaries, and one of the most original of American painters, was Albert Ryder, born in New Bedford, Massa-

Sloan. *Sixth Avenue Elevated at Third Street. Whitney Museum of American Art, New York. The flashing train overhead, and life under the old "El," by the foremost painter of Greenwich Village.*

chusetts, the descendant of mechanics and sea-faring men. After a little schooling with local artists he began to draw from nature, and he believed that he had a great work to perform. "I saw that my pictures were clean and strong," he said, "when I found the sea springing to life on my dead canvas." The sea was his birthright. New Bedford was the whaling port of the world, and he watched the ships that proudly rode out of the harbor in a fair wind; and he noted, too, with a sense of the terror and mystery of the sea, that some of the ships never returned. When the family fortunes declined and the Ryders departed for New York, the painter, then in his twenties, was dependent on his brother. He studied at the National Academy and eventually became a member of that august body, exhibiting with his associates and not much concerned over their opinion of him.

Ryder lived as simply as a monk, and the income from his painting was sufficient for his needs. "Give me a rain-tight roof, some colors and God's sunlight through clear windows," was his prayer, "and keep my soul attuned and my body vigorous for daily work." In his attic studio he worked in blue jeans and a sailor's

Ward. *Statue of Washington. Sub-Treasury Building (now Federal Hall Memorial), New York. A noble, masculine figure, the most convincing and heroic statue of Washington thus far achieved.*

Burchfield. *November Evening. Metropolitan Museum of Art, New York. The countryside with false-front stores straggling along the highway—the loneliness and shabby grandeur of rural life.*

blouse, but on the sidewalks of New York he was a gentleman of the old school, with frock coat, silk hat, and cane. "He looked like one of the old apostles," a friend said, "suddenly come to life in the city, a great, rugged, bearded figure, radiating kindliness and peace." It was his custom, before the light faded, to walk to the water-front and sketch the ships, and on clear nights to stroll through the parks or Jersey woods, "to soak in the moonlight," he said.

Ryder gave to American art about 150 small canvases painted and overpainted in grays, blues, greens, and browns, the surfaces glazed again and again in transparent colors until they shone like enamels. He called himself a

Marsh. *The Bowery. Metropolitan Museum of Art, New York. Derelicts of the famous old street by the painter laureate of the seamy side of New York.*

Wood. *Midnight Ride of Paul Revere. Metropolitan Museum of Art, New York. A great designer brings humor into landscape art, as Paul Revere gallops all over the place on a bright midnight.*

Grosz. *The Poet Max Hermann-Neisse. Museum of Modern Art, New York. A probing, uncompromising characterization by the top-flight satirist of modern Germany.*

dreamer, but more precisely, he was a poet with a firm grip on his imagination, a sharp observer of the subjects on which he built his dreams. With his facts in hand he painted the supernatural power of the sea in the *Flying Dutchman,* the *Smuggler,* the *Wreck, Jonah and the Whale,* and the *Lorelei*—some of them fabulous dramas of waters dark as slate and crisscrossed with phantom lights. He was a great designer, working with the utmost simplicity in striking patterns unlike those of any other painter. The ordinary business of life did not move him; always it was pity, horror, and the sea, strange dangers and warnings of death, the intoxications of moonlight, the enchantment of the Forest of Arden (see Plate 31)— these were his themes and these ruled his noble career. His *Death on a Pale Horse* is a parable in paint, inspired by the death of his friend, a waiter, who bet all his savings on a pale horse which ran too slowly, with the result that the waiter killed himself.

If you care for painting that is strong and sensible, without frills or clever flourishes, you will have discovered the realistic art of Thomas

Hopper. *Nighthawks. Friends of American Art Collection, Art Institute of Chicago. The corner lunch-counter long after midnight, precise and stark with a beam of light shooting into the shadows.*

Eakins (1844–1916). This determined, matter-of-fact man went from Philadelphia to Paris and returned home again to practice his craft and to teach the groping youth of Philadelphia, at a time when good teachers were sorely demanded. He was influenced by the scientific spirit of his day, and with his stable, clear-cut brain would have made an eminent medico himself. He observed and painted many kinds of sports but enjoyed none; attended concerts to observe the faces and chests of singers, not to listen; visited clinics, dissected corpses, and painted anatomy lessons with blood running freely—the first of the kind since Rembrandt. Fire and drama and hot energy he did not possess; with him it was solid truth, nothing magical and nothing overlooked; nothing obscure, but nothing less than the best in close modeling. It may well be that his lasting esteem will rest with his portraits, which will certainly be hung in the same room as those of Copley, or in the room next door.

As the twentieth century opened, a number of Americans were having a field day in their own backyards, among them, Henri, Bellows, Glackens, Sloan, Luks, Robinson, Hopper, and Hart, lusty fellows bound together by strong ties of friendship and aspiration. They were not afraid of the plain or even sordid subjects of American cities. When they were denounced as tramps, or social scavengers, Sloan replied, "You are right, we are the charter members of the ash-can school of art."

The death of George Bellows in 1925, at the age of forty-three, was a national calamity. He was the most popular artist—in the right sense—that America has produced, and people loved him because he was one of them, and true to them. He had a genius for the only thing to paint. He never searched for subjects—they crowded his mind—prize fights, political pow wows, dead-end kids bathing in the East River, revival meetings, nudes, portraits, and what we call today "class struggles." He was not stopped by frustrations and was never feeble or boring; he had the exorbitant vitality of the circus poster, and the athletic integrity of the home-run hitter.

His pictures of prize fights are still the best in American or modern art, despite the good-humored criticisms of professional pugilists and French highbrows. Mickey Walker, former middleweight and light heavyweight champion of the world, but now an exhibiting painter in the plush corridors of the New York

Marin. *Lower Manhattan. Philip L. Goodwin Collection, New York. In the artist's words, "Powers are pulling, pushing sideways, upwards, downwards. I can hear the sound of their strife and the playing of great music."*

Curry. *Wisconsin Landscape. Metropolitan Museum of Art, New York. The fertility and splendor of farm land rendered on a magnificent scale.*

market, had this to say about the *Stag at Sharkey's*, as painted by Bellows: "It is terrific in action! I never seen so O.K. a picture of two boys throwing leather, but as a fighter, and one who kept his feet on the ground, I am kayoed by the thing. Look closely. Here is the big guy delivering the knock-out punch, a left-hook on the jaw, and a cross to follow. But the big guy has his right foot up in the air —way up in the air—and nobody could flatten nobody with his right foot up in the air. Ask Jack Dempsey or Joe Louis. Ask me. I'm not complaining. It's a great picture, and as an artist, I'm a bum. Bellows was an artist—there's a big difference. That's why the foot is in the air. I'm a fighter—I can paint—just a little."

John Sloan (1871–1954), for half a century, was a fearless and active figure in American art, as painter, etcher, and fighter. His favorite corner of New York was the locality bordering on Washington Square, which he has kept alive in thousands of etchings, oils, and drawings: life under the elevated railway, shopgirls returning from toil, hot nights on hot tin roofs, the Bohemian joints of Green-

wich Village, old taverns, streets, back yards, and Washington Square. He is the foremost etcher of the last fifty years, a master of his craft. He spurned the smudges and soft scratches of the romantic British school, and dug his needle into the plate boldly and surely, leaving surfaces upon which the history of the older and better Greenwich Village is written.

His friend Edward Hopper, born in 1882, has painted city streets, dilapidated old houses, and also lighthouses on the New England coast, with a style as stark and bleak as a flashlight exposure made stronger by doubling the contrasts between the lights and the shadows.

Some twenty years ago, a number of artists were united in a movement "to paint America first," each within the range of his particular experiences in a given environment. The leaders of the movement were five men whose work lifted them into nation-wide prominence. There was no official organization. The artists, four from the Middle West, the other from New York, were united by a common determination to express the characteristics, the phenomena, the people, the landscape of lo-

Benton. Arts of the West. Mural, Art Museum of the New Britain Institute. Genre scenes of the West transformed into a mural art of dynamic power and movement.

calities in the United States which they knew at first hand, by birth, study, and active participation in special ways of living. Three of the men have died, the two remaining are still strong and productive, but jointly and severally the five produced a body of paintings of remarkable quality and of permanent importance to the best American tradition.

The pioneer of the movement to bring painting down to native earth was Charles Burchfield, born in Ohio in 1893. His early experiences taught him that life in the midlands of America was neither charming nor classical, but he found beneath its rugged and often shabby surfaces a naked, haunting grandeur. He painted the false-front stores straggling on one side of the highways, farmers in Model-T Fords, the shacks by the railroad, and the big General Grant Gothic houses of the upper crust. He took a poetic view of common things and surrounded them with an epic atmosphere, sometimes warm and friendly,

more often bleak and tragic.

John Steuart Curry, born on a Kansas farm in 1897, was the most poetic American painter after the death of Albert Ryder. He lived in a land of sudden and fearful changes of weather: of tornadoes, dust storms, and blizzards; of spring showers and endless vistas of wheat and corn; of long, golden, Homeric autumns with abundant harvests. In his boyhood he saw the battle of the farmers against the hostilities of nature; as a mature artist he returned to those subjects, and while painting them—the big red barns and the corn rows, the grazing cattle and the sweltering July heat—there came into his colors all the feelings and memories, the sympathies and terrors remaining with him through the years. Before his death in 1946, Curry lived in Madison, Wisconsin, as artist-in-residence to the State University, a post he had occupied for a term of years. His landscape, the *Line Storm*, is a masterpiece in which the Midwestern earth is transformed into a terrifying personality; and in his *Wisconsin Landscape,* he brings out the majesty and opulence of beautifully cultivated land with a Venetian serenity.

Grant Wood died in 1942, a man of genius certainly, who left the fingerprints of his style on landscape painting, magazine covers, settings for the stage and movies, and advertising art. He painted *American Gothic,* sold to the Chicago Art Institute for $350, the most popular picture since Whistler's *Mother;* and *Paul Revere's Ride,* bought in 1950 by the Metropolitan Museum for $19,000. Born into poverty on an Iowa farm, and a born craftsman, he could make anything—his house, his furniture, the mailbox at the door, the pictures on the walls, and a birdhouse out of tomato cans, now in a museum. He matured slowly as a painter, going along by exact calculation and depicting the Hawkeyes honestly and calmly in some of the finest portraits of our time. In his own words, he "discovered the decorative quality in American newness," and into the design of his pictures he wove details such as the bright metal of a cookstove, the lace of a baby's bonnet, the shoulder straps

of a man's overalls. His landscapes, so gay and tidy and carefully designed, reveal a new element in this branch of art—a sense of humor.

Reginald Marsh, who died in 1954 at the age of fifty-six, was a metropolitan artist. He really and truly loved New York with its gaudy diversions, its splendor and cheapness, its magnificent vulgarity. He loved New York as Hogarth loved London and Daumier the common folk of Paris. With a first-rate brain he observed life deeply, or that very real segment of it from the shops of 14th Street, to the dance halls and burlesque houses, to the girls of the public beaches and the girls of Harlem. He was an artist of power and one of our best craftsmen; and for the vitality and technical mastery of his beautifully drawn, full-bodied, large-hipped working girls out for a frolic, you will have to go back a long way in art—back to Rubens.

Thomas Hart Benton, born in Missouri in 1889, has always been active and fearless and troublesome. Recently he completed a painting of Burt Lancaster as Daniel Boone for movie exploitation—and put the final touches to a conception of Abraham Lincoln for a

Rivera. *The Assembly Line. Central panel, south wall, Detroit Institute of Arts. The industrial machinery of America depicted with phenomenal organizing genius—and a new form of mural art.*

Barnard. *Statue of Abraham Lincoln. Cincinnati. The American of sorrows—unsoftened and tragic, the emblem of the struggle for humanity.*

but since his return to America forty years ago, he has been a tireless exponent of American life from the industrial centers to the mountains and backwoods. (See Plate 32.)

Besides his easel pictures, lithographs, water colors, and book illustrations, he has executed four large murals: one in New York, one in New Britain, Connecticut, the third in Indiana, and the last in Missouri—wall decorations standing out, with those of the Mexicans, as the most original on the American continent. He has caught and depicted the turmoil, the raw struggle, the riotous energy of American industrialism; and at the other end of the scale, the loneliness, poverty, and sharecropping pathos of the hillbillies and underprivileged.

Epstein. *Oriel Ross. Museum of Modern Art, New York. The rough medium of bronze shaped into a head of startling reality.*

Negro college in Missouri, a large mural done with somber reverence for Lincoln and those emancipated, a work of power and understanding of the hard glory of the Civil War days. Benton is the descendant of Missouri politicians, and is an artist trained in Paris,

E 31. ALBERT PINKHAM RYDER. *The Forest of Arden*. STEPHEN C. CLARK COLLECTION, NEW YORK

PLATE 32. THOMAS HART BENTON. *Roasting Ears*. METROPOLITAN MUSEUM OF ART, NEW YO

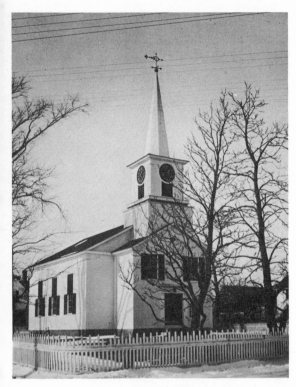

New England Church. Martha's Vineyard, Massachusetts. The little white church, one of the architectural landmarks of New England, with the doors, windows, and spire in perfect proportion.

Johnson Wax Administration and Research Center. Racine, Wisconsin. A vertical unit, only thirteen feet at ground level, seems to rise and hover above the flattened forms around it.

I should include, along with Benton, another American generally classified as one of the great artists of modern Germany. I call him an American because, like Albert Einstein and others exiled by Hitler, he has found a home in the United States and has worked unceasingly for democratic causes. George Grosz, born in Berlin in 1893, came to America in 1932, to begin life all over again. His early life had been hard, and his experiences in World War I left upon him scars that will never be healed. Before he came to New York he depicted the Nazi forces in pictures so dreadful that we cannot describe them, but living for years in America, as a citizen, he abandoned the merciless technique of his earlier years. Grosz is a pitiless portrait painter of the old German tradition, a book illustrator, stage designer, and a master of water

Mt. Vernon. Home of George Washington. Fairfax County, Virginia. The model plantation house erected by the first President with a southern bow to the classical tradition, and a cupola besides.

Orozco. *Zapatistas. Museum of Modern Art, New York. Mexican insurrectionists on the march—an example of Orozco's savage rhythms and originality in design.*

color, perhaps the best since Turner. And as an observer of the American way of life, he is sharper than most of our native artists.

Another water colorist of the most subtle fluency was John Marin (1870–1953) famed for his pictures of the Maine coastline. Trained abroad and influenced by Whistler's etchings, Marin found a sudden release for his talents in the unorthodox practices of French modernism. Every year, on New England's rock-ribbed shores, he produced paintings which seemed to be magically washed on the paper. He looked at nature with a poet's

eye, setting down the forms that most impressed him—at first with close regard for the realistic appearance of trees, rocks, and water, but as he grew older, in brilliant shorthand symbols that are hard to follow.

Some of the most influential and significant painting of the present century has come from South of the Border in the murals of Diego Rivera and José Clemente Orozco. The two artists—poles apart in temperament—have penetrated to the springs of Mexican life with its mixture of the savage and the civilized, the religious and the revolutionary. Both have been active figures in the struggles of the peons and industrial workers against political tyrants, and both have depicted the insurrectional passions of their people on the walls of public buildings.

Rivera (1886–   ) is the more prominent because of his battles with the press and the police. After his student days in Paris, he returned to Mexico equipped technically and physically for leadership. He developed an amazing fresco style, and the public screamed, or condemned, as tremendous murals rolled off his brushes. He covered vast wall spaces, as other men filled little canvases. He worked with a revolver at his belt, as he constructed scenes of violence and bloodshed and satires on capitalism, and in quieter vein, fiestas and local customs. Examples of his mural art may be seen in California, Detroit, and New York.

Orozco (1883–1954), a modest man, has been somewhat obscured by the public attention lavished on his picturesque rival, but as the years go by, his position as one of the most original artists of the twentieth century grows the more secure. Orozco recovered for modern painting the grim conviction, the profound search into religious feelings, and the cries of suffering humanity lost to mural art since the early Italians. He portrayed not only the revolutionary slaughter but the spiritual ferment of his people—inward struggles as old as the ancient gods—and composing his figures in unexpected postures and strange

Rotunda, University of Virginia. Charlottesville. Thomas Jefferson, architect. Practical demonstration of Jefferson's classical preferences in architecture—his own design adapted from the Pantheon of ancient Rome.

Independence Hall. Philadelphia. The Georgian style in America, stately and uplifting, after the genius of Sir Christopher Wren.

Vanderbilt House. Fifth Avenue at 58th Street, New York. The elegance of the French château, with the Plaza Hotel to the right—built in the days when a millionaire could still afford a private house on Fifth Avenue.

Rockefeller Center. New York. The skyscraper center of upper Manhattan—with art, industry, and commerce concentrated into vertical forms.

rhythmical combinations that give dramatic energy to his murals. In this country, his mural art may be seen in New York and at Dartmouth College.

In the field of sculpture, the Colonial period produced nothing comparable to the work of our portrait painters, but after the Civil War our carvers began to find themselves. As the century turned, we could name with pride Ward, Rimmer, Saint-Gaudens, Barnard, and the two Borglums. Among these, Augustus Saint-Gaudens, trained in France, was the most accomplished modeler and is remembered by his monuments to Sherman and Farragut in New York, the

mourning figure in Rock Creek Cemetery, Washington, the Shaw group in Boston, and the Lincoln in Chicago. John Quincy Adams Ward (1830–1910) will live in the hearts of his countrymen as the creator of the greatest, by far the noblest and most heroic, statue of Washington thus far achieved—with all deference to Houdon's work in Richmond, Virginia. The figure stands on the steps of the Sub-Treasury in downtown New York—but the stock gamblers are too busy to notice it.

George Grey Barnard (1863–1938) was one of the Titans of modern sculpture, a man whom Michelangelo would have greeted as a brother, incredibly gifted, physically powerful, incessantly industrious, carving all his works single-handed or with the minimum of assistance. At the age of twenty-two, in Paris, he finished the great work of his youth, *I Feel Two Natures Struggling Within Me,* now in the Metropolitan Museum of New York, and worthy to stand with the statues of the Renaissance masters. His figure of Abraham Lincoln, in Cincinnati, is the most original piece of sculpture in American art and one of the most forceful portrait monuments ever conceived—a man of sorrow, positive, unsoftened, tragic, the symbol of the pioneer civilization in America, and of all modern civilization—so Barnard said.

Jacob Epstein, born in New York in 1880, has lived in London most of his working life and has forced the Britishers, often against their will, to take notice of his sculpture. They have not only taken notice of it; they have damned and defaced it, but he has kept his head and is now honorably accepted by those in authority as an ornament to his art. His early monuments, influenced by the ancient races, are hard for Anglo-Saxons to stomach, but his portraits in bronze are vividly alive

Nebraska State Capitol. Lincoln. The new look in State Capitols—no obsolete domes but a skyscraper standing out as a monument to the pioneering enterprise of America.

Interior, Johnson Wax Administration and Research Center. Racine, Wisconsin. Furniture designed by Frank Lloyd Wright. The mushroom columns, called "golf tees," are reinforced concrete and designed to bolster up a working room flooded with light and air.

and original. He has portrayed servant girls—Negro and white—lords and ladies, dukes, soldiers, authors, and children, all of them flesh-and-blood likenesses in the rough medium of bronze, and all of them representative of various classes of human beings.

In the development of architecture, the Americans have been influenced by many foreign styles: by the British in New England; by the Dutch in Pennsylvania and New York; by the Greek and Roman, in our old municipal buildings, in the city of Washington, and in Virginia under the authority of Jefferson; by the French and Spanish on the Gulf Coast; by the Spanish in the Southwest and by the Spanish today in ranch houses springing up in every nook and corner from Martha's Vineyard to San Diego.

The most attractive domestic architecture is still to be found in New England, where one may see comely little towns, clean and white and tidy, with admirably preserved old houses. Some of them are in seventeenth-century style—salt-boxes, or many-gabled structures with long-pitched roofs and overhanging second stories—and many more of the later classic type, that is, with a few touches of the Greek temple used to break the severity of the corners and doorways. And in a broad lawn stands a church, spotlessly white, with beautifully proportioned windows and doors and a spire suggestive of Wren's British designs. There is no reason why we should imitate the Colonial builders, but the mass production of split-level bungalows and sprawling, one-story ranch houses is not the answer.

The classical influence, partly by the example of Jefferson, who designed his own home and planned the University of Virginia, and partly from the styles imported from Europe, in its first operations left us many fine public buildings and many imposing homes, such as the plantation houses of the South. But as wealth accumulated, a profusion of garbled

styles appeared, and at the close of the nineteenth century, most of our architecture, private and public, was not to be admired. The shops in our cities had façades of Greek, or Gothic, or Georgian imitation; our railway stations were Roman baths; every Statehouse and courthouse had its useless dome; and our houses were General Grant Gothic, with jigsaw ornamentation all over the place.

Today, American architects are the leaders and pioneers in new methods of construction and in new materials. We gave to the world the most original and arresting form of building since the Renaissance—the skyscraper, made possible by the steel skeleton. After a period of unbecoming ornamentation, Greek and Gothic, the modern skyscraper is un-

Temple B'nai Amoona, Temple and Community Center. Model, St. Louis. Eric Mendelsohn, architect. Model of a functional development, a temple and community center organically united in a place to worship and a place for relaxation.

Lever House. Park Avenue between 53rd and 54th Streets, New York. Steel for the skeleton, stainless metals to hold the walls of glass, air-conditioned, as bright as sunlight—the new office building.

adorned like the State Capitol of Nebraska, or like the Lever Brothers building in New York, is all glass and metal.

The most distinguished of living architects is Frank Lloyd Wright, of Wisconsin, whose structures, private and public, have influenced the course of building in every quarter of the world. Wright, our foremost advocate of functional architecture, believes that the form is dictated by the purpose—that every part of a building should express its use, its reason for being, that nothing unnecessary should be added, and that superfluous decoration should be eliminated. In other words, a filling station should be a simple, straightforward building for the dispensing of gasoline, and not an imitation temple or Indian wigwam.

Wright's daring geometrical designing and his extensive use of the cantilever, as exemplified in the office building of the Johnson Wax Company and in the "Falling Water House" of Pennsylvania, have inspired a new school of architecture with results in evidence from coast to coast. The idea behind it is sound and civilized: light, air, and the maximum of hu-

Esso Service Station. Merrick Road, Merrick, Long Island. A functional filling station—simple, straightforward, easy on the eye, the adaptation of form to purpose.

A. Conger Goodyear House. Westbury, Long Island. The modernist house, in exquisite taste, the outside and the inside conjoining harmoniously.

"Falling Water House." Home of Mr. and Mrs. Edgar J. Kauffman. Bear Run, Pennsylvania. Frank Lloyd Wright, architect. A sensational private house fastened to a site above a flowing stream by projecting cantilevers for sun decks and porches.

man comfort in the workrooms of factories and in schoolhouses; and in private houses, glass everywhere with patios and porches to bring mother nature right into one's living room. This is fine and salubrious and soul-stirring, if one lives in Florida or California, but not so practicable in Martha's Vineyard, where I happen to live. My old house is getting feeble, but for a century and a half it has withstood the gales and hurricanes—a fortress against the elements—and after all, a man's house is his castle, not his show window.

Index

Page numbers in roman type refer to the text. *Page numbers in italics refer to the illustrations.*

Acknowledgments

The author and The World Publishing Company herewith thank the following individuals and institutions whose co-operation has made possible the preparation of *The Rainbow Book of Art*.

All possible care has been taken to trace the ownership of every picture included and to make full acknowledgment for its use. If any errors have accidentally occurred they will be corrected in subsequent editions, provided notification is sent to the publisher.

Black and white illustrations on the following pages (These abbreviations are used: L—Left, R—Right, T—Top, B—Bottom):

ACL, Brussels, for 116(T), 118(TL), 118(BR), 119, 120(B), 121, 123, 124(T), 132(B), 134(T), 135(T); Alinari Photo, for 58(TL), 77(B); Alinari Photo, by courtesy of ENIT, New York, for 60, 62(B), 63, 66, 68(TL), 70(T), 73(B), 76(T), 82, 86(B), 87(B), 89(TR), 98(BR), 99(TL), 100(TR), 101(T), 102(T), 110(B); American Museum of Natural History, New York, for 15; Avery Library, Columbia University, New York, for 56, 58(B); Baltimore Museum of Art, for 222(T); Belgian Government Information Center, New York, for 116(B); Bettmann Archive, New York, for 200(T); Boatmen's National Bank of St. Louis, for 229(T); Adrien Boutrelle, New York, for 126(B); British Information Services, New York, for 80, 184(T), 186; Brooklyn Museum, New York, for 192(T); Camera Clix, New York, for 79, 104(B), 128(B), 148, 160(B), 162(B), 199(B), 213(T), 216; Capitan Breuil & Peyrony, in *La Caverne de Font-De-Gaume*, for 12, 14(T); Art Institute of Chicago, for 176(B), 211(T), 212(T), 218(T), 236(T); Museum of the City of New York, for 243(BR); Cleveland Museum of Art, for 193(B), 231(T), 233(T); Detroit Institute of Arts, for 239; Duveen Brothers, Inc., New York, for 140(T); Eastern National Park and Monument Association, for 243(BL); ENIT (Italian State Tourist Office), New York, for 37(TR), 45(T), 62(T), 78, 86(T), 97(BL), 98(BL), 98(TL), 109(T); Federal Hall Memorial Associates, Inc., New York, for 234(T); Museum of Fine Arts, Boston,

for 16, 19(TL), 46(B), 198(T), 228, 232(TR); Fogg Art Museum, Harvard University, Cambridge, Mass., for 105(B); Frans Hals Museum, Haarlem, for 126(T); French Embassy Press and Information Division, New York, for 192(B), 197(B), 199(T); French Government Tourist Office, New York, for 45(B), 48, 58(TR); Frick Collection, New York, for 103, 113(B), 125(B), 167, 198(B), 202(BL), 211(B); Ewing Galloway, New York, for 30, 39, 161(T), 191(B), 202(TL), 232(TL); Philip Gendreau, New York, for 46(T), 136; German Tourist Information Office, New York, for 130, 134(B); Bill Hedrich, Hedrich-Blessing, Chicago, for 248; Erich S. Herrmann, Inc., New York, for 25(T), 175; S. C. Johnson and Son, Inc., for 241(TR), 245(B); Lincoln Chamber of Commerce, Lincoln, Neb., for 245(T); Lever Brothers Co., New York, for 247(T); Marsh Photographers, Inc., for 240(L); Shirley W. Mayhew, for 241(TL); Eric Mendelsohn, for 246; Metropolitan Museum of Art, New York, for 20(TL), 21(BL), 22(B), 23, 29, 33, 34, 36(B), 37(B), 40(T), 41, 44, 47, 69, 84(T), 96, 110(T), 117(B), 120(T), 124(B), 137, 140(B), 144(B), 146, 150(T), 151, 154(B), 161(B), 163(T), 165(T), 166(T), 170(T), 171(T), 174(B), 177, 178(B), 182, 183, 185(B), 194, 195, 196(TL), 196(BR), 203, 204(BL), 205(TL), 206(TL), 206(B), 207(B), 208, 212(B), 214, 217(T), 220(B), 224, 229(B), 234(B), 235(TL), 235(B), 237; Museum of Modern Art, New York, for 218(B), 219, 221, 223, 225, 235(TR), 236(B), 240(BR), 242; More Memorial Library, Columbia University, New York, for 51, 52, 55, 73(T); Mount Vernon Ladies' Association, Mount Vernon, Va., for 241(B); National Gallery, London, for 100(BL), 127(TL), 127(B), 157(B), 176(T), 187; National Gallery of Art, Washington, D.C., for 92(B), 99(B), 111(B), 112(B), 114, 142(T), 149, 178(T), 205(B), 207(T), 210, 213(B), 220(T); Nelson-Atkins Gallery of Art, Kansas City, Mo., for 204(BR); Netherlands Information Service, New York, for 127(TR), 129(R), 141, 143; Art Museum of the New Britain Institute, for 238; New-York Historical Society, New York, for 230(T); New York Public Library Picture Collection, for 36(T), 230(B); Oriental Institute, University of Chicago, for 27; Pennsylvania Academy of the Fine Arts, Philadelphia, for 226; University of Pennsylvania, Philadelphia, for 231(B); Philadelphia Museum of Art, for 188, 217(B), 222(B); Pictura Films Corp., for 102(BR); Pierpont Morgan Library, New York, for 135(B), 154(T); Raymond and Raymond, New York, for 122; Rijks Museum, Amsterdam, for 129(L), 142(B), 144(T), 145; Standard Oil Co., New Jersey, for 247(BL); Ezra Stoller, New York, for 247(BR); Taft Museum, Cincinnati, for 232(B); Tate Gallery, London, for 185(T); Taylor and Dull, New York, for 233(B); Thomas Airviews, New York, for 244; Ralph Thompson, for 243(TL); Three Lions, Inc., New York, for 101(BR), 160(T), 193(T), 196(BL), 202(BR); Trans World Airlines, Inc., for 22(T), 24, 57, 190, 191(T); University of Virginia, Charlottesville, for 243(TL); Wallace Collection, London, for 174(T).

Color Plates:

The author and The World Publishing Company herewith thank Simon and Schuster, Inc., and The Condé Nast Publications Inc. for the color plates appearing in this book.

About the Author

THOMAS CRAVEN has spent more than forty years as a student and critic of art. Born in Kansas, he has traveled extensively, all through the United States and in foreign lands, making the acquaintance at firsthand of art and artists. This constant contact with the makers of great art and with their works has given him an insight unequaled in modern art criticism—and this deep knowledge of their aims and achievements is reflected in his writing. As commentator and interpreter of the artist and his work to the public, Mr. Craven has had a large part in the widening of America's cultural horizons in his books *Men of Art, Modern Art,* and *The Story of Painting.* His editorial accomplishment in *A Treasury of Art Masterpieces* and *A Treasury of American Prints* has been widely acclaimed for its scope and imagination.

10 11 12 13 14 74 73 72